Fields of Linguistics –
Aktuelle Fragestellungen und Herausforderungen

Band 10

Herausgegeben von
Joanna Szczęk, Anna Dargiewicz
und Mariusz Jakosz

Advisory Board:
Marisol Benito Rey (Autonome Universität Madrid, Spanien), Maria Biskup (Universität Warschau, Polen), Anna Chita (Nationale und Kapodistrian-Universität Athen, Griechenland), Martine Dalmas (Universität Sorbonne Paris, Frankreich), Jarochna Dąbrowska-Burkhardt (Universität Zielona Góra, Polen), Peter Ernst (Universität Wien, Österreich), Csaba Földes (Universität Erfurt, Deutschland), Beata Grzeszczakowska-Pawlikowska (Universität Łódź, Polen), Małgorzata Guławska-Gawkowska (Universität Warschau, Polen), Anna Jaroszewska (Universität Warschau, Polen), Sabine E. Koesters Gensini (Universität La Sapienza in Rom, Italien), Renate Link (Technische Hochschule Aschaffenburg, Deutschland), Magdalena Lisiecka-Czop (Universität Stettin, Polen), Heinz-Helmut Lüger (Universität Koblenz-Landau, Deutschland), Jacek Makowski (Universität Łódź, Polen), Simon Meier-Vieracker (Technische Universität Dresden, Deutschland), Carmen Mellado Blanco (Universität Santiago de Compostela, Spanien), Daniela Pelka (Universität Oppeln, Polen), Joanna Pędzisz (Maria-Curie-Skłodowska-Universität Lublin, Polen), Georg Schuppener (Universität Leipzig, Deutschland / Universität der Hl. Kyrill und Method in Trnava, Slowakei), Anna Sulikowska (Universität Stettin, Polen), Janusz Taborek (Adam-Mickiewicz-Universität in Poznań, Polen), Joanna Targońska (Warmia und Mazury-Universität Olsztyn, Polen), Claudia Wich-Reif (Universität Bonn, Deutschland), Mariola Wierzbicka (Universität Rzeszów, Polen), Beatrice Wilke (Universität Salerno, Italien)

Die Bände dieser Reihe sind peer-reviewed.

Nataliia Holubenko / Bożena Iwanowska / Yan Kapranov

Linguistic Representations of the Conceptual Sphere of the American South in Literary Translation

Strategies and Tactics for Rendering Ethnoculturally Marked Concepts from English into Ukrainian

V&R unipress

Bibliografische Information der Deutschen Nationalbibliothek
Die Deutsche Nationalbibliothek verzeichnet diese Publikation in der Deutschen
Nationalbibliografie; detaillierte bibliografische Daten sind im Internet über
https://dnb.de abrufbar.

© 2024 Brill | V&R unipress, Robert-Bosch-Breite 10, D-37079 Göttingen, ein Imprint der Brill-Gruppe
(Koninklijke Brill BV, Leiden, Niederlande; Brill USA Inc., Boston MA, USA; Brill Asia Pte Ltd,
Singapore; Brill Deutschland GmbH, Paderborn, Deutschland; Brill Österreich GmbH, Wien,
Österreich)
Koninklijke Brill BV umfasst die Imprints Brill, Brill Nijhoff, Brill Schöningh, Brill Fink, Brill mentis,
Brill Wageningen Academic, Vandenhoeck & Ruprecht, Böhlau und V&R unipress.
Alle Rechte vorbehalten. Das Werk und seine Teile sind urheberrechtlich geschützt.
Jede Verwertung in anderen als den gesetzlich zugelassenen Fällen bedarf der vorherigen
schriftlichen Einwilligung des Verlages.

Druck und Bindung: CPI books GmbH, Birkstraße 10, D-25917 Leck
Printed in the EU.

Vandenhoeck & Ruprecht Verlage | www.vandenhoeck-ruprecht-verlage.com

ISSN 2941-7465
ISBN 978-3-8471-1798-8

Contents

Introduction 9

Chapter 1. Theoretical and Methodological Fundamentals on Rendering the Linguistic Representations of the Conceptual Sphere of the American South in Literary Translation 13
  1.1 Translation Studies and Cognitive Science: Areas of Intersection . . 13
      1.1.1 Linguistic and Conceptual Worldviews as Components of National Culture in Translation Studies 14
      1.1.2 Conceptualization of the Worldview in the Consciousness of the Individual in the Translation Process 18
  1.2 The Concept in the Contemporary Paradigm of Translation Studies 22
      1.2.1 The Concept in Cognitive Translation Studies 24
      1.2.2 Linguistic and Conceptual Factors of Asymmetry in Translation 28
      1.2.3 The Problem of Translatability of Linguistic Representations of Ethnoculturally Marked Concepts 33
  1.3 Methodological Principles for Rendering Linguistic Representations of Ethnoculturally Marked Concepts in Literary Translation 38
      1.3.1 Strategies and Tactics for Rendering English Representations of Ethnoculturally Marked Concepts in Literary Translation . 40
      1.3.2 Research Stages and Steps for Rendering English Representations of Ethnoculturally Marked Concepts of the American South into Ukrainian 42
  Conclusions to Chapter 1 45

Chapter 2. Rendering of English Linguistic Representations of Historical
and Social Concepts of the American South into Ukrainian 49
   2.1 Rendering of English Linguistic Representations of the CIVIL WAR
      Concept of the American South into Ukrainian 51
      2.1.1 Rendering the Core Components of the Concept of the CIVIL
           WAR Concept 52
      2.1.2 Rendering the Peripheral Components of the CIVIL WAR
           Concept in Primary and Secondary Texts 60
   2.2 Rendering of English Linguistic Representations of the SOCIAL
      STRUCTURE Concept of the American South into Ukrainian 67
      2.2.1 Rendering the Core Components of the Concept of the
           SOCIAL STRUCTURE Concept 67
      2.2.2 Rendering the Peripheral Components of the SOCIAL
           STRUCTURE Concept in Primary and Secondary Texts 78
   2.3 Rendering of English Linguistic Representations of the SLAVERY
      Concept of the American South into Ukrainian 81
      2.3.1 Rendering the Core Components of the Concept of the
           SLAVERY Concept 82
      2.3.2 Rendering the Peripheral Components of the SLAVERY
           Concept in Primary and Secondary Texts 92
   Conclusions to Chapter 2 98

Chapter 3. Rendering of English Linguistic Representations of Ethically
Marked Concepts of the American South into Ukrainian 101
   3.1 Rendering of English Linguistic Representations of the SOUTHERN
      LADY and SOUTHERN GENTLEMAN Concepts of the American
      South into Ukrainian 102
      3.1.1 Rendering the Core Components of the Concept SOUTHERN
           LADY and SOUTHERN GENTLEMAN Concepts 102
      3.1.2 Rendering the Peripheral Components of the SOUTHERN
           LADY and SOUTHERN GENTLEMAN Concepts in Primary
           and Secondary Texts 108
   3.2 Rendering of English Linguistic Representations of the WHITE
      TRASH Concept of the American South into Ukrainian 113
      3.2.1 Rendering the Core Components of the WHITE TRASH
           Concept 114
      3.2.2 Rendering the Peripheral Components of the WHITE TRASH
           Concept in Primary and Secondary Texts 120

3.3 Rendering of English Linguistic Representations of the BLACKS
    Concept of the American South into Ukrainian 121
    3.3.1 Rendering the Core Components of the BLACKS Concept . . . 122
    3.3.2 Rendering the Peripheral Components of the BLACKS
          Concept in Primary and Secondary Texts 130
Conclusions for Chapter 3 136

Conclusions 139

References 143
    Lexicographic Sources 158
    Illustrative Sources 159

Introduction

The contemporary stage of translation studies is characterized by a focus on critical concepts in linguistic science, including the "conceptual picture of the world" (O. Kubryakova, O. Selivanova) and the *"linguistic worldview"* (Yu. Karaulov, O. Kubryakova, O. Selivanova), *the concept* (M. Alefirenko, N. Arutyunova, S. Zhabotynska, V. Karasik, V. Maslova, Yu. Stepanov), and *the conceptual sphere* (D. Likhachov, O. Selivanova). These concepts convey one of the most significant aspects of human existence, enabling translation scholars to concentrate on the deep processes of interaction between language, thought, and reality and the role of language in shaping the inner world of individuals. This directs contemporary translators towards achieving adequacy in reproducing the representational imagery parameters of phenomena that collectively create a unique world picture of a particular linguaculture.

The conceptual sphere is studied in a socio-cultural context since it responds sensitively to changes in society and the life of a particular ethnicity. Every social modeling within a linguistic community causes linguistic modeling, whereby the content of a concept may change depending on specific circumstances and the receptivity to change among the speakers of a particular language. Understanding *a literary text* as a conceptual whole requires the translator to engage in a high level of abstraction during the analysis, as the concept, as a unit of world cognition, can have varying degrees of informational saturation while remaining an integral entity capable of being supplemented, altered, and reflecting human experience. The goal of the conceptual approach to translation is to preserve the basic cultural concepts in the target text.

The relevance of this monograph is driven by the orientation of contemporary translation studies towards the comprehensive assimilation of knowledge, extensive engagement with the achievements of linguistic cultural studies, cognitive science, and the anthropocentric paradigm in the study of language, as well as addressing the issue of adequately reproducing the linguistic representations of a literary work's concept sphere, precisely the concept sphere of the American

South – the southern states of the USA, which have long been distinguished as a distinct historical, cultural, and even socio-psychological hub.

This study aims to identify the challenges of rendering English-language representations of the American South's concept sphere in literary translation.

The monograph formulates and addresses the following **objectives:**
- to differentiate the concepts of the worldview, the conceptual picture of the world, and the linguistic worldview within the framework of translation analysis;
- to outline the translation parameters of the concepts "conceptual sphere" and "ethnoculturally marked concept";
- to develop a comprehensive methodology for reconstructing and interpreting the concepts of the American South in the context of the cognitive approach to translating literary works and determining the specifics of their verbalization in target texts;
- to determine the realization of the concepts of CIVIL WAR, SOCIAL ORDER, SLAVERY, and their characteristics in diachrony and synchrony;
- to identify common and distinctive means of verbalizing concepts in the compared linguacultures;
- to define the strategies and tactics for reproducing the linguistic representations of the concepts of the American South in translation;
- to identify and systematize the translation challenges in reproducing the dominant features of the concept sphere of the American South.

The research hypothesis is that the adequate reproduction of English-language representations of the concept sphere of the American South in the analyzed works is achieved through the use of appropriate translation strategies (domestication and foreignization) and tactics: translators employ intratextual explanations, descriptive translation, semantic development, generalization, and omission. In translation, linguistic representations of concepts may be reproduced fully – in cases where the cognitive background of the original and translation receivers coincides, partially – when adequate conveyance of linguistic expression does not ensure specific-contextual meaning, and deformatively – when excessive explication of the original content introduces information not present in the text into the translation.

The monograph's object is ethnoculturally marked concepts as components of the world picture of the American South in the works of the most prominent writers of this sector of American literature and their Ukrainian translations.

The monograph focuses on the strategies and tactics for reproducing in Ukrainian translations of the English-language representations of the concept sphere of the American South based on the original texts by R. P. Warren, H. Beecher-Stowe, H. Lee, M. Mitchell, M. Twain, and W. Faulkner.

The material for the *monograph* includes the literary works of W. Faulkner: "The Reivers" – "Крадії" (translated by R. Dotsenko, 1972); M. Twain: "The Adventures of Tom Sawyer" – "Пригоди Тома Сойєра" (translated by Yu. Koretsky, 1982), "The Adventures of Huckleberry Finn" – "Пригоди Гекльберрі Фінна" (translated by I. Steshenko, 1984); M. Mitchell: "Gone with the Wind" – "Звіяні вітром" (translated by R. Dotsenko, 1992); H. Lee: "To Kill a Mockingbird" – "Убити пересмішника" (translated by M. Kharenko, 1997; translated by T. Nekryach, 2015); "Go Set a Watchman" – "Іди, вартового постав" (translated by T. Nekryach, manuscript); R. P. Warren: "All the King's Men" – "Усе королівське військо" (translated by V. Mitrofanov, 2010); H. Beecher-Stowe: "Uncle Tom's Cabin" – "Хатина дядька Тома" (translated by L. Kuznetsova, 2012; translated by V. Mitrofanov, 2006) in the original and their Ukrainian translations.

The theoretical and methodological basis of the monograph comprises studies by domestic and foreign scholars: in translation studies – L. Barkhudarov, L. Venuti, V. Vinogradov, V. Komissarov, V. Koptilov, I. Korunets, A. Lefevere, Yu. Nida, T. Nekryach, A. Popovich, O. Rebriy, M. Rylsky, M. Snell-Hornby, A. Fedorov, O. Cherednychenko, K. Chukovsky; in text interpretation – W. Iser, V. Kukharenko; in the world picture – H. Brutyan, A. Gurevich, Yu. Karaulov, O. Kubryakova, R. Pavilionis, D. Raevsky; in linguistic, cultural studies – M. Alefirenko, V. Vorobyev, V. Maslova; in the linguistic-cultural approach to defining the concept – S. Vorkachov, V. Karasik, G. Slyshkin, Yu. Stepanov; in semiotics – Yu. Lotman, U. Eco; in cognitive science – L. Belekhova, O. Vorobyova, S. Zhabotynska, Yu. Karaulov, V. Nikonova, I. Tarasova; in literary studies – T. Denisova, Ya. Zasursky, M. Mendelson, R. Orlova.

The goal and tasks of the study determine the choice of **research methods.** The proposed methodology is based on *a comparative-translation analysis* – for studying the original texts and their translations with the interpretation of the linguistic representations of the concept sphere of the American South; *a contrastive-translation analysis* – for identifying linguistic and conceptual asymmetry in the original and translated texts; *the transformational method* – for elucidating translation transformations that enable adequate reproduction of the literary text; *the method of translation adequacy evaluation* – for defining the criteria of adequate translation, which include ensuring the pragmatic goals of the translation act; *the method of translation quality assessment* – for identifying, describing, and characterizing translation errors and achievements; *the contextual-interpretive method* – for establishing the status of the text in the sociocultural context and immersing in the cultural universe of the respective reality; *the continuous sampling method* – for forming the research corpus; *elements of conceptual analysis* – for modeling and describing concepts to delve into the deep semantics of the work for its adequate translation. Additionally, *the field struc-*

turing method was employed – for systematizing linguistic means in terms of their proximity/distance; *the componential analysis method* – for determining the conceptual features of ethnoculturally marked concepts in both languages; *the distributional analysis method* – for identifying the linguistic environment of concept names in context. *The quantitative calculation method* was also applied to determine the frequency of various translation strategies and tactics.

The theoretical significance of the monograph results is associated with the expansion of the theoretical and methodological foundations for studying the national specificity of the concept sphere of different cultures in the translation aspect, as well as the improvement and specification of the conceptual apparatus of the theory of literary translation, mainly through the study of the world picture, concept sphere, and ethnocultural concepts as categories of translation studies.

The practical significance of the monograph lies in the fact that the materials and results of the study can be used in linguodidactics and the theory and practice of translation for studying pre-translation interpretation (section "Translational Text Analysis"), analyzing and reflecting on the literary text (section "Text Interpretation"), practical application of methods for reproducing the linguistic representations of the concepts of the American South – the semantic foundation of the entire literary work, for creating adequate translations of literary texts.

Dr. Nataliia Holubenko

Chapter 1.
Theoretical and Methodological Fundamentals on Rendering the Linguistic Representations of the Conceptual Sphere of the American South in Literary Translation

This chapter presents the theoretical principles underlying the critical concepts of the monograph research, precisely the relationship between translation studies and cognitive science in contemporary linguistic inquiries; the specifics of literary translation, particularly achieving adequacy in reproduction; identification of linguistic and conceptual factors of asymmetry affecting the quality of literary translation; and the definition of cognitive linguistics concepts within the scope of translation studies, such as linguistic and conceptual worldviews, conceptualization and categorization, conceptual sphere, and concept.

1.1 Translation Studies and Cognitive Science: Areas of Intersection

In the history of translation, literary translation has long held a central position, with critical issues being (and still considered) all problems of language and thought, language and culture, the national and individual conceptual and linguistic worldviews, the creation and perception of text, and issues of creativity and stereotypes in thinking and speech activities. According to the general postmodernist tendencies in translation theory, prerequisites for development in a post-linguistic direction have emerged, with the central operative unit being the concept: L. Alexeyeva, N. Galiyeva, G. Lakoff. With the departure from the denotative function of language (direct reflection of objective reality), doubts arise regarding the adequate translatability of a literary text as a product of individual consciousness representing a worldview shaped by ethnocultural traditions. Hence, a broad spectrum of research on cognitive processes allows for the establishment of the cognitive paradigm in the theory of intercultural communication (V. Karasik [82], O. Kornilov [95], V. Krasnykh [98], Y. Stepanov [168], S. Ter-Minasova [174]) and in one of its varieties – translation. The foundation of the cognitive approach in translation studies lies in interdisciplinary research that examines human thinking, cognitive activity (cognitive psychology, psycholinguistics, cognitive linguistics), and the role of ethnosociocultural factors in individual speech behavior (ethnolinguistics, cultural anthropology). This complex scientific discipline in Western literature is called cognitive studies (cognitive science). In contrast, in domestic tradition, the term "cognitive science" is prevalent, operating with concepts important for contemporary translation studies, particularly such as linguistic and conceptual worldviews (henceforth LWV and CWV), the reproduction of which poses challenges for the translator, as both the internal processes in human consciousness and their realization in language and culture are considered. Therefore, studying such cognitive linguistics concepts as linguistic and conceptual worldviews in the context of literary translation is relevant and essential.

1.1.1 Linguistic and Conceptual Worldviews as Components of National Culture in Translation Studies

Contemporary translation studies view translation not merely as the reproduction of a text in another language but as a complex communicative process and a field of cultural interaction. In culture, meanings are generated and reproduced from one language to another. K. Levi-Strauss sees translation as the translator's analysis of a foreign cultural system [111, p. 80], which requires more work to reproduce in translation adequately. Culture is interpreted not only as an explicit expression in the text but also as a particular mental, worldview, and axiological manifestation of the author or depicted subject, representing a model of interpreting reality. According to D. Tannen, "it is important to consider the interaction of not only multiple languages but also the cultures and conceptual spheres associated with these languages" [248, p. 343]. H. Vermeer asserts that any translation is culturally conditioned and relative [253, p. 9], as an adequate translation must consider the cultural factors of a particular society, complicating the translator's task.

The dialectical interrelation of the three phenomena "(ethno)culture – (ethno)consciousness – language" is defined by the independently existing world surrounding humans, human consciousness representing this world, and language representing the conceptualization of the world by humans, since "language structures are referentially related to the world of consciousness in which the real world – both physical and ideal – is represented" [89, p. 12]. Language, as a reflection of national ways of perceiving reality, is closely linked to memory. Considering that the national element is a collection of collective memory, translation, viewed as a means of describing national cultures, especially literary translation, involves the ability to interpret, filter, and transform information stored in national memory.

N. M. Nesterova notes that the new paradigm has turned reality into a sign system, placing it on par with language, text, and culture [129]. According to Y. M. Lotman, semiotics should form the basis of cultural theory and the methodology of any cultural studies, as culture, in general, can be viewed as a text [115, p. 72]. These considerations have led to understanding culture as a text and the possibility for translation studies to apply linguistic methods to cultural, cognitive, and anthropological research fields.

Creating a literary text is primarily a cognitive process, clearly illustrating the penetration of individual thought into broader spheres of human activity. However, reading and evaluating a literary text is a much more complex inter-cognitive action of revealing its meanings [98]. A literary text is a center for transmitting and storing information, a form of existence of a particular culture, and an embodiment of personal representations. It is primarily a model of the author, indicating the level of their intellectual, moral, and other qualities. In this sense, the text transforms linguistic signs regarding their cognitive and axiological representation. The conceptual approach to objects in the surrounding world allows for identifying figurative nominations that create new representations, characteristics, and features in the description of an object. Therefore, the interest of translation scholars in concepts introduced by cognitive scientists, such as worldview, linguistic, and conceptual worldviews, in the context of adequacy issues, allows for more precise identification of the difficulties that hinder the complete reproduction of the semantic and symbolic components of the author's intent.

The term "worldview", fundamental in modern humanities research, is used by scholars to reflect human existence, interaction with the world, and the essential conditions of existence, and is actively studied and often used by G. Brutyana [25], M. Heidegger [190], Y. Karaulov [83], B. Kedrov [85], O. Kubryakova [103], O. Selivanova [161], and others – representatives of various sciences: philosophy, psychology, cultural studies, epistemology, cognitive science, linguistics.

In modern science, "worldview" denotes a holistic image of the world – a set of value representations that reveal the peculiarities of an individual's worldview. The worldview includes value-oriented knowledge about the world arising in a person due to their entire spiritual activity [199, p. 95]. A vital definition proposed by B. M. Kedrov states that "the human consciousness integrates the results of various experiences, sensations, and logical cognition, generalizing information from different sources, which are organized into a system of views, reflections, and representations about the world. Socially significant representations of reality create the worldview in individual consciousness" [85, p. 17]. Therefore, adequately reproducing representations of a particular society's worldview and the accurate conveyance of its experience and perceptions requires a thorough study of the history and culture of this society.

Since each individual's worldview is formed during socialization, it inevitably bears a national cultural imprint. In this regard, global science has recently recognized the relevance of studying the national-cultural specificity of the worldview, aligning well with the general trend of various disciplines, including translation studies, where the study of culture plays a significant role [73, p. 39]. These postulates about the importance of culture's influence on individual consciousness and thinking confirm the necessity of considering cultural factors when translating literary texts.

Analyzing the problems of knowledge representation in human consciousness, a distinction is made between *the conceptual system* as an organized combination of concepts in human consciousness and the mental lexicon as a system of verbalized knowledge (internal lexicon, internal word, linguistic memory, thesaurus) [158, p. 71], which appeal not to the individual consciousness of a specific speaker, but to the general vision of the world by all language speakers. Important observations by G. A. Brutyana suggest that the worldview in our consciousness can be represented in the form of conceptual and linguistic models.

The conceptual worldview is considered a broader concept, forming the basis for the linguistic worldview. The conceptual worldview is associated with knowledge about the world and is identical to the conceptual sphere of an ethnic group. The linguistic worldview, in turn, is created in the nomination process, with its crucial element being the lexical unit. The linguistic image of the world serves as a means of explaining the knowledge that constitutes the conceptual sphere of an ethnic group [72, p. 51]. The concept of the linguistic worldview is one of the most important in linguoculturology. As O. I. Cherednichenko notes, "the peculiarities of linguistic worldviews are revealed not only in the designations of common and different denotations but also in the different metaphorization of words with specific semantics, which can become cultural symbols <...>" [199, p. 5]. The linguistic worldview is a system of images reflected in linguistic semantics that interpret the experience of the people who speak this language. The study of the linguistic worldview has been the focus of many scientific inquiries, including those by I. Golubovska [60], O. Kornilov [95], O. Kubryakova [101], L. Lysychenko [112], O. Selivanova [161], and other scholars.

O. S. Kubryakova asserts that conceptual and linguistic worldviews correlate as a whole to a part [103, p. 107]. The linguistic worldview is part of the conceptual worldview, but it is much narrower since the conceptual worldview involves the individual's cognitive activity [174, p. 47]. Emphasizing the leading role of language in understanding reality, E. Sapir noted that "the real world is to a large extent unconsciously built up on the language habits of the group. We hear, see, and otherwise experience very largely as we do because our community's language habits predispose certain interpretation choices" [163, p. 135]. Defining the linguistic worldview as a materialization of human perception of the world and, simultaneously, a collective and individual formation in human consciousness, necessarily determined by culture, is essential for modern translators striving to reproduce not just ordinary words and expressions but the essence of an individual's consciousness within a particular society, as represented in language.

Due to its epistemological function, language is directly linked to cognitive processes of perception, information processing, and thinking. Therefore, it is reasonable to agree with G. V. Kolshansky, who believes it is linguistically correct to speak not of a linguistic but of a linguistic-cognitive worldview without equating language and thinking but placing cognitive foundations under the linguistic model [91, p. 37]. In general, language and thinking always appear in dialectical unity, each with its characteristics, but in the inseparable connection of a single whole. Form cannot exist without content, and content, in turn, always has a formal expression [29, p. 34]. Language reflects the features of non-linguistic activity relevant to the speakers of a particular language and culture. Mastering a language, especially the meanings of words, a speaker begins to perceive the world through the lens of their language and with the conceptualization of the world characteristic of the corresponding culture. Therefore, when considering the literature of the American South in the context of translation studies, it is essential first to research and study the conceptual and linguistic worldviews that reflect the central traditional, stereotypical, and cultural representations of the inhabitants of this region.

For practicing translators, it is crucial to know that the linguistic worldview develops through identifying and naming new phenomena and deepening knowledge about the properties of already known phenomena and concepts. In this case, synonyms arise in the language, fixing the refined meaning. The emergence of new words and meanings does not exhaust the language's possibilities. In the linguistic worldview, semantic transformations of linguistic units and the differentiation of meanings in polysemantic lexemes, synonymic differentiation, and synonymic convergence in the structure of synonymic series, desemitization of linguistic units occupy an essential place [135, p. 190]. The richness of a language is determined not only by the richness of its vocabulary and grammatical constructions but also by the richness of the conceptual world, the conceptual sphere of a particular nation. The conceptual sphere in which any national language exists is a dynamic formation that is constantly changing and enriching. Thus, language is a specific concentration of the nation's culture and its embodiment in various social strata and individuals [113, p. 286]. Based on such postulates, the linguistic worldview is a verbal reflection of the conceptual one. Moreover, since the conceptual worldview (and consequently, the linguistic one) constantly evolves, translators must study specific linguistic and conceptual elements synchronically and diachronically.

Translation practice proves that despite numerous differences between languages and cultures, it is still possible to adequately convey the ethnocultural information encoded by the author in the source text. As noted by I. S. Shevchenko, "the translator's activity involves paraphrasing, reinterpreting the lacunar places of the original, applying techniques that allow compensating for, supplementing, or annulling the lacunar fragments in the translated communication through various signs" [203, p. 7].

Thus, in scientific literature, the linguistic worldview is understood as the nature of reflecting the conceptual worldview in language. The linguistic worldview is a global image of the world, a reflection of human consciousness created due to diverse experiences and the spiritual activity of an individual and a nation. This interpretation of facts is a progressive step in the development of translation studies, as it signifies a rejection of the naive notion of different languages as identical ways of expressing the same thought yet does not dismiss the possibility of translation. Therefore, for an adequate translation of a literary text, it is necessary to possess a specific cultural fund since the author builds communication with the reader based on knowledge of the artistic, aesthetic, and ideological characteristics of a particular ethnic group.

1.1.2 Conceptualization of the Worldview in the Consciousness of the Individual in the Translation Process

As a type of translational activity, literary translation expresses spiritual culture and should be regarded as an essential functional component of its complex system. Its primary role lies in identifying multifaceted connections and relationships with the individual's surrounding environment. It should be noted that translation is maximally "factual", yet its essence lies in "relations": balancing between similarities and differences of languages and cultures, it becomes a "third side" that acquires traits of both linguistic and mental structures, harmonizing them [1, p. 92]. Thus, the primary task of the translator is to identify and correctly understand the author's cognitive space, that is, the set of the author's knowledge and perceptions of the world, reflected at the mental level of the semantics of linguistic units.

N. M. Lyubimov rightly observed that a person's knowledge is unified into a whole, creating cognitive units. As a result, perceiving the world reflects information received through sensory channels on relevant schemas stored in memory [118, p. 142]. Reality is reflected in human consciousness, forming a conceptual worldview. As a subject of cognition and a linguistic personality, an individual adapts their internal conceptual system to the real world by dividing it into separate fragments and encoding them through language. Thus, the conceptual worldview is reflected in the linguistic worldview. The linguistic worldview is not a mirror reflection or a photograph but the result of a complex and multifaceted interpretation of its fragments and elements [26, p. 62; 29, p. 40; 175, p. 81]. Therefore, the translator must adapt their internal conceptual system to the culture from which the literary work is translated, accurately reproducing the verbal units of a particular ethnocultural community and the internal system of characters and the author, illuminating their thoughts and images formed in their consciousness. This process in contemporary linguistic science is called "linguistic localization", or the cultural adaptation of a product to the peculiarities of a country, region, or group of people. Z. Bauman [13], R. Robertson [243], Y. Roshchupkina [152], and others have studied this phenomenon. Adaptation involves a thorough study of both the source and target cultures to create the most accurate and communicatively equivalent text.

In general, one of the central problems of localization and translation is the issue of equivalence. Identifying the nature and conditions of equivalence has been one of the main tasks throughout the development of linguistic translation theory. A distinctive feature of translation, setting it apart from other forms of intercultural communication, is creating a text that will replace (represent or substitute) the original in the corresponding linguistic and cultural environment [201, p. 75]. This definition reflects the essence of translation and localization, characterizing translation as a process crossing both linguistic and cultural boundaries, encompassing both linguistic and extralinguistic aspects. Hence, translation today is not limited to resolving narrow linguistic tasks but is characterized by interdisciplinarity, grounded in the achievements of linguoculturology and cognitive science, where the translation process cannot be seen purely as a linguistic operation.

In localization, two types of equivalence are realized. The first type is translational equivalence, concerning the selection of functional equivalents in the target language. The other type of equivalence is related to the internationalization process. It involves preparing the source text for translation by generalizing the content to explain meanings at various levels – from individual terms to syntactic constructions [210, p. 49]. Thus, at the level of the source text, conditions are theoretically created that enable the establishment of equivalence between the elements of the original and the translation before work begins, regardless of the target language.

For the linguistic theory of localization, the pragmatic dimension of "receptor orientation" is critical, introduced in the concept of dynamic equivalence by E. Nida and C. Taber [239]. This dimension contrasts "dynamic equivalence" in translation with the idea of "formal correspondence", where the forms of the source text are mechanically reproduced in the target language, often distorting the message and leading to incorrect perception. Thus, one of the main factors in localizing linguistic representations of a concept is the alignment and total reproduction of the secondary communicative situation according to the primary one, ensuring that all text elements are harmonized in form and content not only about the original but also to each other and the context.

Knowledge in human consciousness is organized through the crucial cognitive process of conceptualization. Conceptualization in cognitive linguistics is "conceptual classification, which involves understanding certain information based on identifying semantic components in human consciousness, leading to the formation of concepts, conceptual structures, and the entire conceptual system" [135, p. 81]. After reading the original work, the translator's consciousness gradually conceptualizes new representations, images, and knowledge. The translators become characters in the literary work and members of the same linguocultural community. Only after conceptualization and categorization, one of the main ways of organizing knowledge reflected in linguistic categorization, can the translator reproduce the organization of the individual's thinking and linguistic expression since linguistic categories also undergo reinterpretation and, from a cognitive perspective, reflect the human experience.

R. I. Pavilonis, studying conceptualization, found that the results of cognitive activity can be associated with forming a system of meanings, or concepts, concerning information about the actual or possible arrangement of objects in the individual's consciousness [134, p. 102]. Researching the idea as an object of cognitive linguistics, linguoculturology, and a translational unit involves analysis at both semantic and cognitive levels. However, while the semantic level of researching the meanings and content of linguistic units is limited to their structural characteristics, the cognitive level implies going beyond linguistic meaning to analyze the relationship between linguistic meaning and conceptual content conveyed by individual words within the language and speech system [21, p. 13]. Studying language at the cognitive level is linked to examining human mental and cognitive processes.

One can agree with O. L. Bessonova, who notes that "the cognitive approach assumes that the meaning of a word includes not only the features sufficient for word identification but also the entire complex of knowledge and extralinguistic experience of the linguistic community, a combination of linguistic and extralinguistic information" [17, p. 36–37]. More than simply translating linguistic units is required for the reader's adequate perception of the translated text since extralinguistic information, experiences, and knowledge of the people are not conveyed, failing to evoke emotions, experiences, and representations in the reader of the translated text. Therefore, spiritual exchange between different ethnicities enriches humanity's overall achievements. It should be noted that translation continues the existence of the work and culture, serving as a form of their development.

However, more than understanding and perceiving cognitive models and conceptual schemes is required for adequate reproduction and transmission of the required literacies. The issue of ethnolinguistic differences in worldviews, repeatedly addressed in the research by S. Vorkachov [38], O. Selivanova [158], P. Sysoev [166], and others, is caused by the existence of linguistic worldviews with distinctive features for speakers of different languages. Therefore, "the national-linguistic worldview is a certain expression of an ethnic group's perception and understanding of the world, verbalized interpretation by the linguistic community of the surrounding world and themselves in this world" [60, p. 6], reflecting the peculiarities of mentality and culture. Linguistic localization of representations of each specific concept is integral to the theory and practice of literary translation. Adapting and modifying their reproduction to meet national requirements is crucial, preserving the original's communicative effect in the translation. Generalizing similar messages and reducing them to the most acceptable form of expression correlates with the concept of "functional relationships" between linguistic units, described by E. Nida [241]. According to E. Nida, the translation process involves the procedure of "restructuring" and reducing words and phrases to "core" or "near-core" elements, which are "the simplest in terms of structure and most evident in terms of semantics" [241, p. 159]. To adequately reproduce a literary text, the linguistic representations of ethnoculturally marked concepts should be divided into core and peripheral elements. This division helps penetrate the deep structure of the scholarly work and the culture of the corresponding ethnic group.

Literary translators must understand that the carriers of concepts, representing knowledge about the world depending on their language, unite into ethnic groups. This happens thanks to cultural models denoting society's conditional cognitive resources [169]. Concepts at the ethnic group level do not retain all the variations of an individual's concept, leaving the most general representations of the phenomenon's essence. Simultaneously, such a concept has pronounced national character and mentality traits and, despite being formed by individuals, also shapes the person's conceptual worldview [33, p. 20], whose correct understanding and interpretation enable the adequacy of literary translation.

Thus, literary translation is a tool for cultural assimilation of the world, expanding humanity's collective memory and a factor in the culture itself. Therefore, the cognitive approach to language analysis involves identifying, explaining, and predicting categorization and conceptualization processes reflected in language and reconstructed as a conceptual system. These are essential factors for adequately translating literary works while preserving the text's style and intention.

1.2 The Concept in the Contemporary Paradigm of Translation Studies

The shift in translation's status as a research object at the turn of the 20th and 21st centuries has transformed translation studies from a linguistic discipline into an interdisciplinary one. As N. M. Nesterova notes, it is now difficult to name a science that remains "indifferent" to translation and does not find its "point of intersection" within it [128].

Over the past few decades, translation theory has developed in a direction encompassing a broader range of aspects than merely linguistic problems and formal relations between source and translated texts. It actively integrates the latest achievements in text linguistics and discourse analysis and pays special attention to cultural and ethical issues. The perception of translation has long since ceased to be associated with "replacing" one language with another at the sentence level. The development of translation studies fields such as descriptive analysis and multi-system theory proposed in the works of G. Vermeer [253], I. Even-Zohar [215–216], J. Lambert [231], and "Skopos theory" as presented by K. Reiss and H. Toury [251], among others, have highlighted issues of interpersonal dynamics, social relations, and interlingual interaction, and directed attention to various cultural specifics. I. Even-Zohar notes that "translation is no longer a phenomenon whose nature and borders are given once and for all, but becomes an activity dependent on the relations within a specific cultural system" [215, p. 51]. Translation is recognized as a complex, multifaceted, and multi-component type of activity that involves not only interlingual but also intercultural mediation.

In this context, a systematic approach to linguocultural research, particularly in translation studies, which is crucial for our work, can be adopted based on the view of S. G. Vorkachov using two phenomena – the (national) linguistic personality and the (linguocultural) concept, as they reflect "the mentality and mindset of the generalized speaker of a natural language" [38].

In many studies on intercultural communication issues, the unit of knowledge is considered a concept whose definition is notably variable. In recent years, the field of cultural concept research has been intensively developing: M. Alefirenko [4], S. Vorkachov [36; 37; 38], V. Karasik [82], L. Kovalova [87], G. Slyshkin [167], Y. Stepanov [168], I. Sternin [171], and others. Cultural concepts are "symbolically charged signs of a particular culture". M. F. Alefirenko states that a cultural concept constitutes a synergistic subcategory formed by different semiotic systems – language and culture [4, p. 11]. G. G. Slyshkin notes that the theory of cultural concepts provides excellent opportunities for understanding the communication process as an appeal to various concepts [167, p. 81]. For translation, the specificity of cultural concepts and conceptual spheres is highly relevant today, as it intersects with one of the most challenging issues in translation – the transmission of culturally specific information from the source text using another language. Given that the conceptual system of each nation is unique, causing significant difficulties for translators in reproducing linguistic representations of cultural concepts integral to literary works, the adequacy of literary translation depends on understanding and interpreting concepts and selecting the most accurate equivalent during translation.

V. N. Komissarov defines *literary translation* as "the translation of literary works, that is, texts whose main function is the artistic and aesthetic impact on the reader" [92, p. 414]. It is important to note that "the function of influence in a literary text is mostly not self-sufficient; it is aimed at forming an emotional and intellectual attitude towards certain phenomena, facts, and events" [156, p. 231]. The significance of literary translation for the culture of people who exchange aesthetic experiences through it is undeniable. As N. L. Galeyeva points out, "without textual activity, <…> linguistic contacts, the exchange of value orientations and norms within a monolingual community, and the achievement of national-cultural specificity of other language collectives are impossible" [43, p. 17]. Literary translation involves, first and foremost, the translator, then numerous readers who, through the translator's activity and their own (reading), analyze, interpret, and immerse themselves in the world of values and national uniqueness of another people, enabling a deeper understanding of their spiritual orientations. This results in mutual cultural enrichment. G. Gachechiladze, emphasizing the need to create a theory of literary translation, notes that "literary translation, as the highest form of translation, can encompass all forms of life, all shades of living activity" [46, p. 50]. Applying this assertion to our material, we see that cultural concepts are reflected in the literary text, and reproducing their linguistic representations requires the translator to apply both classical and contemporary theoretical translation models to achieve overall adequacy in literary translation. These models include the situational-denotative, transformational, semantic, semantic, and semantic-semiotic models, O. Kade's triphase, the interpretive theory of translation, the theory of equivalence levels, and the theory of regular correspondences. Each proposed model is essential for translating specific segments of a literary text. However, in modern translation studies, the most common type of translation process model is the interpretive model, based on the idea that the translation process relies on the mental processes of text interpretation. For example, the model proposed by the English-Arabic translation theorist Omar Sheikh Al-Shabab [207], which is based on the conceptual notions of J. Catford's linguistic translation theory [219]: source language, source text, translator, translation text, target language, target text.

This translation process consists of five stages: editing the source text, interpreting the source text, interpreting in the new language, formulating the translation text, and editing the formulated text.

Translation enriches culture and language with new motifs, images, genres, stylistic techniques, concepts, and shades of meaning; it catalyzes ethnocultural and conceptual influences and revitalizes the internal life of its linguistic environment. Translation is the re-expression of concepts, ideas, beauty, and spirit materialized in language, as the union of the literary work with a mobile extralinguistic context provides the content with ever-new structures and meanings.

1.2.1 The Concept in Cognitive Translation Studies

Translation is the intersection point where practically all problems of language and thought, language and culture, national and individual in conceptual and linguistic worldviews, genre and style issues, text creation and perception, text and intertext issues, and the importance and secondary nature of textual activity and the text itself converge. Additionally, it addresses problems of creativity and stereotypes in thinking and speech activity. This list of issues present in the phenomenon of translation needs to be more comprehensive. An essential problem for translation is the relationship between language and culture, which is closely related to the search for universal and specific elements in the perception of reality by speakers of different linguocultural traditions. Studying languages and cultures allows revealing their peculiarities, as "comparing one's native language and 'own' culture with another language and 'foreign' culture helps to highlight their dissimilarity with 'one's own' culture, offering a new understanding of the surrounding world, eliminating the illusion of a single possible worldview, and enriching and expanding one's worldview and perception" [62, p. 10]. As L. V. Kovalova notes, "the concept becomes verbalized and becomes part of the semantic space of the language, using the system of linguistic signs. Language can represent all the information acquired by a person and the accumulated experience of society" [87, p. 55]. Therefore, in the theory and practice of translation, there is a notion of the "cognitive function of translation", which is closely related to its communicative function, as the purpose of this type of communication is to transmit information and thereby enrich and expand the background knowledge of the recipient. Ethnospecific fragments of the conceptual worldview, reflecting a nation's mental and cultural uniqueness, become accessible to speakers of other languages through translations.

The views of cognitive linguistics representatives R. Langacker and G. Lakoff have significantly influenced the development of the mental aspect of the intercultural communication theory. To understand the cognitive processes occurring in human consciousness during interaction with the surrounding world, G. Lakoff proposed the concept of idealized cognitive models – mental structures through which we organize our knowledge about the world.

In the early 21st century, a cognitive direction in translation emerged, known as "Cognitive Translation Studies" (Cognitive Translatology): works by S. Halverson [218], D. Kiraly [227], V. Komissarov [92], M. Munoz [235], V. Khairullin [191], M. Tsvilling [196]. The prevailing idea is that the translation process at all stages is heuristic and intuitive, involving the sequential selection of different possibilities. However, heuristic operations to choose a translation invariant are based on complex cognitive processes. The translator's intuition relies on their professional knowledge, skills, and abilities and can suggest quick, unexpected, and successful solutions to complex translation problems. Intuitiveness in translation is only one aspect of the translator's professional competence. Thus, the translation process combines logical, algorithmic operations and intuitive-heuristic actions, meaning that unpredictable insights, guesses, and associations observed during translation are based on the translator's cognitive experience thesaurus.

An exciting aspect of studying the cognitive element of translation is the organization and functioning of knowledge during translation. As practice shows, the success of intercultural communication largely depends on the presence of specific shared knowledge among communicants belonging to different linguo-cultural communities. Investigating the nature of cultural and cognitive factors in translation, V. I. Khairullin concludes that "utterances in translation are structured based on certain cognitive schemes" [191, p. 9]. The author believes that for solving translation tasks, it is essential to structure knowledge reflecting the relationships between primary cognitive categories: material object (animate and inanimate), space, time, and action.

Before translating a literary text, the translator must study the cultural concepts of the society in which the text was created, determine how they are reflected in the text's fabric, and outline strategies for reproducing the linguistic representations of these concepts in translation. Accordingly, analyzing the idea allows for identifying the peculiarities of the linguistic worldview, embodying the human perception of real-world phenomena, and forming the foundation of the general spiritual worldview.

The convergence of conceptual and linguistic worldviews through disseminating shared knowledge via translations leads to the constant renewal of nominative resources. Despite discrepancies in the verbalization of concepts, their quantity significantly exceeds the number of ethnospecific concepts, creating conditions for achieving semantic equivalence in translation [199, p. 64]. The contradictions related to the perception of primary information can be resolved through the translator's interpretive activity.

The ethnocultural marking of the conceptual sphere is confirmed in studies by S. G. Vorkachov, who proposes understanding the concept as a unit of collective knowledge that directs towards the highest spiritual values, has a linguistic expression, and is connected with ethnocultural specificity [36, p. 47]. Ethnocultural concepts repeatedly observed in the works of M. Alefirenko [4] and I. Serebryanska [165] reflect ethnic worldview and mark the linguistic worldview, defined as a verbally expressed content unit of consciousness enriched with cultural meanings and individual associations, reflecting the main stages of the development of a particular language and culture.

The problem of individual-author interpretation of the world in concepts is fascinating and under-researched. "On the one hand, the writer is a representative of a certain ethnic group with characteristic spirituality, and on the other hand, the clearly expressed creative potential of a talented author manifests itself in their specific worldview and, consequently, in the verbalization of concepts" [113, p. 283]. It is generally recognized that the national-cultural specificity of the meanings of different types of words is due to their unique status and national originality, influenced by individual-author perception and the peculiarities of the dentate itself, which belongs to the-unique phenomena and therefore evokes high emotional tension and a range of positive emotions. Thus, the monograph research focuses on the linguistic representations of ethnoculturally marked concepts of the American South, i.e., those that are colored and marked by the corresponding ethnocultural context and are not identical to ethnocultural concepts.

Ethnoculturally marked concepts combine people's personal, historical-cultural, social, and traditional values. They are determined by ethnocultural content and denote phenomena with a specific linguistic code of the ethnic group and society.

For accurately reproducing the linguistic representations of ethnoculturally marked concepts of a particular nation in another language, it is necessary first to examine their model and structure, after which they can be interpreted. S. G. Vorkachov distinguishes two complementary models describing the relationship between "concept vs. its linguistic representation" – archetypal and invariant [38]. In the archetypal model, the concept is considered as something generalized but sensually imaginary, hidden in the depths of consciousness, embodied in a reduced form in the concept represented in the word's meaning. In the invariant model, the concept is presented as the boundary of generalizing the content plan of linguistic units representing a particular semantic field [38]. The concept here is perceived not as innate but as formed by the subject's mastery of language and extralinguistic reality.

The stylistic significance of concepts is still exhausted by the diversity of feelings in the reader, reactions, and human emotions. The idea attracts the writer with its vast possibilities for interpretation and the variety of traditional and new means of semantic filling. The writer forms expressive semantic associations through the metaphorical expression of thought, as in creating a true masterpiece, the artist is simultaneously a philosopher, and thought is equated with the image. However, not all linguistic representations of concepts are fully reproduced in translations.

The concept's organization is crucial from a translation perspective: the idea consists of a core, a basic layer, and a periphery. "The concept's core is a certain image surrounded by a basic cognitive layer reflecting the object's features. The periphery consists of weakly structured conceptual layers that reflect the interpretation of some features and their combinations in the form of statements and consciousness guidelines derived in a particular culture from the mentality of different peoples. This layer is called the 'interpretative field of the concept', containing conclusions from the concept of various groups of people. The interpretative field of the concept is weakly structured but extremely important for understanding national mentality, and therefore should be reproduced in translation" [205, p. 23].

Ethnoculturally marked concepts of each nation and linguistic community are distinct and unique, complicating the problem of reproducing their linguistic representations in translations. The closer the cultural areas of the communicative act participants (the process of perceiving and understanding the literary text by the reader) are, the less significant the differences in their linguistic worldviews are. Conversely, representatives of significantly distant cultures will have more significant discrepancies, complicating the translator's task.

A concept is a multidimensional semantic formation with figurative, conceptual, and value components [82, p. 127]. The symbolic element in the idea includes visual, auditory, tactile, and taste characteristics of objects, phenomena, and events reflected in our memory, as well as relevant features of practical knowledge. The conceptual component represents the linguistic fixation of the concept, its designation, description, feature structure, definition, and comparative characteristics of a particular concept concerning a series of concepts. The value component is inherent in any mental formation, linking human spiritual life with the phenomenon of culture. The main feature of the lexical expression of these components is that they are not only thought but also emotionally experienced. In translation, all concept components – figurative, conceptual, and value – must be reproduced as fully as possible, as the worldview is created from a combination of figurative, conceptual, and value dominants. Inaccurate reproduction of any component can lead to distortion of the original worldview.

Scientists are working on compiling a complete list of cultural concepts, or, according to V. I. Karasik, the "conceptual apparatus of culture" [82, p. 126]. V. I. Karasik distinguishes units through which the concept expresses a multi-component network of meanings in linguistic consciousness [82, p. 137]. These include lexical, phraseological, and paremiological units, precedent texts, etiquette formulas, and speech-behavioral tactics reflecting recurring fragments of social life, according to Y. M. Vereshchagin and V. G. Kostomarov [6, p. 12]. This is quite important in the context of our research, as the study of the American South SOCIAL STRUCTURE, detailed in the practical sections, reflects the main stereotypical behaviors and perceptions of the residents of the southern United States.

The concept of culture is essential for translation studies because this interdisciplinary field of science is also based on cultural facts. Translation studies border on philology and cultural studies, as translation facilitates linguistic and artistic dialogue. In the process of translation, we deal with texts, so the specificity of culture can manifest in two ways: "culture in language" (a specific linguistic worldview) and "culture described by language" (presentation of cultural artifacts in text content). These two aspects create two levels of translation problems. Transitioning from text to text means transitioning not only from language to language but also from culture to culture, as emphasized by A. Lefevre [233].

Summarizing a brief overview of the concepts underlying the cognitive approach to studying intercultural communication and translation as its variety, we note that the mental approach to studying the space of the translation process contains significant potential for defining the mechanism of achieving and conveying the meaning of a foreign language text during translation. The emergence of many translation studies from the cognitive science perspective indicates the strengthening of the cognitive paradigm's position in translation studies in recent years. Given its interdisciplinarity, the mental approach to studying various types of verbal communication can unite diverse translation studies (linguistic, psycholinguistic, linguocultural, linguosemiotic) into a single independent scientific discipline with a clearly defined object and research subject.

Ultimately, the translator constantly overcomes the contradiction between the individual and the general, trying to recreate the holistic aesthetic impact and preserve all the stylistic features of the original. This interpretation of facts is a progressive step in the development of translation studies, as it signifies the rejection of the naive notion of different languages as identical ways of expressing the same thought yet does not dismiss the possibility of adequate translation. Considering the achievements of these translation approaches allows for identifying specific factors that cause asymmetry in translation, particularly in literary translation.

1.2.2 Linguistic and Conceptual Factors of Asymmetry in Translation

The relationship between the original text and its translation depends on many factors, including the text's genre, the translation's purpose, the translation method, translation tradition, country, era, the author's personality, and the translator's personality. Today, alongside numerous theoretical works on translation that thoroughly investigate the main linguistic factors of discrepancies in translation, such as the works of L. Barkhudarov [12], T. Kazakova [79], V. Komissarov [92], Y. Retsker [149], O. Schweitzer [202], there is a growing number of studies examining the cultural factors of discrepancies in translation. These studies rely on related knowledge from semiotics, cognitivism, pragmatics, and psycholinguistics (works by S. Bassnett [208], A. Lefevere [233], M. Munoz [235], E. Roche [244], S. Savory [246]). O. D. Schweitzer rightly notes that translation's linguistic and extralinguistic determinants form a series of interconnected filter chains (selectors) that influence the final version of the translation [201, p. 125]. The central place among them belongs to the text itself, which appears in two guises – the source text in the primary communicative situation and the translated text in the secondary communicative situation. Therefore, the main factors of asymmetry in translation are the language system, language norm, translation norm, literary tradition, national color, differences in the conceptual spheres of the original and translated cultures, the primary communicative situation, and the secondary communicative situation.

In modern translation studies, primary attention is given to the role of the anthropocentric factor in the creative process of both original and translational works. Researchers in translation increasingly refer to critical concepts of linguoculturology, such as worldview and concepts, which help develop an integrated approach to translating literary works and reduce the gap between theory and practice in translation studies.

Knowledge and understanding of the main factors of asymmetry in translation – both linguistic and conceptual – are practical tools for the translator of literary works. The writer moves from reality and its perception to a word-fixed image. On the other hand, the translator moves from the existing text and the reality recreated by the author's imagination through its secondary perception to a new imaginative embodiment fixed in the translated text. D. S. Likhachev outlined the main difficulties in studying translations: "When studying translations, the possibilities of using content to establish the history of the text are minimal" [113, p. 283]. Although the translator's activity is ontologically secondary, it requires significant creative efforts. Translation is a complex and differentiated phenomenon, the essence of which lies in the comparative reproduction of the main invariant, necessary background information, and stylistic functions of the text through adequately transforming linguistic structures and meanings using another language in the translated text.

In the translation process, two languages and two cultures interact, each having general and national specificity. The presence of a universal human element is because thinking in people who speak different languages remains generally the same. N. G. Valeyeva explains this by humans' physical nature, brain functions, and higher nervous system [28]. Specific external conditions of existence for a particular ethnic group (geographical, physiological-anthropological features, cultural traditions) form certain peculiarities in perceptions that define the basis of the national conceptual and linguistic worldviews [28]. Today, it is undeniable that languages reflect reality differently and asymmetrically. When languages come into contact during translation, and the meaning of one language is defined through the meaning of another while describing any fragment of reality, asymmetry becomes more pronounced. This is not only because certain elements present in one ethnic culture may be absent in another (i.e., lacunarity) but also because the relationships between specific objects present in universal human culture may differ. These objects can evoke different associations, thus relating differently to the people's cultural experience.

L. V. Kushnina addresses the issue of resolving contradictions caused by interlingual asymmetry in translating literary texts in her studies. In her concept, the text is considered a node where languages and cultures intersect as an intertextual dialogue phenomenon, where meanings clash and are actualized. The core of this concept is the understanding of translation as "a system of transposing meanings from one culture's text into another culture's text, governing deep gestalt-synergetic processes aimed at harmonizing texts from different cultures" [106, p. 4]. Thus, in literary translation, it is essential to consider the author's concepts of the original work and accurately reproduce extralinguistic phenomena as components of the overall contextual system of the original.

As previously mentioned, during translation, the interaction of two linguocultural communities reveals both the universal and the specific of each culture as a system. O. V. Orishak emphasizes that "the objective property of translation is only partial transmission of the content of the original message, which is due to the inevitable asymmetry of any pair of language systems that come into contact during translation and the asymmetry of linguistic worldviews" [133, p. 3]. Therefore, the possibility and necessity of analytical and critical comparison of foreign culture with one's own culture are essential conditions for the professional training and activity of the translator. In this process, the primary attention, according to O. V. Orishak, should be paid to two aspects: national and international. "Critical attitudes towards any cultural traditions, positive and negative, are possible only if one is well-versed in universal and generally accepted cultural norms and values" [133, p. 4]. This is particularly relevant to the verbal representation of cultural concepts that belong to the linguistic level of consciousness. In contrast, the images and notions they denote belong to the cognitive level of consciousness.

The incompatibility of linguistic worldviews of representatives from different cultures requires significant efforts from the translator to adapt the author's information in the original text for complete comprehension by the foreign-language recipient. This causes asymmetry during the translation of ethnoculturally marked concepts. O. I. Bykova notes that the degree of adequacy in conveying the connotative content of the translation variant in the translated text is inversely proportional to the ethnocultural markedness of the original text units. A high volume of ethnocultural connotation in the original text units limits the adequacy of content reproduction in the translated text [18, p. 162], as in literary translation, aimed at accurately "reflecting the thoughts and feelings of the author of the prose or poetic original through another language, transforming their images into the material of another language" [93, p. 3], the ideological and imaginative structure of the original may not be fully reproduced if the translator is unaware of the social and cultural environment in which the work was created.

The asymmetry of linguistic worldviews lies in the absence of equivalents and complete correspondences of some nationally marked or ethnoculturally marked concepts in one culture in another culture, or they may only have partial equivalents. On the other hand, both cultures may have corresponding lexemes, but the concepts they denote differ in content. Moreover, the translator must possess intercultural competence, which includes knowledge of culture and cultural universals, the mechanism of reflecting culture in language and speech, adaptation to the phenomena of another culture, an empathetic attitude towards its speakers, and the ability to determine the cultural component of the meaning of realities and behavior patterns.

The degree of preservation of the original text's informativeness depends on the translator's personality, who, being fully aware of the possible semantic incompleteness of text recoding, strives to maximally demonstrate or not demonstrate all the peculiarities of the original [87, p. 85]. The translated work is reborn in another linguistic medium thanks to the translator's abilities and talent.

The literary text should be conveyed in another language "not from sound to sound, not from word to word, not from phrase to phrase, but from the link of the ideological and imaginative structure of the original to the corresponding link of the translation" [93, p. 260]. According to V. V. Koptilov, the translator must go "broad and deep" – attracting new wide layers of readers to the masterpieces of world literature and delving into the poetic spaces of their authors' worlds [93, p. 261]. Translation belongs to the sphere of genetic contacts, as it maintains connections between Ukrainian or any other literature and many world literatures.

It is worth emphasizing that literary translation is, on the one hand, a product of interlibrary communication and, on the other hand, a particular cognitive intermediary between two languages, an essential source of cultural information that largely determines and directs the directions of intercultural communication. Modern scholars say translation is primarily "a process of constant mutual interpretation of signs" [92, p. 78]. In the cognitive dimension, translation is the primary and central aspect of intercultural communication. It plays a vital role in human mental abilities, i.e., those mechanisms that provide an everyday basis linking the cognitive structures of the languages involved in the translation. It activates linguistic influences and interactions that stimulate linguistic shifts, which is especially noticeable in the lexical composition enriched with toponyms and anthroponyms, realia words borrowed from other ethnocultures. Through translation, languages interact, enrich, and change each other. Numerous studies, including works by D. Gudkov [61], A. Pym [242], S. Ter-Minasova [174], N. Fenenko [181], dedicated to intercultural communication and translation, are noted for their clear orientation towards communicative strategies. This approach reveals that several patterns influencing the creation of an adequate communicative situation in the translation field primarily depend on the specificity of the reproduced text.

However, the most significant difficulties in translation arise not only from differences in the content of the consciousness images of individuals belonging to different linguocultural communities but also from substantial discrepancies in the ethnic consciousness of communicants. As N. V. Ufimtseva notes, the system and composition of the core of linguistic consciousness reflect the system and composition of ethnic constants present in the collective unconscious [179, p. 217]. It is understood that communication between representatives of different linguocultural communities [61, p. 117] is possible with a standard sociocultural code.

American researcher of translation issues S. Bassnett emphasizes the importance of a dual statement according to which translation presupposes the correctness of the assertion that language is "the core of culture", i.e., linguistic categories of meanings being transformed are only part of the translation process; "a whole set of extralinguistic criteria must also be considered" [208, p. 92]. At the same time, the researcher notes that "attempting to fit the value system of the source text culture within the bounds of the translation text culture is a dangerous endeavor" [208, p. 98]. However, it can be done if linguistic and conceptual asymmetry factors are considered when translating literary texts. Such a result reflects the conscientiousness and erudition of the translator.

Therefore, the idea of asymmetry of concepts underlying linguistic forms, as the primary cognitive categories reflecting the cultural experience of a particular ethnic group, holds undeniable interest for modern translation theory. In translation, there is a collision between the general categorical and the nationally specific. During professional activity, the translator, based on their individual and acquired interpretative abilities, strives to adequately translate one of the most challenging texts – literary. The idea of asymmetry of concepts in translation is especially relevant to this study.

1.2.3 The Problem of Translatability of Linguistic Representations of Ethnoculturally Marked Concepts

The principle of translatability is fundamental to the translator's professional worldview and is a significant focus in the development of modern translation studies. Dante Alighieri wrote about the impossibility of reproducing the music of poetry in another language, and Miguel de Cervantes compared translation to the reverse side of a tapestry. Since then, doubts about the possibility of full-fledged translation have persisted, although the search for ways to achieve adequate reproduction has continued. Thus, on the one hand, "translatability" refers to the fundamental possibility of translating from one language to another. On the other hand, it concerns the ability to select an equivalent for a specific linguistic unit of the source text in the target language. Solving the problem of translatability in translation theory depends on how the relationship between linguistic and extralinguistic aspects of translation is interpreted, what requirements are set for translation, and what normative criteria are used for its evaluation.

A unique worldview, thinking, behavior, and a stable system of spiritual values characterize an ethnocultural community. Ethnic consciousness implies the identification of the individual with this community's historical past; in the development process of national spirituality, constants are produced and verbally embodied in literary works. Therefore, an objective condition for adequately translating a literary text is the reproduction of linguistic representations of ethnoculturally marked concepts.

It is essential to assert that each concept contains the imprint of the ecosystem within which it was formed. Equally significant is the issue of reproducing the amount of information embedded in a specific idea of the source culture during translation. If we define culture as "the history of man's awareness of his place in the world" [155, p. 3], it can be concluded that culture is reflected in concepts through language. Thus, language expresses the sensory, implicit level of world perception. The conceptual (or symbolic) function of language allows the speaker to "embody their perception of phenomena of real reality in language" [194, p. 129], so the translated work, like the original text, should affect the mind and feelings of readers.

An ethnoculturally marked concept reflects a country's history, experience, and culture or a specific region. Its linguistic representations should maximally reflect the internal state, thoughts, and images that arise in the consciousness and associations of the region's inhabitants. Therefore, increasing attention is being paid to the adequacy of translation, which expresses the same communicative attitudes and intentions as the source text.

Within the general communication theory, there is a notion of functional-communicative adequacy in translation. This entails reproducing the dominant function of the text based on the sender's communicative intention, aiming to ensure the communicative effect on the recipient. An adequate translation can be considered one that reproduces the functional dominance of the source message according to the communicative intention of the original text sender [156].

L. K. Latyshev believes that the source and translated texts should evoke the same reactions in their respective audiences [109, p. 126]. Only by analyzing linguistic material and the extralinguistic conditions of text creation can the translator understand the author's communicative intention and subsequently create a translated text that considers this intention. Specific cognitive structures reflect the environment, spiritual life, and people's behavior in the individual's consciousness, which are then realized and restructured in linguistic categories and forms.

The adequacy of literary translation is thus determined not only by knowledge of the "foreign" culture's algorithms but also by the collision of the author's and translators' worldviews or mental planes, that is, their individual-personal perceptions of objective and subjective reality [184, p. 146]. Therefore, translation activity is defined by two semiotic worldviews: national (ethnic) and individual.

Recently, translation studies have emphasized the activity-based approach to the translation process, which differs from the traditional substitution-transformational ontology of translation regarding the actor and activity. In the substitution-transformational ontology, activity is reduced to optimizing the system of transformations and substitutions. In contrast, in the cognitive-activity ontology, translation is not limited to manipulating different linguistic means but is an activity according to the original's program [42, p. 18]. Thus, the scientific focus shifts from seeking necessary substitutes and transforms to studying the author's original program, determining the translator's subsequent activity with the source text, and creating a translated text as close as possible in form and content to the original.

Within the activity ontology developed by N. L. Galeyeva, translating a literary text involves "culturally appropriate material transformation", that is, the multi-step transformation of the original material from condensed cognitive activity into a non-material form – understanding, then the transition of the understood ideal into new materiality in the form of the translated text [42, p. 14]. In other words, the cognitive-activity direction, unlike the traditional one, which studies translation as a process of achieving linguistic and informational equivalence, examines it as a type of human cognitive activity aimed at understanding and transforming the result of understanding the source individual knowledge into the translated text.

However, there is no doubt that all practical achievements made within the framework of traditional linguistically oriented ontology should be applied in the translation process. The cognitive-activity ontology of translation does not contradict previous theories but complements and develops the ideas of past scholars. Thus, being modern, cognitive, and anthropocentrically oriented, the cognitive-activity theory does not reject the postulates of V. Komissarov or Y. Retsker but approaches the problem from a different perspective at a different conceptual level.

The application of these achievements shows that the new paradigm retains some terms widely used in the past. These are, of course, the basic concepts of traditional translation theory – equivalence and adequacy.

Proponents of traditional theory consider adequacy one of the primary outcomes of the translation process. Y. I. Retsker defines an adequate translation as the unity of form and content on a new linguistic basis [149, p. 64]. A satisfactory translation often involves deviations from formal equivalence and adaptive strategies.

The adequacy of translating literary texts within the cognitive-activity theory lies in the translator not altering the original content but creating conditions for the recipient of the translation to perceive the same content information as the original recipient [43, p. 14]. Moreover, it is necessary to convey the content and the understanding of the ideological and aesthetic features inherent in the primary culture.

The term "adequacy" in most of its definitions has an evaluative, even normative, character. Yet, its usage is debated since it is sometimes used synonymously with "equivalence" and sometimes in contrast to it. It is worth noting that when these two terms are used together, adequacy generally refers to a more accessible, less absolute correlation of the original and translated texts than equivalence. The term adequacy belongs, in particular, to the "skopos" theory by K. Reiss and H. Vermeer, who denoted it as the relationship between the original text and the translated text concerning the purpose of the message, reproduced in the translation process [162, p. 145]. O. D. Schweitzer, adhering to the traditional view that equivalence is an absolute criterion, defines adequacy through the translator's reaction to the communicative situation. As the researcher notes, one of the main criteria of adequacy is that any deviation from equivalence must be motivated by an objective need, not the translator's whim [202, p. 96]. Adequacy stems from the assumption that the decision made by the translator is often a compromise, that translation requires sacrifices, and that certain losses are necessary to convey the main aspects of the source text.

G. I. Bogin notes that understanding a text follows a specific scheme *of cognitive activity* [19, p. 4]. Understanding without a scheme, without rational categorization, is either misunderstanding or not understanding at all. This is a process devoid of the normative action feature. The author believes that translation is impossible without proper understanding and interpretation of the text, achieved through the cognitive activity process and the translator's interpretation of the literary text, conditioned by understanding the content, constructed to facilitate the recipient's comprehension of the text as a coherent structure of reality-building means and reflection on one's categorization method.

The correlation of translation with intercultural communication classifies it under the cultural paradigm, oriented towards sociocultural factors determining the possibility of translating original signs into different signs.

The correlation of translation with inter-conceptual communication allows it to be viewed as specific cognitive strategies used by the translator to identify the author's model of the studied phenomenon. The conceptual model of translation, developed by T. O. Fesenko based on literary texts, is founded on the idea of translation as "the verbal projection of the ethnomental experience of one linguocultural community through the integration of the translator's mental planes as a representative of another linguocultural community" [183, p. 45; 184, p. 68]. The conceptual translation model reflects the main trends in modern translation studies, which view translation as a type of cognitive activity. Cognitive translation studies explore translation as an integral interaction process between cognitive, communicative, and semiotic factors.

French linguist S. Savornin, in addition to reproducing the linguistic representations of the basic concepts of the original text in the translation, also emphasizes the role of the translator and their ethics in the translation process: "Thus, the process of translation, being a creative process, besides the close ties between languages and cultures, requires linguistic competence, as it plays the most important role in creating identifiable constructions, also requiring the translator to be aware of the responsibility of this role along with developing and deepening the practice of ethics" [246]. Therefore, the translated text results from re-perception, and the translator acts as a mediator in the dialogue of cultures [144, p. 124]. The translator recreates linguistic representations of the concept from one sociocultural plane to another, relying on their cultural memory, which is inseparable from the cultural memory of their people.

A foreign language is considered the primary tool of intercultural communication [174, p. 23], translation is the channel through which languages and cultures interact [181, p. 199], and the translator is a bicultural mediator who helps fill cognitive and communicative gaps that arise during the overlapping of the sender's and recipient's linguistic worldviews [38]. The discrepancy between the original and the translation arises due to differences between the sender's culture, to which the original belongs, and the recipient's culture, to which the translation is created. Under such conditions, the text emerges as a double parallel perception of one's own and another's system of views on the phenomena of the material world [40, p. 68]. The translator's skill as a linguistic personality lies in how skillfully and accurately they bring two different languages and cultures closer together. Remembering that a concept is verbalized in the text through logical relations is essential. Thus, if the logical relations between the concepts identified by the translator are preserved in the secondary text, it can be considered that the translator understood the overall meaning of the concept.

The concept of functioning in a particular culture's conceptual sphere is determined by its ability to develop its dynamic nature [170, p. 609]. The multifacetedness and multilayeredness of the concept can be explained by its dual nature: firstly, it is diachronically and historically conditioned; secondly, it is synchronically conditioned by the numerous simultaneous representations in different syntagmatic contexts. Moving from one cultural layer to another, cultural archetypes determine the dynamic development of culture itself [40, p. 68]. At the same time, the translator, like the author, is a particular individual with a specific worldview, imagery, and emotionality. Therefore, they must understand the cultural background of the original language and realize their way of conveying the author's communicative intention.

The pragmatic information of a linguistic sign is related to its expressive and illocutionary functions. Precedent properties of the concept include the ability to associate with verbal, symbolic, or life phenomena known to all members of the ethnocultural community [167, p. 64]. Besides, the pragma-stylistic features of lexical-grammatical units are realized exclusively against the background of the synonymous row, that is, based on intra-system relations [38].

The ways to overcome obstacles to translatability and the nature of these obstacles affect the very essence of the concept of translatability and its relation to equivalence and adequacy. Just as complete equivalence, complete translatability is only sometimes achievable. Partial losses to achieve the main pragmatic goal necessitate translation at the level of partial equivalence but with the mandatory condition of adequacy in the translator's decision. It should be noted that the principle of translatability, which allows certain losses, assumes that these losses concern less significant elements of the text and require the preservation of its functional dominants and "rational informational content" [225, p. 26]. This constitutes one of the main principles of translation strategy in general and the reproduction of linguistic representations of ethnoculturally marked concepts in particular.

Each language has many intralingual lacunae, that is, empty, unfilled places in the lexical-phraseological system of the language. If a concept becomes a topic of discussion in society, its communicative relevance is being formed. In this case, the lacuna will inevitably be filled in one way or another. Lexically unexpressed concepts represented by intralingual lacunae exist in national consciousness because they reflect the denotations of national reality [171, p. 11]. I. A. Sternin and G. V. Bykova [171] distinguish between intralingual (mentioned above) and interlingual lacunae. Intralingual lacunae are the absence of a word in the language, revealed by semantically close words within a particular linguistic paradigm. In contrast, interlingual lacunae are the absence of a linguistic unit in one language but its presence in another. Interlingual lacunae are divided into motivated and unmotivated. Motivated ones can be explained by the absence of the corresponding object or phenomenon in national culture (e. g., *борщ* (lit. borscht), *кутя* (lit. kutya), *вишиванка* (lit. vyshyvanka)). In contrast, unmotivated ones cannot be explained by the absence of an object or phenomenon (e. g., *доба*, the evening after work) [171, p. 16].

As S. G. Vorkachov notes, when reproducing a linguistic analog of the corresponding concept in a foreign language, only the latter's "semantic shell" is transmitted, formed by its definitive features that allow distinguishing this concept from adjacent specific formations [37, p. 91]. All ethnocultural information – the totality of particular worldview representations of the linguistic personality – remains within the specific ethnic language.

Despite the presence of conceptual lacunae in both linguocultures and the continuous enrichment of the dictionary with neologisms, such texts can be adequately translated, provided the main functions of the original are preserved in the translation. The hypothesis of translatability implies promoting the processes of active search and the creation of equivalents in the target language for new terms and concepts of the original text. Therefore, to adequately reproduce the linguistic representations of ethnoculturally marked concepts, it is necessary to consider primarily the multi-component nature of the idea and the specificity of conceptualization in a literary work.

1.3 Methodological Principles for Rendering Linguistic Representations of Ethnoculturally Marked Concepts in Literary Translation

Given the monograph's topic, the primary specialized method of our scientific work is the comparative-translational analysis. This method involves analyzing the original texts and their translations and addressing translation studies problems such as general lexicological and grammatical issues with a detailed examination of linguistic questions related to interpreting the linguistic representations of the conceptual sphere of the American South. When reproducing linguistic representations of concepts, the translator must convey them at the same stylistic and pragmatic level, effectively using the target language's resources to achieve the sender's objectives. Neglecting the communicative functions of the text during translation undermines all efforts to adequately reproduce the linguistic representations of the conceptual sphere realized in the original. It destroys the perception of the literary text's integrity.

The comparative-translational analysis of English literary texts and their Ukrainian translations necessitated examining the main lexical, grammatical, and lexico-grammatical translation means – translation transformations. The primary method here is transformational analysis.

Transformation analysis involves identifying and describing the translator's transformations to achieve equivalence between the source and target texts. This method is essential for understanding how translators adapt source text elements to fit the norms and conventions of the target language. Key transformations include lexical shifts, grammatical adjustments, and syntactic changes that preserve the original's meaning and effect in the target language.

The contrastive-translational analysis of the original and translated texts involves examining English and Ukrainian linguistic and speech norms. To adequately reproduce the conceptual information encoded in literary texts, the translator must consider the target language's linguistic factors, which necessitate applying translation transformations when reproducing linguistic representations of concepts. These factors include differences in the target audience's linguistic worldview, usage norms, and cultural stereotypes.

The method of evaluating translation adequacy, whose criteria stem from V. N. Komissarov's approach to adequate translation "as a translation that ensures the pragmatic tasks of the translation act", focuses on determining how well the translation fulfills its intended purpose and meets the communicative needs of the target audience. This method assesses whether the translation maintains the original's pragmatic potential and effectively conveys the intended message.

The translation quality assessment (TQA) method involves describing, highlighting, and characterizing translation errors and considering these errors when determining the translation's degree of correspondence to the original. This method helps identify areas where the translation may have deviated from the original's meaning or failed to maintain its communicative effectiveness, allowing for a more objective evaluation of its quality.

The selection of research methods is determined by the monograph's goals and objectives and the specific nature of its subject matter. An adequate translation must account for the fact that the source language units should be communicatively equivalent to the target language units. The translator's task is to understand and preserve the pragmatic potential of the linguistic representations of concepts in the translation text and reproduce their informational core and peripheral elements within the norms of the target language and speech. This is achievable only by correlating the text's meaning with the speech situation and applying appropriate methods.

1.3.1 Strategies and Tactics for Rendering English Representations of Ethnoculturally Marked Concepts in Literary Translation

A broad range of scholars is interested in the national peculiarities of worldview, mentality, and ethnospecific language communication, which are reflected in the linguistic picture of the world of a particular ethnic community: N. Arutyunova [6], G. Brutyan [25], G. Gachev [45], I. Holubovska [60], O. Zalevska [73], G. Kolshansky [91], O. Kornilov [95], O. Kubryakova [100], S. Ter-Minasova [174]. An ethnoculturally marked concept reflects the history, experience, and culture of a country or a specific region; therefore, its linguistic representations should maximally convey the internal state, thoughts, images, and associations of the region's inhabitants. Consequently, more attention is being given to factors that ensure translation adequacy. However, to accurately reproduce a literary text, the translator must follow a translation strategy, a concept widely understood by scholars as either a general or an idea for translating a specific text.

The problem of defining the term **"translation strategy"** has been studied by both domestic and foreign researchers such as S. Bassnett [208], T. Kazakova [79], V. Komissarov [92], G. Krings [230], and V. Sdobnikov [156]. A critical analysis of the scientific literature shows that different scholars define translation strategies based on various judgments.

For instance, G. Hennig and P. Kusmaul, in their textbook "Translation Strategy", consider strategy from a practical perspective: "To achieve the goal, we need a translation strategy that shows the optimal way to solve translation problems. Like any strategy, a translation strategy should be based on facts. In this respect, it is comparable to a chess player's strategy, where the player in the game's development phase must consider time and the opponent's strategy. The consistency with which the player follows their chosen strategy is reflected in the placement of the chess pieces, which only becomes clear to professionals. Therefore, an amateur or beginner in this field needs expert commentary to recognize the strategy underlying the game" [220, p. 112].

One of the first to conceptualize translation strategy theoretically was G. Krings. He defines translation strategies as "potentially conscious plans of the translator aimed at solving a specific translation problem within a specific translation task" [220, p. 74]. G. Krings distinguishes between two categories of translation activity analysis: micro-strategy – ways to solve a series of translation tasks, and macro-strategy – ways to solve a single task.

V. N. Komissarov, in his work "Modern Translation Studies", defines *strategy* as "a kind of translational thinking that underlies the actions of the translator" [92, p. 356] and identifies three groups of principles for carrying out the translation process, forming the basis of the translation strategy. The principles proposed by the scholar cover the entire range of linguistic and extralinguistic factors: some initial settings, the choice of the general direction of actions that the translator will follow when making specific decisions, and the selection of the nature and sequence of actions during translation.

A translation strategy (especially for literary texts) involves deciding which aspects of the original should primarily be reflected in the translation. Adequately reproducing all aspects of the original is only sometimes possible, leading to certain losses in translation. Therefore, the translator must determine the priority scale in advance and create a hierarchy of values that will highlight the main features of the original.

According to the chosen general translation strategy, the translator then determines the specific ways to implement the communicative intent (O. D. Schweitzer includes translation transformations here, which are components of the translation technology), considering linguistic and extralinguistic determinants of translation [202]. Therefore, translation tactics are steps and methods for implementing the corresponding strategy.

Moreover, when recognizing, evaluating, and reproducing the artistic images of the source text, the translator must interpret them, going beyond the translated text and considering it in the context of the tradition and peculiarities of the source language to restore the concept with all its historical, cultural, and aesthetic significance based on this interpretation.

T. A. Kazakova's theory, which proposes her strategies for solving tasks in literary translation, is also of considerable interest. The author calls them heuristic, contrasting the term "heuristic" with "algorithm", as there is no algorithm in literary translation as a set of rules that allows for mechanically solving any specific task from a class of similar tasks [79, pp. 64–65].

L. K. Latyshev's position is worth noting: "By neutralizing the linguistic and ethnic barrier, translation provides speakers of the source language (SL) and speakers of the target language (TL) with only objectively equal opportunities to perceive and interpret the message in its source and translated versions, including the ability to respond to it similarly; but what the actual reaction (communicative effect) will be depends on the individual and personal qualities of each separate recipient of the original and translation" [109, p. 21].

In literary translation, a strategy aimed at achieving equivalence of impression ("impressive equivalence" by N. A. Fenenko) plays an important role [181]. Implementing this strategy, the translator chooses between conventional, usual unconventional, and occasional linguistic means [181]. Implementing the first means group helps the translator "maintain loyalty to the SL culture and thus make the TL text somewhat exotic for the TL culture bearers". In contrast, the second group "maintains loyalty to the TL culture and thus meets the expectations of TL culture bearers, but at the expense of neglecting the cultural specificity of the SL" [181, p. 56]. Therefore, when reproducing linguistic representations of ethnoculturally marked concepts, the specificity of conceptualization in a literary work must be considered.

The linguistic picture of the world of the American South's linguistic-cultural community is a multidimensional formation that verbalizes the corresponding conceptual sphere containing ethnoculturally marked concepts. These concepts determine the ethnic characteristics and worldview of the mentality shaped by unique historical, social, and cultural conditions. The historical stage of a nation's development, language, and culture is considered exceptional, which means that the reality of its existence is conceptualized. Accordingly, the study of conceptualizing knowledge about the world is based on conceptual analysis – a methodology for modeling knowledge representation structures.

1.3.2 Research Stages and Steps for Rendering English Representations of Ethnoculturally Marked Concepts of the American South into Ukrainian

In the context of this research, the theory of the essence of the concept developed by representatives of the linguistic and cultural direction is found to be relevant for studying the value load of the text, as culturally significant, culturally specific, dominant formations can serve as markers of the text's value. The idea of linguocultural representatives regarding the limited number of concepts is also pertinent. Fundamental concepts can only reflect the evolution of the most essential worldview ideas in human consciousness and the people's spiritual experience. The quantitative composition of these concepts changes over time, possibly due to changes in sociocultural settings, leading to the displacement of some ideas and the actualization of others.

V. I. Karasik, considering concepts from the standpoint of linguoculturology, distinguishes three components: conceptual, imaginative, and value-based. The last of these is dominant because it serves the study of culture based on the value principle. Therefore, studying basic cultural concepts is critical because they correlate the text with reality and organize its value structure.

This means that the methodology for researching the reproduction of ethnocultural concepts of the American South in translation has a comprehensive nature and involves several stages since it is based on a comprehensive comparative and contrastive translation analysis and the model of conceptual analysis of the literary text based on the methodology of V. A. Maslova and L. G. Babenko. The application of the latter will help identify the conceptual space of the text, the basic concepts, and the adequate reproduction of linguistic representations, which enables the correct interpretation of not only the literary text but also the uniqueness, culture, and behavioral codes of the inhabitants of the

American South in the late 19th – early 20th century, or other words, *a cultural-historical analysis:*

Collection of Preliminary Data involves highlighting pretextual presuppositions necessary for forming the conceptual space of the text: the time of its creation, information about the authors, and their style. This step is crucial as the Southern literary school formed during the American Romanticism period. Its specificity was due to a complex of material factors and the mentality they generated: settlement peculiarities, a significant contingent of French-speaking residents, and climatic conditions favoring the cultivation of cotton and tobacco, which were productive only in large areas and required a large workforce. This led to the importation of enslaved people.

In the 19th century, certain stereotypes that contributed to creating the legendary image of the heroic, tragic, and noble South emerged. In this regard, a specific place as a socio-political-geographical entity transforms into a generalized image: 1) racial issues; 2) depiction of tragedy, crime, and violence; 3) detective plots; 4) heightened attention to local color, folklore, nature; 5) symbolism as a dominant means of artistic generalization.

Analysis of the Lexical Composition of the Text aims to identify critical words – representations of the concept. In novels such as Harriet Beecher Stowe's "Uncle Tom's Cabin", Harper Lee's "To Kill a Mockingbird", Margaret Mitchell's "Gone with the Wind", Mark Twain's "The Adventures of Tom Sawyer" and "The Adventures of Huckleberry Finn", Robert Penn Warren's "All the King's Men", and William Faulkner's "The Reivers", frequent lexemes include lady and gentleman, negroes, white trash, Yankee, Civil War.

Identification of Basic Ethnoculturally Marked Concepts of the American South includes SOUTHERN LADY and SOUTHERN GENTLEMAN, WHITE TRASH, BLACKS, SOCIAL STRUCTURE, CIVIL WAR, and SLAVERY according to the frequency of keywords in literary works.

For example, semantically, a *lady* is 1) a woman who is polite and behaves very well; 2) a woman of a good family or superior social position, while a gentleman is 1) a man of a high social class, especially one whose family owns much property; 2) a man who is always polite, has good manners, and treats other people well.

Description of Basic Concepts:
a) Identifying a synonymic series of the keyword of the concept with varying degrees of expressiveness. For example, besides the lexeme *negro*, synonyms with more or less emotional coloring include *nigger, darky, servants, enslaved people, field hands, house negroes, home-coming hands, valet, black wench, wench* (before the Civil War), and *colored people, black, lower class, black fellow, degraded race, house full, black man-of-all-work* (after the war).

Comparing the linguistic units of the original and translated texts allows for emphasizing the differential features of the concept.

b) Identifying conceptual features that form the structure of the American South concepts in English and Ukrainian. For example, the phrase *a cornfield nigger*, used by R. P. Warren with a negative connotation, is translated by V. Mitrofanov into Ukrainian as *перший-ліпший чорношкірий з плантації*, highlighting the positive traits of black people and endowing them with positive attributes.

c) Creating a field model of the concept to identify the core (basic cognitive-propositional structures and central lexical representations), which includes representations of keywords, their synonyms, and the periphery (associative-imaginative representations) in the compared languages. The concept's core is the central, relevant universal feature for different ethnic communities. The periphery includes everything contributed by culture, traditions, folk, and personal experience, representing subjective experience and various pragmatic, connotative (imaginative, evaluative, expressive), and associative characteristics.

Authors employing ***analysis of behavioral codes*** often speak about the ethno-cultural uniqueness of the relevant concepts and their specific place in the concept sphere of the American South culture bearers. For example, *Harriet Beecher Stowe* depicts the courage of the black character Lucy using the metaphorical phrase *with a haughty, negligent air*, which the translator reproduces in the target language through stylistic neutralization – *зневажливо усміхаючись*. This loses the imagery and meaning of the message: *and with a haughty, negligent air, delivered her basket* [BS, p. 560] – *і, зневажливо усміхаючись, поставила свій кошик на ваги* [Kuznetsova, p. 366]. The sentence shows that Lucy's behavior reflects a contemptuous, hateful attitude of blacks towards whites.

At this stage, the search for nationally specific traits of the Southern ethnos is conducted, demonstrating the uniqueness and originality of the linguistic thinking of this linguistic-cultural community, explicitly and implicitly reflecting the specific cognitive experience of the society and its worldview, determined by the historical, political, and cultural characteristics of the region.

Studying the ***mechanism of applying translation strategies*** in the given examples, translators use the strategy of naturalizing meaning (bringing the text closer to the target language) and employ two opposing principles – the law of translation dispersion and the law of translation convergence. For instance: *negro* – *негри / темношкірі / челядники*; *field hands* – *негри / раби на плантаціях*; *white trash* – *біла голота / білі злидарі / білі безземельні / білі голодранці / біле бидло* – <u>translation dispersion</u> (scattering of the original) and *enslaved people/servants* – *челядь*; *white mind / white folks* – *білі люди* – <u>trans-</u>

lation convergence, which creates a kind of hyperonym that accumulates several meanings. It can be concluded that the translator's aim for the maximum possible transmission of the original's linguistic features requires minimizing the action of the translation dispersion law and avoiding the convergence of different concepts in one equivalent. A high coefficient of translation dispersion and translation convergence leads to the loss of the imaginative basis of a foreign subculture, affecting the perception of the cross-cultural reader.

Identifying Dominant Translation Strategies and Tactics in Reproducing Linguistic Representations of Ethnoculturally Marked Concepts of the American South: Determining translation difficulties in reproducing the English representations of the conceptual sphere.

Thus, a conceptual analysis, which is based on a comprehensive contextual, componential, and distributive analysis of original texts, aims to investigate the linguistic and cultural realization of the basic concepts of the unique area of the American South. This, combined with comparative and contrastive translation analysis, allows for a deeper understanding of the value of ethnoculturally marked concepts of the American South. Reproducing their linguistic representations in Ukrainian contributes to the adequate comprehension by cross-cultural readers of literary works, revealing the historically and culturally conditioned peculiarities of the worldview and lifestyle of the inhabitants of the Southern United States.

Conclusions to Chapter 1

A distinct philosophical and cultural approach to literary translation is evident in translation studies at the end of the 20th and the beginning of the 21st century. Adequate translation in the modern era is attainable with the insights of linguocultural studies and cognitive linguistics, with the concept being a central notion. The reproduction of linguistic representations of concepts in literary texts is closely linked with cognitive translation studies and the cognitive-activity theory of translation, a novel approach in the field. Cognitive translation studies encompass a multifaceted examination of linguistic, psycholinguistic, linguocultural, and linguosemiotic perspectives.

During translation from one language to another, the worldviews of the source and target languages overlay. These worldviews simultaneously infiltrate and influence each other. Their interaction results in a translation variant representing the uniqueness of the worldview depicted in the original text and elements characteristic of the translator's native language.

Concepts are components of the conceptual worldview, which reflect the world on a mental level. The linguistic worldview, in turn, is a set of knowledge about the world encoded in vocabulary and phraseology. Different languages reflect particular ways of conceptualizing (perceiving and organizing) the world; thus, each language has specific ethnospecific properties that verbalize distinct cultural features.

When representatives of two different peoples interact, different languages and other cultures collide. This collision reflects the discrepancy between the linguistic and conceptual worldviews of two linguocultural communities, resulting in linguistic and conceptual asymmetry. The cause of this asymmetry lies, on the one hand, in the complete absence of certain nationally specific notions and concepts in one of the cultures. On the other hand, interacting languages may have corresponding lexemes, but the mental concepts they verbalize differ in scope. Linguistic and conceptual asymmetry in translation leads to difficulties reproducing the author's information in the original text for the foreign recipient.

Translation creates necessary prerequisites for studying the linguistic and conceptual worldview of a particular people, as well as those of the author and translator. The interpretative mode of verbal meanings is correlated with the socio- and ethnocultural competence of the bearers of conceptual systems.

The methodology for studying the translation of linguistic representations of ethnoculturally marked concepts involves the unity of general scientific, linguistic, and translation methods. The most effective methods have been continuous sampling, conceptual analysis, comparative-translation analysis, and contrastive-translation analysis.

Combining conceptual analysis with contrastive-translation analysis enables the identification of verbalized concepts in literary works written by Southern American authors of the 19th and 20th centuries. This combination allows for identifying the main features of the Southern American mentality and analyzing the strategies translators use to adequately reproduce the linguistic representations of ethnoculturally marked concepts. Typical and atypical features in the compared languages are identified, and the factors and chosen translation strategies that influence foreign readers' understanding of basic ethnoculturally marked concepts of the American South are traced.

To adequately translate a literary text, a translator must follow a translation strategy, a concept understood broadly by scholars as either the overall concept of translation or the concept of translating a specific text. Translation strategies encompass all linguistic and extralinguistic factors, including initial assumptions, the choice of the general direction of actions the translator will follow when making specific decisions, and the nature and sequence of actions in the translation process.

The translator's inclination towards "exoticization" or, conversely, "naturalization" of the translated text may require the simultaneous application of translation strategies that are dialectically opposed in nature. This includes translation dispersion, which involves scattering the original, and the principle of translation convergence, which creates a hyperonym that accumulates several meanings.

The application of translation strategies and tactics, along with the appropriate research methods, allows for the elucidation of the specifics of verbalizing particular meanings unique to each language. It also helps to identify similar and distinct features in the conceptual systems of the source and target cultures, which are determined through translation transformations.

Chapter 2.
Rendering of English Linguistic Representations of Historical and Social Concepts of the American South into Ukrainian

The culture of each nation forms its conceptual sphere, represented by a national-linguistic worldview. Therefore, when we speak of the conceptual sphere of a people's language, we mean the conceptual sphere of their culture. The worldview of an individual or a nation results from the long historical development of an ethnic group. What is the "American South", the southern states of the USA, as a unique and distinctive society? If it exists, it is verbalized in a certain way. This is particularly relevant for the verbal representation of cultural concepts, which belong to the linguistic level of consciousness, and the images and ideas behind them, which belong to the cognitive level of consciousness. A concept is information in an imagistic form, while the conceptual sphere is a collection of mental images that constitute structured knowledge of people and their informational base.

The cultural and literary boom in the South during the 1920s–1930s was a true revival of the intellectual and spiritual life of the region, which had been devastated by the Civil War in the United States from 1861 to 1865. It established a strong tradition of the "Southern school" in American literature, which was so influential that it elevated regional literature to a level of national and even global significance. The Southern literary tradition, which formed in the 19th century through the works of George Washington Cable and Mark Twain, continued in the 20th century in the works of Southern writers such as Tennessee Williams, Ellen Glasgow, Harper Lee, Margaret Mitchell, William Styron, Robert Penn Warren, William Faulkner, and others.

In the 19th century, certain stereotypes emerged in literature and linguistic consciousness, creating the legendary image of a heroic, tragic, and noble South. These stereotypes are best utilized in Margaret Mitchell's somewhat apologetic novel "Gone with the Wind", which contains the archetypal features of the Southern myth: the noble lady and her devoted gentleman, slaveholders as "fathers of the Negroes", their "loving children" – the Negroes, the arrogant and greedy Yankees, and the brave Southerners who valiantly overcome all adversities.

The Southern tradition has its value foundation. It is based on patriarchal relationships, hierarchy, and slave-owning, where the tragedy of slave life and the lack of homogeneity among the white population were evident. Alongside the aristocratic caste, there existed a stratum of pioneer farmers who worked hard on the land and those contemptuously referred to as "white trash". The patriarchal lifestyle associated with slavery led to the illegitimate but constant intermingling of all races and peoples, creating a unique community in the South that was not present in other American territories. The community, a human collective in contrast to Northern individualism, is the core of the Southern tradition, somewhat mythologized and exaggerated.

The lives and works of writers were closely connected to the South. The decline of the South is seen as punishment for its "sinfulness" for rejecting one of its own – the black person. This is why the South must submit to the North. The victory of the North in the Civil War not only brought the declared emancipation of the Negroes from slavery but also signified the triumph of capitalism over the old patriarchal order of small Southern towns. The North was filled with utopian hopes for bourgeois democracy, which opened unprecedented opportunities for anyone with energy, persistence, and resourcefulness. The "aristocratic" South mourned its past with its established order and old plantation family traditions.

In the literary texts written by Southern authors at the turn of the 19th and 20th centuries, a structured set of basic concepts reflecting the mental space is actualized and mirrored in various signs and forms. These concepts define the national characteristics of mentality, worldview, and character of the inhabitants of the Southern United States, shaped by unique historical, social, and cultural conditions. The national character of Southerners is a unique mindset, psychology, and behavior, a set of social-psychological traits, national-psychological attitudes, and stereotypes that help distinguish representatives of the American South from other communities, particularly the residents of the Northern USA. Therefore, studying primary historical and social concepts – SOCIAL ORDER, CIVIL WAR, and SLAVERY – represents a new step in developing translation studies. This allows for a more objective discussion of various translation strategies and tactics in solving the main task of achieving adequacy in literary translation and provides an objective basis for comparative analysis of translations to understand the ethnospecificity of conceptualization, categorization, and verbalization of reality in the American South.

2.1 Rendering of English Linguistic Representations of the CIVIL WAR Concept of the American South into Ukrainian

By the mid-19th century, tensions between the two regions of the United States, the North and the South, had begun to escalate. The South was interested in developing international trade – selling cotton and food products at high prices to Europe and purchasing imported industrial goods cheaply. The North, on the other hand, was interested in curtailing trade with Europe. This would allow the North to process the South's agricultural raw materials in Northern factories and offer industrial products to the Southern states. The antagonism between the regions lay in the fact that the socioeconomic system of the South was based on slavery, whereas the North relied on free labor. The struggle of the Southern states to maintain slavery led to the Civil War from 1861 to 1865, in which the Republican North emerged victorious.

American criticism highlights one of the critical failures of American literature: the inability, despite numerous efforts, to produce a "great book" based on the pivotal events in the nation's history – the Civil War. However, it is worth mentioning the numerous works in American literature that address the theme of the Civil War, including "Gone with the Wind" by Margaret Mitchell and "All the King's Men" by Robert Penn Warren. Literary interpretations of Civil War events continue to this day. The war initiated a period of intense socialization and the communal sharing of tools, resources, and efforts. Individuals became much more dependent on one another: "In modern societies, war is a unique moment of concentration and intense absorption of all that usually seeks to maintain a certain zone of independence" [84].

Translating texts dealing with the Civil War requires understanding the profound historical, social, and cultural implications embedded in the original language. Translators must convey not only the literal events but also the cultural connotations and the emotional weight carried by terms and phrases specific to this historical period. This involves carefully considering how concepts such as slavery, freedom, and regional identity are represented linguistically in both the source and target languages. Translators must navigate the complex interplay of these factors to produce a translation that resonates with the target audience while preserving the integrity of the original text.

2.1.1 Rendering the Core Components of the Concept of the CIVIL WAR Concept

The primary theme of the novels above is war. Thus, in this context, it is essential to 1) examine the socio-cultural and psychological aspects of the concept of CIVIL WAR, which constitute the core of the analyzed concept; 2) analyze the representation of this concept in the novels; and 3) determine how these aspects are realized in the Ukrainian translation.

Critical linguistic units that present the concept's core include the lexemes *Civil War* and *Yankee*. Therefore, the meaning of the Civil War and other related elements characterizing the concept of CIVIL WAR in the 19th and early 20th centuries should be considered dynamically. At the initial stage of the war between the industrial northern states and the slaveholding southern states of the USA, the concept signifies the confrontation between two systems – slavery and free labor.

From the analyzed material, it is evident that the structure of the concept of CIVIL WAR is formed by such conceptual features that characterize the beginning and progress of the war, such as "ideological opponents", "Yankee treachery", "humiliation of Southerners by Yankees", "Southern patriotism", and "land". The semantic content of the concept at the initial stages of the war (1861–1865) is formed by components that reflect the characteristics of representatives of two ideologically opposing systems, i.e., the feature "ideological opponents" is actualized.

> *It is a long and hard-fought battle* [Mark Twain: HF, p. 22]

> *– запеклий тривалий бій* [Steshenko, p. 17].

The Civil War disrupted American society, sowing seeds of treachery and evil in the hearts of Americans and becoming a cornerstone of the emotional oppression of Southerners, plunging society into a chasm of poverty and suffering. This is seen in Margaret Mitchell's novel "Gone with the Wind". Translator R. Dotsenko conveys this atmosphere in the Ukrainian version of the story:

> *In that section, the Confederate sympathizers were in the minority and the hand of war fell heavily upon them, as it did on all the border states, neighbour informing against neighbour and brother killing brother* [Mitchell, p. 239].

> *– У тих суміжних з Північчю околицях прихильники Конфедерації були в меншості, і важка рука війни далася їм взнаки найдошкульнішим чином, бо сусід доносив на сусіда, а брат убивав брата* [Dotsenko: ZV I, p. 270].

The war caused the decline of the state in all aspects of its organization and had a significant impact on the consciousness and moral state of citizens, which may be implied in the novel but must be adequately reproduced in translation:

> *I **execrate** these **vampires** who are sucking the lifeblood of **the men** who follow Robert Lee – these **men** who are making the very name of blockader a stench in the nostrils of all **patriotic men** [Mitchell, p. 224].*
>
> *– Я шлю прокляття на голови цих упирів, що смокчуть кров **воїнів**, очолюваних Робертом Лі, на цих **недолюдів**, через яких сама згадка про проривників блокади відгонить смородом для кожного **щирого патріота** [Dotsenko: ZV I, p. 253].*

Indeed, when describing the Northern and Southern soldiers, the author uses the repetition of the neutral, stylistically unmarked noun "men", which is translated as "воїни" and "недолюди". M. Mitchell does not separately highlight Southerners and Northerners, as the hateful attitude of the former towards the latter is self-evident. The translator explains the implicit yet understood meanings: "men" – "воїни" when referring to Southerners, and "недолюди" when referring to Northerners. R. Dotsenko "improves" (according to U. Eco) the original, striving to convey explicitly to the target reader what is implied. Such situational enrichment seems acceptable in this case, as it corresponds to that time's historical and social realities.

Southerners "execrate these vampires" – "шлють прокляття на голови цих упирів" (Northern soldiers). In translation, the phrase is rendered with the addition "на голови цих упирів". The expression "make the very name of blockader a stench in the nostrils of all patriotic men" – "згадка про проривників блокади відгонить смородом для кожного щирого патріота" undergoes domestication, as the lexeme "nostrils" is omitted from the phrase "a stench in the nostrils" – "відгонити смородом", since the words "відгонити смородом з ніздрів" does not exist in Ukrainian. The translator amplifies the image of Southerners, who in the original are depicted as "all patriotic men", adding the adjective "щирий" – "кожний щирий патріот" in the translation.

In M. Mitchell's novel, Southern and Northern soldiers are vividly described, presenting a real challenge for the translator to reproduce in Ukrainian adequately:

> *They loved their men, they believed in them, they trusted them to the last breaths of their bodies. How could disaster ever come to women such as they when their **stalwart gray line** stood between them and the Yankees? [Mitchell, p. 88].*
>
> *– Вони любили своїх коханих і кревних, вірили й покладалися на них до останнього подиху. Хіба може щось загрожувати цьому жіноцтву, коли між ними та янкі стоять **незламним муром воїни в сірих уніформах?** [Dotsenko: ZV I, p. 183].*

The translator, reproducing the image of the "stalwart gray line" as "незламний мур воїнів в сірих уніформах", resorts to semantic development and addition, which helps maintain the visual concreteness and necessary connotations. Indeed, not everyone knows that during the Civil War, Southerners wore gray uniforms while Northerners wore blue. Thus, the "gray line", which means "the Confederate army in the Civil War, or a member of that army" [OGBACLE, p. 1087], metonymically indicates, through color designation, the Southern soldiers. Intratextual explanation in translation is necessary.

Color reproduction in translation is a real challenge for the translator; relying on personal interpretation of color is not advisable – one must consider the specificity of color designations in the culture to which the original belongs. Therefore, translating the Confederate uniform "butternut" is difficult, as it can be interpreted in various ways. In one Ukrainian translation, "butternut" (M. Mitchell) is rendered as "жовтувата" (R. Dotsenko) uniform. In the following description, the translator conveys a different shade:

*The army in **butternut** were now **seasoned fighters**, their generals had proven their mettle, and everyone knew that when the campaign reopened in the spring, the Yankees would be crushed for good and all* [Mitchell, p. 238].

*– Недавні новобранці в **сірій формі** перетворились на **загартованих вояків**, генерали засвідчили свою енергію, і всі були певні, що з розгортанням військових дій навесні північан розіб'ють остаточно* [Dotsenko: ZV I, p. 268].

It is incorrect to say that the translation of "butternut" as "сірий" is wrong, as in the previous example, it reproduces a shade rather than a color, as "butternut" means "a North American walnut tree that bears oblong sticky fruits. Its light-colored, soft timber is useful primarily for making furniture and cabinetry" [OGBACLE, p. 784], which translates into Ukrainian as "горіх сірий каліфорнійський". There are shades of gray and yellowish colors. Moreover, in colloquial language, "butternut" is also used to denote "a Confederate soldier or supporter (so called because the fabric of the Confederate uniform was typically homespun and dyed with butternut extract)" [WTNIDELU, p. 978].

Southerners at war became "seasoned fighters," which is rendered in translation as "загартовані вояки".

As in the previous example, the verb used in the form of a participle, employed in describing the actions of the blue ranks: "to strike", used in the sense of "to attack someone, especially suddenly" [OGBACLE, p. 1123], i.e., to attack. The verb is used twice in one sentence: *On came the blue lines, relentlessly, like a monster serpent, coiling, striking venomously, drawing its injured lengths back, but always **striking** again* [Mitchell, p. 281]. *– Сині лави невблаганно насувалися, звиваючись, мов страховинні змії, – вони люто нападали, зазнавши втрат, відступали, але щоразу **атакували** знову* [Dotsenko: ZV I, p. 314–315]. The participle "striking" is translated with two synonymous verbs – "нападати" and "атакувати".

Despite not all Southern soldiers being at the front, they still defended their people – children, women: *Greybeards in the Home Guard and members of the* state militia, **safe** in Atlanta, insisted they could have managed the campaign better and drew maps on tablecloths to prove their contentions [Mitchell, p. 282]. – *Сивобороді діди з внутрішньої гвардії та міліції, сидячи в Атланті, **як у Бога за пазухою**, твердили, що вони провели б цю кампанію набагато успішніше, на доказ чого креслили на скатертинах карти військових дій* [Dotsenko: ZV I, p. 315]. Thus, the meaning of the adjective "safe" in this context – "(of a place) affording security or protection" [DCE, p. 1165] – corresponds to the meaning of the Ukrainian saying "як у Бога за пазухою" – to be in safety.

One of the most relevant features of the concept of CIVIL WAR is the semantic component **Yankee.** It is known that the meaning of the word "Yankee" has changed over time, but the exact origin of the term is still unknown. Some researchers suggest that the word has Native American roots – "Yankee" in the Cherokee language means "coward". By the end of the 18th century, the fixed expression "damned Yankees" had appeared. During and after the Civil War, Confederates referred to their Northern enemies this way. Senator J. William Fulbright from Arkansas wrote in 1966: "The very word 'Yankee' still evokes in Southerners historical memories of defeat and humiliation, of the burning of Atlanta, Sherman's march, and the destruction of the ancestral estate" [200]. Accordingly, for Southern residents of the USA, the word "Yankee" is associated with the feature "Yankee treachery".

R. Dotsenko uses the technique of differentiation, translating the lexeme "rascal" as "ниций", which adequately reflects the somewhat conditional image of a Yankee, as inferred from Scarlett's conversation with Rhett Butler: *"I think you're a mercenary **rascal** – just like the Yankees"* [Mitchell, p. 98]. – *Те, що ви **ниций** користолюбець, не кращий за янкі* [Dotsenko: ZV I, p. 203].

The following passage does not cause translation difficulties, as **"damned Yankees"** has a direct equivalent in Ukrainian – **"кляті янкі"**: *"They aren't anything but **damned Yankees!**"* [Mitchell, p. 640]. – *Вони **кляті янкі**, та й годі!* [Dotsenko: ZV I, p. 181]. To influence the cross-cultural reader, the translator appeals to emotional perception by using expressive and stylistically colored linguistic means in the translated text – the colloquial expression "якого чорта," used to convey great dissatisfaction and irritation: *"**What devils** the Yankees were to set them free, free to jeer at white people!"* [Mitchell, p. 558]. – ***Якого чорта** ці янкі дали їм волю, дали змогу насміхатися над білими!* [Dotsenko: ZV I, p. 83].

R. Dotsenko often resorts to direct translation – "lured by the bounty money" / "спокусившись на щедру платню": *"The North could call on the whole world for supplies and for soldiers, and thousands of Irish and Germans were pouring into the Union Army, **lured by the bounty money** offered by the North"* [Mitchell, p. 75]. – *Північ могла з усього світу діставати техніку й солдатів, тисячі ірландців та німців вливалися в армію північан, **спокусившись на щедру платню…*** [Dotsenko: ZV I, p. 156].

The conceptual feature "humiliation of Southerners by Yankees," represented in literary works, is crucial for revealing the semantic component of Yankee, which characterizes the attitude of Northern residents toward Southerners. The South suffers from Northern intimidation and attempts to resist its system, which in translation is conveyed through direct translation: "whether the South would stand for further insults from the Yankees" / "допоки Південь терпітиме образи янкі", as illustrated in the description: *he supper things cleared away, Gerald resumed his oration, but with little satisfaction to himself and none at all to his audience. His thunderous predictions of immediate war and his rhetorical questions as to **whether the South would stand for further insults from the Yankees**...* [Mitchell, p. 33]. – *Коли прибрали зі столу, Джеральд знов заходився просторікувати, хоч і мав невелику від цього втіху, а його аудиторія – ще меншу. На грізні його передбачення неминучої війни та риторичні запитання, **допоки Південь терпітиме образи янкі**...* [Dotsenko: ZV I, p. 75].

In translation, transformations of meaning differentiation often occur – "grind into the dirt" / "утоптати у багно" – to achieve the most accurate reflection of the worldview. However, the Ukrainian translation of the verb "to trample" – "глумитися" does not reflect the reality of the relations between the North and the South, as "to trample" means "to behave in a way that shows that you do not care about someone's rights and feelings" [DCE, p. 1765], i. e., to treat with contempt and disdain, while the translation "глумитися" means to mock or ridicule someone: *The South was too beautiful a place to be let go without a struggle, too loved **to be trampled** by Yankees who hated Southerners enough to enjoy grinding them into the dirt, too dear a homeland to be turned over to ignorant negroes drunk with whisky and freedom* [Mitchell, p. 617]. – *Південь занадто прекрасний, щоб віддати його без боротьби, занадто люблений, щоб дозволити **глумитися** з нього янкі, ладних утоптати південців у багно, занадто дорогий їм як рідний край, щоб відступити його неукам-неграм, сп'янілим від горілки та волі* [Dotsenko: ZV I, p. 153–154].

The "patriotism of Southerners" (love for the homeland, which implies readiness to defend it and act in its interests) is vividly portrayed in the novel "Gone with the Wind". The Civil War in the USA repeatedly showcases the courage of Southerners, who are not afraid to take up arms and defend their native land. This is observed in the following excerpt from the novel: *"God's nightgown, man! Pray for a peaceable settlement with the Yankees after we've fired on the rascals at Fort Sumter? Peaceable? **The South should show by arms** that she cannot be insulted and that she is not leaving the Union by the Union's kindness but her own strength!"* [Mitchell, p. 55]. – *А хай їм чорт, чоловіче! Напрошуватись на мирне залагодження суперечки з янкі? Після того, як ми витурили цих негідників з Форту Самтер? Мирне залагодження? Ні, **Південь повинен зі зброєю в руках показати**, що не потерпить образ, що ми вийдемо* з *Союзу не з його ласки, а зі своєї власної волі* [Dotsenko: ZV II, p. 115]. The sentence includes the phrase *"the South should show by arms"*, where *"arms"* means *"weapons and ammunition; armaments"* [LDELC, p. 224]. The translator employs semantic development to render this expression – "Південь повинен зі зброєю в руках показати", preserving the connotation of the original message, as "зі зброєю в руках" means "to take personal part in the war" [VTSSUM, p. 627].

"They might be dying in thousands but, like the fruit of the dragon's teeth, thousands of fresh men in grey and butternut with **the Rebel yell** *on their lips would spring up from the earth to take their places"* [Mitchell, p. 242]. – *Вони можуть гинути тисячами, але, мов ті казкові драконові зуби, постануть з-під землі на їхнє місце тисячі нових вояків у сірих та жовтуватих уніформах і* **з войовничим кличем** *на устах ринуть у бій* [Dotsenko: ZV II, p. 273]. Indeed, the patriotism and courage of Southerners are confirmed by the phrase "Rebel yell", which was typical for the soldiers of the Southern states during the Civil War, as it means "a shout or battle cry used by the Confederates during the American Civil War" [NWDTEL, p. 1116]. The Ukrainian equivalent "войовничий клич" is used with equally heroic and patriotic connotations.

In the Ukrainian fragment of the novel "Gone with the Wind", R. Dotsenko omits the adjectives "the pleasantest and the most reassuring things". It refers to the Southerners' belief in the most favorable and desirable military action. In translation, it is simplified to "сприятливий перебіг військових дій": *Scarlett, though filled with the universal Southern desire to believe only* **the pleasantest and the most reassuring things** *about the progress of the fighting, felt cold as she watched the motley ranks go by* [Mitchell, p. 295]. – *Скарлет, попри властиву всім південцям готовність вірити лише в* **сприятливий перебіг військових дій**, *відчувала, як у неї холоне на душі, коли вона дивилась на цю строкату колону* [Dotsenko: ZV II, p. 329].

The repetition of the noun "rejoicing" in the sense of "great joy or delight" is a deliberate technique, as it emphasizes the patriotism and faith of the Southerners who genuinely rejoice in the successful progress of the military actions. The Ukrainian translator avoids repetition, replacing the noun with the verb "радіти": *There was universal* **rejoicing** *in that holiday season,* **rejoicing** *and thankfulness that the tide was turning* [Mitchell, p. 238]. – *На різдвяних святах усі* **раділи**, *серця людей були сповнені вдячності, що військовий талан обернувся лицем до південців* [Dotsenko: ZV II, p. 268]. Such a translation does not convey all the features of the author's style on the one hand, but on the other, it presents a comprehensible picture of the mood and faith of the Southerners to the cross-cultural reader.

The dedication of Southerners to their cause will never allow them to switch sides for material gain, as exemplified by the character Gerald O'Hara in "Gone with the Wind":

"*That was what she was countin' on, that he would take the **Iron-Clad oath** and not even know it*" [Mitchell, p. 666]. – *Якраз на це вона й розраховувала – що він підпише **присягу на вірність Сполученим Штатам**, навіть не тямлячи, що робить* [Dotsenko: ZV II, p. 212]. The historicism "Iron-Clad oath", used to represent the concept, means "a 19th-century warship with armor plating" [OGBACLE, p. 272], which assures the refusal to aid enemies, i. e., it is "an oath of allegiance to the United States." This semantics is represented through descriptive translation into Ukrainian.

To reproduce the courage of Southerners as accurately as possible, R. Dotsenko employs amplification by adding the phrase "привчившись ніколи не втрачати бадьорості". The original mentions that the soldiers "still had the energy" – "у них ще ставало духу": *Johnston's veterans, however, went by with the tireless, careless step which had carried them for three years, and they **still had the energy** to grin and wave at pretty girls and to call rude gibes to men not in uniform* [Mitchell, p. 304]. – *Джонсонові ветерани, на відміну від інших, ішли, не показуючи втоми й виснаження, за три роки війни **привчившись ніколи не втрачати бадьорості**, – **у них ще ставало духу** підморгувати й махати рукою гарненьким дівчатам або підпускати шпильки на адресу чоловіків, які досі були не у військовій формі* [Dotsenko, p. 340].

In the novels, the Civil War has a negative connotation – evil, devastation, fear, and death – and is associated with the symbol of land. The conceptual feature "land", as a fragment of the image of the American South, denotes the native home and territory where plantation slavery thrived. The disruption of such an idyll in the South provokes outrage and dissatisfaction.

M. Mitchell makes the post-war years in the Southern states visible to the cross-cultural reader, vividly depicting every detail of the environment and the actions of military and civilians. This creates a unique picture of that locality, the accurate reproduction of which enables the reader of the translation to perceive it as precisely as possible:

*The city ringed with **red-clay** rifle-pits, the monotonous booming of cannon that never rested, the long lines of ambulances and ox-carts dripping blood down **the dusty streets** toward the hospitals, the overworked burial squads dragging out men when they were hardly cold and dumping them like so many logs in endless rows of shallow ditches* [Mitchell, p. 324].

*– Тільки тридцять днів, протягом яких у місті, оперезаному кільцем **шанців у червоній землі**, безугавно бухали снаряди, нескінченно вервечкою тяглися до шпиталів санітарні карети й запряжені волами вози, скроплюючи **курні дороги** кров'ю, а перевтомлені похоронні команди волокли на кладовище не охололі ще трупи й скидали їх, немов колоди, у довжелезні ряди абияк викопаних неглибоких ровів* [Dotsenko: ZV I, p. 361].

At the beginning of the sentence, the author briefly acquaints the reader with the environment, noting that the city is surrounded by earthworks in "red-clay" or "червоній землі" as stated in the translation. However, the translator resorts to the generalization of the term "clay", which denotes clay, using the hypernym "земля" (earth). Changes also occur in the phrase "dusty streets", which means "covered with, full of, or resembling dust" [NWDTEL, p. 734], and is translated as "запорошені дороги" (dusty roads). The translator employs semantic development, possibly somewhat specifying the adjective "dusty streets" to "курні дороги" (dusty roads).

> It was **a savagely red land**, blood-coloured after rains, brick dust in droughts... [Mitchell, p.4].

> – *Ця* **ясно-червона земля**, *що ставала криваво-багряною після зливі перетворювалася на цеглисту пилюгу впосуху...* [Dotsenko: ZV I, p. 12].

To render the phrase "savagely red land", the translator chooses the equivalent "ясно-червона земля" (bright-red land), which means "cruel and vicious; aggressively hostile; (of a place) wild-looking and inhospitable; uncultivated"[NWDTEL, p. 1458]. The adverb "savagely" does not directly connect with color but suggests that the author aimed to convey the land's distinctiveness rather than its color. In translation, only the color aspect is reproduced. Furthermore, different ethnic groups have varied reactions influenced by conventional, typical collocations in their languages. For example, Ukrainians associate red with love and blood, while Americans might link it to skin colour.

While M. Mitchell's novel frequently uses the adjective "red" to depict the post-war environment, M. Twain's novel The Adventures of Tom Sawyer often employs the adjective "grey", providing a neutral reflection of the world: *It was the cool grey dawn* [Mark Twain: TS, p. 96] – *був холодний сірий світанок* [Koretskyi, p. 74]; *The sky was beginning to get a little grey in the east* [Mark Twain: TS, p. 80] – *небо на сході вже почало сіріти* [Koretskyi, p. 47].

Thus, the core components of the CIVIL WAR are the lexemes **Civil War** and **Yankee**. The conceptual features such as *"ideological opponents"*, *"Yankee treachery"*, *"Yankee humiliation of Southerners"*, *"Southern patriotism"*, and *"land"* are explained at the conceptual level within the socio-cultural and historical context. At the lexico-semantic level, these features are fixed in the semantics of direct nominations of the concept of CIVIL WAR. The core components of the concept are reproduced in all examined sources with a domestication strategy, which aims to bring the text closer to the reader's culture. Given the pronounced national characteristics of the concept, difficulties are overcome through translation transformations or tactics such as addition (*all patriotic men – кожний щирий патріот*); specification of meaning (*men – воїни, men – недолюди*); descriptive translation (*Iron-Clad oath – присяга на вірність Спо-*

лученим Штатам); semantic development (*shallow ditch – абияк викопані рови*).

2.1.2 Rendering the Peripheral Components of the CIVIL WAR Concept in Primary and Secondary Texts

Peripheral elements closely related to the core are significant for representing the concept and, thus, must be adequately reproduced in the translation. The periphery of the concept of figurative-value features, metaphors, stable comparisons, and idiomatic expressions represent CIVIL WAR. Adequate translation of these into Ukrainian requires substantial effort, erudition, and knowledge of the culture of the American South.

Metaphors, formed on an associative-figurative basis, are crucial for accurate translation, as analyzing them can reveal aspects of the worldview that directly penetrate the structure of linguistic units. This is evident in descriptions where metaphorical nominations denote "decline":

In that section, the Confederate sympathizers were in the minority and **the hand of war fell heavily upon them***, as it did on all the border states, neighbour informing against neighbour and brother killing brother* [Mitchell, p. 239]. – *У тих суміжних з Північчю околицях прихильники Конфедерації були в меншості, і важка рука війни далася їм взнаки найдошкульнішим чином, бо сусід доносив на сусіда, а брат убивав брата* [Dotsenko: ZV II, p. 270]. Comparing the beginnings of the original and Ukrainian sentences, it is evident that the descriptive translation conveys the metaphorical expression *"the hand of war fell heavily upon them"* – *"важка рука війни далася їм взнаки найдошкульнішим чином"*, reflecting a sense of decline, tragedy, and anxiety.

The consequences of war – poverty, hunger – are depicted in the novel to make the reader feel the situation, using the metaphor *"hunger rode the winds"*, which associatively relates to the factual information *"hunger spread"*, fixing in the recipient's mind connotations of rapidity:

The rutted red roads were frozen to flintiness, and **hunger rode the winds** *through Georgia* [Mitchell, p. 445]. – *Вибоїста червінь шляхів затужавіла на кремінь, і над Джорджією розпростер свої крила голод* [Dotsenko: ZV II, p. 492]. The translator uses semantic development – *"розпростер свої крила голод"* (hunger spread its wings), in the translation, notable for the poetization of the bird and its negative attributes through the associative connection with the concept CIVIL WAR.

In the following fragment, R. Dotsenko employs demetaphorization:
The dark sky became pink and then dull red, and, suddenly above the trees, she saw a huge **tongue of flame** *leap high to the heavens* [Mitchell, p. 353]. – ***Темне***

небо порожевіло, далі взялося ясно-червоною барвою, і врешті понад деревами фахнув у небо величезний омах полум'я [Dotsenko: ZV I, p. 392]. The metaphor *"tongue of flame"* – *"язик полум'я"* – is translated as *"фахнув у небо"*. The imagery is lost in Ukrainian, as it is rendered with the archaic term *"омах"* (a sudden blaze).

The Civil War instilled in Southerners a "devotion" to a sacred cause, metaphorically represented in the language:

Even now, the Southern ranks might be falling like grain before a hailstorm, but the Cause for which they fought could never fall [Mitchell, p. 241–242]. – *Лави південців, може, навіть у цю хвилину падають під градом куль, але Справа, за яку вони борються, ніколи не може зазнати поразки* [Dotsenko: ZV II, p. 272–273]. The original indicates that Southern ranks fall to the ground, dying from the numerous shots. As a hidden mechanism of associative thinking, the figurative metaphor *"Cause could never fall"* relates to the implied subtextual information: faith, victory, dream, and patriotism, explicitly conveyed in the Ukrainian translation.

The cause to which Southerners were passionately devoted is also mirrored through a metaphor repeated twice:

*The Cause they had thought could never **fall had fallen** forever* [Mitchell, p. 462]. – *Та Священна Справа, що здавалася їм навік-віків непохитною, пішла як за вітром* [Dotsenko: ZV II, p. 511]. The original employs a wordplay – the repetition of *"fall"* and *"fallen"*, expressing an emotionally charged reaction – devotion, sadness, disappointment. The figurative metaphor *"the Cause could never fall"*, associatively linked to the factual information – *the Cause is lasting, durable*, is translated as *"Справа, яка здавалася непохитною"*, maintaining the same implied information as the original – faith, patriotism, hope. The second metaphor, *"the Cause had fallen forever,"* meaning *the Cause had not been realized*, is presented in the translated text with the idiom *"піти за вітром"* (gone with the wind), creating a different figurative microsystem, correlating with the novel's title.

The fragment describes people's pride in the brave fight of Southern soldiers. In the source text, this is conveyed by the phrase *"the tide was turning"* meaning *"to reverse the trend of events"* [OGBACLE, p. 392], analogous in Ukrainian to *"зміна перебігу подій, переломний момент"* [ААРЛС, p. 846]. However, the translator opted for semantic development *"військовий талан обернувся лицем до південців"* (military luck turned to favor the Southerners), using a figurative metaphor that enhances the depiction of loyalty, heroism, and patriotism of the Southern soldiers.

The driving force of Southern society was the "dream" of a bright future, great victory, and the hope that the best is yet to come, which is a semantic component of the concept of CIVIL WAR – confidence in the future:

True, grim determination had taken the place of **high-hearted hopes,** *but people could still find a silver lining in the cloud* [Mitchell, p. 262]. – *Єдине, що легковажну самовпевненість заступила похмура рішучість, люди повторювали, що нема лиха, яке не вийшло б на добро* [Dotsenko: ZV I, p. 295]. Peripheral elements of the concept explicate features expressed through the metaphorical phrase *"high-hearted hopes"*, associatively linked to *"great hopes"* and implied subtextual information: faith, hope, confidence, and expectation. In the translated text, *"high-hearted hopes"* is rendered as *"легковажна самовпевненість"* (reckless self-confidence), which carries a different connotative meaning since confidence (a component of hope) and self-confidence are two different notions. Confidence means strong belief in something, faith in something, whereas self-confidence implies excessive confidence in oneself, one's capabilities, and abilities. The translator resorts to semantic development – *"легковажна самовпевненість"* (reckless self-confidence).

Comparisons authors use to actualize the concept of CIVIL WAR at the lexico-semantic level generally do not engage in complex metatextual relations, as they mainly convey visual impressions more clearly and usually do not carry hidden or additional meanings. However, losses during translation are considered inevitable. They are explained by discrepancies in the systems of the SL and the TL, the asymmetry of cultural realities, and the peculiarities of usage. These factors are objective and significantly influence translation decisions. Conversely, translation decisions are also influenced by subjective factors: the translator's ability to understand the meaning embedded in the source text and the skill to implement the necessary interlingual transformations to convey it using the means of the TL.

Peripheral features, actualized in comparisons, characterize Northern soldiers:

Moreover, England was coming in to help the Confederacy win the war because the English mills were standing idle for want of Southern cotton. Naturally, the British aristocracy sympathized with the Confederacy, **as one aristocrat with another,** *against a race of dollar lovers like the Yankees* [Mitchell, p. 89]. – *Та й Англія допоможе Конфедерації виграти війну, адже англійські фабрики припиняють роботу через брак південської вовни! І взагалі британська знать, безперечно, співчуває Конфедерації, будучи* **споріднена з нею по духу,** *і відчуває неприязнь до цих доларолюбців-янкі* [Dotsenko: ZV II, p. 184]. The phrase "as one aristocrat with another" is translated into Ukrainian with the corresponding contextually relevant equivalent "споріднена по духу", which changes the value basis of this expression, shortening the associative chain for the reader of the translated text.

Northern soldiers are compared to "like a monster serpent", translated into Ukrainian with meaning differentiation – "мов страховинні змії", which evokes and instills feelings of "fear", terror:

The blue lines came relentlessly, **like a monster serpent,** *coiling, striking venomously, drawing its injured lengths back, but always striking again* [Mitchell, p. 281].

– Сині лави невблаганно насувалися, звиваючись, ***мов страховинні змії****, – вони люто нападали, зазнавши втрат, відступали, але щоразу атакували знову* [Dotsenko: ZV II, p. 314–315].

In translation, it is essential to find equivalents that are adequate in meaning, imagery, internal form, and stylistic coloring and that convey the connotative and pragmatic characteristics of the expression:

However, hideous rumors that Lee was killed, the battle lost, and enormous casualty lists coming in flew up and down the quiet streets **like darting bats** [Mitchell, p. 241]. *– Але зловісні чутки про те, що генерала Лі вбито й битву програно, що завдано величезних втрат, носилися по всьому притихлому місту,* ***мов знавіснілі від страху кажани*** [Dotsenko: ZV I, p. 272]. The author uses the comparison "like darting bats" to convey the despair and hopelessness of Southerners who learn from rumors (as they previously believed) about the defeat in the war. In folk beliefs, bats are considered friends of the devil or even his embodiment. In the Bible, they are mentioned as "unclean" animals. The Ukrainian variant of the comparison "мов знавіснілі від страху кажани" creates the image of frenzied, frightened bats that do not know where to fly. The translator uses semantic development, emphasizing the emotion of fear in Southerners. The original "darting bats" denotes bats flying very quickly, as the verb "to dart" means "to move suddenly and quickly in a particular direction" [LDELC, p. 396].

The emotion of "fear" in Southerners towards Northerners is traced in the following comparison:

And if the Yankees can take the railroad there, they can pull up the strings and have us, **just like a possum in a poke** [Mitchell, p. 314]. *– Якщо янкі захоплять там залізницю, вони затягнуть поворозки й* ***придушать нас, як опосума*** [Dotsenko: ZV I, p. 350]. In the conversation about the Yankees taking the railroad and "have us, just like a possum in a poke", the Ukrainian translator simplifies this expression, not fully conveying its meaning, translating it as "придушать нас, як опосума". R. Dotsenko, first, removes the word "poke", which means a bag or sack. Second, for the Ukrainian reader, the expression "придушити, як опосума" does not contain the full range of associations, as the marsupial animal possum does not live in Ukraine. However, this decision is justified: the estrangement helps to convey the desired local color.

*The Yankees cleaned us out like a **swarm** of locusts* [Mitchell, p. 426]. – *Янкі обчистили нас, як сарана, **геть дочиста*** [Dotsenko: ZV II, p. 471]. The translator intensifies the emotionality of the description by adding "геть дочиста", which compensates for the omission of the lexeme "swarm" – "рій" in the translation.

For a clear visualization of the situation in the Southern USA, comparisons reflecting the concept sphere of the American South during the Civil War represent the "courage" of Southerners:

Even now the Southern ranks might be falling like grain before a hailstorm, but the Cause for which they fought could never fall [Mitchell, p. 241–242]. – *Лави південців, може, навіть у цю хвилину падають під градом куль, але Справа, за яку вони борються, ніколи не може зазнати поразки* [Dotsenko: ZV II, p. 272–273]. The original suggests that the Southern ranks fall to the ground one after another like grain before a hailstorm, with the pace of falling rapidly increasing. The Ukrainian translator omits the comparison and translates it such that the Southerners fall under a hail of bullets. This means they die from numerous shots. R. Dotsenko conveys clear visual impressions by simplifying the comparison and looking at it differently.

The courage of Southerners is represented by the comparison "like the fruit of the dragon's teeth", which alludes to an ancient Greek myth. The dictionary of ancient mythology explains that by the oracle's command, Cadmus, a hero of Theban myths, killed a dragon and sowed its teeth, from which warriors grew. Cadmus threw a stone at the warriors, who then began to fight each other; as a result, only five warriors remained. Together with Cadmus, they founded Thebes and became the ancestors of the noble Theban families. In a figurative sense, "to sow dragon's teeth" means "to breed enmity" and "to foster numerous monsters":

*They might be dying in thousands but, **like the fruit of the dragon's teeth**, thousands of fresh men in grey and butternut with the Rebel yell on their lips would spring up from the earth to take their places* [Mitchell, p. 242]. – *Вони можуть гинути тисячами, але, **мов ті казкові драконові зуби**, постануть з-під землі на їхнє місце тисячі нових вояків у сірих та жовтуватих уніформах і з войовничим кличем на устах ринуть у бій* [Dotsenko: ZV II, p. 273]. The comparison "like the fruit of the dragon's teeth" is rendered in Ukrainian as "мов ті казкові драконові зуби". The translator employs semantic development by adding the modifier "казкові" (fairy-tale), although it is clear without this addition that it is not about natural dragon teeth. However, omitting the lexeme "fruit", meaning "descendant", does not create a discrepancy in the connotations of the two comparisons, as the original implies that thousands of new warriors will rise from the ground, ready for victory.

Some comparisons are culturally and historically specific, requiring the translator to know ethnostereotypes and Biblical stories. The atmosphere of "decline" and people's despair is embodied in the comparison "as poor as Job's turkey":

*Wasn't everybody **as poor as Job's turkey**, and weren't the streets full of men, some of them formerly rich, who were without work?* [Mitchell, p. 631]. – *Чи ж не бачиш на кожному кроці **бідних, наче Йов**, чи ж не повно на вулицях чоловіків, які колись були заможні, а тепер потребують роботи?* [Dotsenko: ZV II, p. 170]. The author says that in the post-war years, people became as poor as Job's turkey or, in translation, "наче Йов". The first part of the comparison is correctly rendered, as Job is the Old Testament patriarch, also called Righteous Job, the Long-suffering. This means, on the one hand, renouncing luxury and overeating and, on the other, constant faith in God's goodness and mercy. The comparison "poor as Job" also signifies Southerners' faith in a better future. However, the original text mentions not only Job but also Job's turkey, which the translator disregarded.

Reproducing conceptual elements actualized in idioms demands translational skill and a well-developed linguistic sensitivity. The equivalent is always singular; if the translator knows it, translation becomes straightforward. Idiomatic expressions are realized by the feature of "hunger", which actualizes the concept of the CIVIL WAR:

*Don't tell me **the wolf is still at the door** of Tara* [Mitchell, p. 595]. – *Тільки не кажіть мені, що **злидні** й досі під дверима Тари* [Dotsenko: ZV II, p. 128]. According to K. T. Barantsev's English-Ukrainian phraseological dictionary, the Ukrainian equivalent of the English fixed expression "wolf at one's door" is "голод, злидні" [AUFS, p. 673]. This means the entire phrase signifies "poverty", but the translator only rendered the lexeme "wolf" as "злидні".

The nature of idiomatic expressions is closely connected with the background knowledge of native speakers and the people's cultural-historical traditions, consolidating people's life experiences in the language. Just as a painter's work conveys a mood in addition to thought, most idioms that preserve imagery also convey feelings, moods, and an expressive evaluation of the subject of thought, which is correlated in language with the expression of the entire utterance. The "fear" of Southerners towards Northerners as a characteristic feature of the concept of the CIVIL WAR is represented by the following idiomatic expressions:

*But if I tried to draw a draft on it, the Yankees would be on me **like a duck on a June bug**, and then neither of us would get it* [Mitchell, p. 553]. – *Бо якби я спробував виписати чек на якусь частку тих грошей, янкі **накинулися б на мене, мов кури на хруща**, і тоді б ні вам, ні мені не побачити з них жодного шеляга* [Dotsenko: ZV I, p. 79]. To reproduce the idiom "to be on smb like a duck on a June bug", the translator finds a partial equivalent, replacing the lexeme "duck" with "кури", and attempts to avoid losing the imagery of the expression – "накинутися, мов кури на хруща". In the target text, the eeriness and sense of fear are conveyed.

However, the same fixed expression is only sometimes translated uniformly, as the context of the idiom's usage is considered. In the target language, it may have several equivalents:

*And if you so much as swear at them, much less hit them a few licks for the good of their souls, the Freedmen's Bureau is down on you **like a duck on a June bug*** [Mitchell, p. 607]. – *А як нагримати на них – я вже й не кажу, щоб шмагонути разок-другий для їхнього ж добра, – то зразу ж **накриє тебе мокрим рядном** Бюро звільненців* [Dotsenko: ZV II, p. 142]. The translator renders the fixed expression "to be down on smb like a duck on a June bug" with the Ukrainian equivalent "накрити мокрим рядном", meaning to attack someone with reproaches.

*Yankee officers who knew nothing of the law and cared less for the circumstances of the crime could go through the motions of holding a trial **and put a rope around a Southerner's neck*** [Mitchell, p. 616]. – *Офіцери-янкі, які не знаються на законах і яких ще менше обходять обставини злочину, залюбки засудять кожного південця і тут-таки **накинуть йому зашморг на шию*** [Dotsenko: ZV II, p. 152–153]. In the original text, M. Mitchell uses the idiom "put a rope around one's neck" to make the expression more expressive, meaning "the power to control or lead someone" [CDIEUS, p. 361] or, according to Barantsev's English-Ukrainian phraseological dictionary, "занапастити, привести до загибелі когось" [AUFS, p. 713]. The translated idiom is rendered with the Ukrainian equivalent "накинути зашморг на шию" (to hang someone). The translation conveys the emotion of fear present in the original.

The concept of the CIVIL WAR is also comprehended through interaction with the universal concept of FAITH, whose periphery consists of part of the idiom "every cloud has a silver lining" – "a silver lining", analogous to the Ukrainian variant "промінь надії". Since the idiom in the original is rephrased to "find a silver lining in the cloud", the Ukrainian translation is also presented in a slightly altered form, "нема лиха, яке не вийшло б на добро". However, the dictionary offers such an equivalent: "нема добра без лиха".

*Pa, I thought that we'd **give the Yanks a taste of their own medicine** but the General says No, and personally I don't care to get shot just for the pleasure of burning some Yank's house* [Mitchell, p. 240]. – *Я гадав, тату, що **ми відплатимо янкі їхньою ж монетою**, але генерал сказав "Ні", хоч я особисто – хай би мене й розстріляли – ладен втішитись тим, що пущу з димом котрийсь будинок янкі* [Dotsenko: ZV I, p. 270–271]. The idiomatic expression "give a taste of their own medicine", meaning "to treat someone as badly as they have treated you" [DCE, p. 1025], which implicitly reflects the intentions of both warring sides, is rendered by the translator with the Ukrainian equivalent "відплатити їхньою ж монетою", which retains both the pragmatic potential of the original expression and its pragmatic coloration.

A comparative analysis of the original and translated works proves that a significant part of the transformations aimed at achieving an adequate translation is semantically and pragmatically motivated since the ultimate goal is the adequate reproduction of the concept of the CIVIL WAR. Descriptive translation, semantic development, addition, and meaning specification are often used to reproduce the core elements of the concept. To adequately reproduce the figurative-value components, it is essential to consider and preserve the national-cultural specificity and historical context.

2.2 Rendering of English Linguistic Representations of the SOCIAL STRUCTURE Concept of the American South into Ukrainian

Each ethnoculture shares similarities and differences with other ethnocultures, which is evident in the network of concepts forming the conceptual basis of any language and in the language itself. Since the conceptual worldview is dynamic, changing primarily under the influence of extralinguistic factors of a socio-historical and cognitive nature, ethnospecific fragments reflecting a nation's mental and cultural distinctiveness become increasingly challenging to translate. Examining the social structure of the American South, whose inhabitants differ from Northerners in their devotion to the land and a set system of values that gradually loses its integrity after the defeat in the Civil War, reveals the Southern efforts to find a model that maintains unity, social order, and moral integrity. Therefore, to achieve a comprehensive understanding of the conceptual sphere of the American South, it is essential to explore the depiction of the main elements of the concept of SOCIAL ORDER and how their specificities are rendered in translations.

2.2.1 Rendering the Core Components of the Concept of the SOCIAL STRUCTURE Concept

This section focuses, first, on the conceptual features of the concept of SOCIAL ORDER that most fully reflect the lifestyle of Southerners in a diachronic perspective – both before and after the Civil War – second, on their implementation in Ukrainian translation, and third, on the strategies and tactics used by translators in conveying the core linguistic representations of ethnoculturally marked concepts. The material is drawn from works that highlight the key moments of the Civil War's impact on readers' perceptions of the social structure of the American South.

Many historians and literary scholars agree that the South's way of life depended heavily on social class. Aristocrats, for example, had time for leisure and various banquets, while enslaved Black people on plantations worked from dawn to late at night without a moment's rest:

> *There was indeed a caste system in Maycomb, but to my mind it worked this way: the older citizens, the present generation of people who had lived side by side for years and years, were utterly predictable to one another: they took for granted attitudes, character shadings, even gestures, as having been repeated in each generation and refined by time* [Lee: KM, p. 147].

> *– В Мейкомбі жителі ділилися на касти – явище закономірне, і суть місцевої кастової системи, на мій погляд, полягала в тому, що сучасне покоління, дорослі люди, які багато років жили поряд, добре знали одне одного: зовнішність, особливості характеру, навіть жести сприймалися як звичайна річ, що переходила з покоління в покоління і відточувалася часом* [Kharenko, p. 77].

> *– У Мейкомі насправді існував кастовий розподіл, але я це розуміла так: старші мешканці, нинішнє покоління людей, що прожили плече-в-плече багато років, були цілком передбачувані одне для одного: їх не дивували нічиї ставлення, ані особливості характеру, ані навіть жести, бо усе це передавалося з покоління у покоління і з роками відшліфовувалося* [Nekryach: UP, p. 100].

Although the narrative is from the perspective of Jean Louise, an eight-year-old girl who witnesses the caste division of white people and the contemptuous attitude towards black people, she intuitively senses the falsehood and injustice of the life surrounding her. Jean Louise is gifted with a great sense of truth and love. This mirrors the influence of Mark Twain, who also depicted a life system based on racial division through a child's consciousness.

In the Southern United States, social stratification was as follows: aristocratic planters, white farmers, poor whites, and black slaves. The lifestyle of Southerners depended on the stratum to which they belonged.

The core of the concept of SOCIAL ORDER includes terms such as aristocratic planters, white farmers, poor whites, and black slaves. Therefore, examining the conceptual features of these lexeme nominations and their reproduction in Ukrainian is appropriate. The caste division of the population is formulated by the boy Jem in the novel To Kill a Mockingbird, explaining the higher society's rejection of the lower classes:

> *There are four kinds of folks in the world. There is the ordinary kind like us and the neighbors, there is the kind like the Cunninghams out in the woods, the kind like the*

> *Ewells down at the dump, and the Negroes. The thing about it is, our kind of folks do not like the Cunninghams, the Cunninghams don't like the Ewells, and the Ewells hate and despise the colored folks* [Lee: KM, p. 255–256].
>
> *– На світі є чотири типи людей. Звичайні – такі, як ми і наші сусіди; потім такі, як Канінгеми, що живуть у глушині; далі йдуть такі, як Юели, що живуть на звалищах, і, нарешті, негри. Вся справа в тому, що нам не подобаються Канінгеми, Канінгемам – Юели, а Юели ненавидять кольорових* [Kharenko, p. 136].
>
> *– У світі існує чотири види людей. Звичайні люди, як ми і наші сусіди, люди на кшталт Каннінгемів, що живуть у лісі, люди типу Юелів, що живуть на звалищі, і негри. Річ у тім, що такі, як ми, не люблять Каннінгемів, Каннінгеми не люблять Юелів, а Юели ненавидять і зневажають негрів* [Nekryach: UP, p. 174].

As seen from the excerpts, one of the social strata is the aristocratic planters. Mostly, these were descendants of French colonists who brought across the ocean not only their way of life and culinary recipes but also the customs and manners of the gallant century; these aristocrats prided themselves on their worldliness and gallant conduct, and their adherence to the chivalric code of honor. Planters in the Southern United States were descendants of former aristocrats who owned lands, and black slaves worked on plantations, growing cotton, and doing all the household chores. Such aristocrats are the Finch, Buford, and Haverford families in To Kill a Mockingbird, and the O'Hara family in Gone with the Wind. All of them have "noble origins":

> *Atticus said one time the reason Auntie's so hipped on the family is because **all we've got's background and not a dime to our names*** [Lee: KM, p. 256].
>
> *– Колись Аттікус сказав, ніби тітка тому пишається своїм родоводом, що у нас уся **спадщина – добре ім'я*** [Kharenko, p. 136].
>
> *– Атикус якось сказав, що тітка так носиться з нашим родоводом, **бо грошей у нас немає, саме лише походження*** [Nekryach: UP, p. 174].

From Jem's description, noting that "all we've got's background and not a dime to our names", it is clear that the planter family has lost almost everything except their house. In the secondary texts, M. Kharenko translates this as "спадщина – добре ім'я" (inheritance – a good name), while T. Nekrych opts for a descriptive translation "бо грошей у нас немає, саме лише походження" (because we have no money, just heritage). Although "background" encompasses more than just origin, as it includes roots, lineage, and the person themselves, both translators correctly convey the general idea.

Atticus Finch also explains to the children that:

> *<...> you are not **from run-of-the-mill people**, that you are the product of several generations' gentle breeding... Gentle breeding... and that you should try to live up to your name...* [Lee: KM, p. 149].

– <...> ви *небезрідні*, що за вами стоять кілька поколінь, невід'ємною рисою яких була бездоганна вихованість...бездоганна вихованість... І ви повинні жити так, щоб бути гідними вашого імені [Kharenko, p. 79–80].

– <...> ви **належите не до пересічної родини**, а є добутком шляхетного виховання кількох полінь... Шляхетного виховання... і ви мусите робити все, щоб не заплямувати своє ім'я... [Nekryach: UP, p. 102].

The phrase "from run-of-the-mill people", which means "ordinary and not special or exciting in any way" [CALDT], is rendered by T. Nekrych as "належите не до пересічної родини" (not belonging to an ordinary family), highlighting the noble origin of the family. M. Kharenko translates it as "не безрідні" (not without lineage), which carries a different semantic meaning – "those who have relatives" [VSUM]. Further, Aunt Alexandra confirms her point by stating that "you are the product of several generations' gentle breeding", which both translators render with synonymous equivalents: M. Kharenko with additional explication "за вами стоять кілька поколінь, невід'ємною рисою яких була бездоганна вихованість" (several generations, an inherent feature of which was impeccable upbringing), and T. Nekrych as "є добутком шляхетного виховання кількох полінь" (the product of several generations of noble breeding).

The "leisurely, unhurried life" is characteristic of Southern planters who had time for both work and rest. They lived off the labor of black slaves, supervised by overseers. Aristocrats sought entertainment: women preferred balls and formal visits, while men enjoyed card games, bar stands, duels, and constant light-hearted conversations. This carefree life of the aristocratic planters is depicted in many works describing both the pre-war and post-war periods in the USA:

*They had money enough and slaves enough to give them time to play, and **they liked to play**. They seemed never too busy to drop work for a fish fry, a hunt or a horse race, and scarcely a week went by without its barbecue or ball* [Mitchell, p. 30].

– *Вони мали достатньо грошей і рабів, тож могли собі гаяти час у розвагах, а хисту й **охоти розважатись їм не бракувало**. Здавалося, будь-якої пори вони можуть кинути все й гайнути на річку по рибу, влаштувати полювання або кінні перегони, і рідко випадав такий тиждень, щоб не було балу чи пікніка* [Dotsenko: ZV I, p. 64].

R. Dotsenko employs semantic development in rendering the phrase "they liked to play" as "хисту й охоти розважатись їм не бракувало" (they had the skill and desire to entertain themselves), describing the leisurely life of planters in the South.

Adequately conveying the way of life of Southerners in artistic images requires the translator to mobilize all their knowledge to construct an accurate interpretation of the text to understand a foreign reader. This is particularly relevant to those aspects of life and routine of the Southerners in the 19th century that are pretty removed from the life experiences of the target reader, especially the relationships between white slave owners, who have nothing to occupy themselves with except entertainment, and black slaves, who, working on plantations, have no free time for rest:

> *He found poker the most useful of all Southern customs, poker and a steady head for* **whisky**, *and it was his natural aptitude for cards and amber liquor that brought to Gerald two of his three most prized possessions, his valet and his plantation* [Mitchell, p. 24].

> – *Він виявив, що покер, а також ясна голова при* **чарці** *можуть стати в неабиякій пригоді, і саме своїй вродженій тямі до карт та вмінню легко поглинати золотавий трунок Джералд і завдячував два з трьох своїх найкоштовніших набутків – служника-негра й плантацію* [Dotsenko: ZV I, p. 51].

The translator employs metonymy in translating the American "whisky" as "чаркою" (a glass). R. Dotsenko's choice to translate "a steady head" as "ясна голова" (clear head) seems appropriate, as both expressions are idiomatic. Additionally, the phrase "aptitude for cards and amber liquor" is translated contextually as "тяма до карт та вміння легко поглинати золотавий трунок". Overall, the translation effectively portrays the leisure activities of wealthy Southerners.

Behavioral models and the lifestyle of Southern planters, as part of their conceptual sphere, are vividly conveyed in the following excerpt:

> *And raising good cotton,* **riding well**, *shooting straight, dancing lightly, squiring the ladies with elegance and carrying one's liquor like a gentleman were the things that mattered* [Mitchell, p. 2].

> – *До таких речей належали вміння вирощувати добрий бавовник,* **зугарно їздити верхи**, *влучно стріляти, легко танцювати, гречно залицятися до дам і не втрачати джентльменських манер навіть під чаркою* [Dotsenko: ZV I, p. 7].

The phrase "riding well" is successfully translated while preserving its semantic component as "зугарно їздити верхи". We see a rather banal evaluative phrase in the original, whereas the translator embellishes the image. There is a noticeable individualized approach to translating "shooting straight", with the selected equivalent "влучно стріляти" being a fitting choice from the lexical wealth available.

The idle life of Southern planters is well reflected in the phrase "as enthusiastic visitors as they were hosts", translated into Ukrainian with the addition of the adjective "щедрий" as "такі ж ревні гостювальники, як і щедрі господарі", which is illustrated in the following passage:

> *When a Southerner took the trouble to pack a trunk and travel twenty miles for a visit, the visit was seldom of shorter duration than a month, usually much longer. Southerners* **were as enthusiastic visitors** *as they were hosts, and there was nothing unusual in*

relatives coming to spend the Christmas holidays and remaining until July [Mitchell, p. 79].

– Коли котрийсь південець розохочувався спакуватись і вирушити за двадцять миль у гостину, то гостина рідко тривала менше місяця, а звичайно затягувалася на багато довший термін. З південців були **такі ж ревні гостювальники**, як і щедрі господарі, і не становило великого дива, що родичі могли завітати на Різдво й засидітись у гостях до липня [Dotsenko: ZV I, p. 164].

This aspect of the life of aristocratic planters is also noted in the 1930s, as depicted in To Kill a Mockingbird, describing Aunt Alexandra's visit, which both translators render literally:

"Well, your father and I decided it was time I came to stay with you for a while". "For a while" in Maycomb meant anything from three days to thirty years [Lee: KM, p. 142-143].

– Ми з вашим батьком вирішили, що мені пора вже деякий час пожити у вар. "Деякий час", як його розуміють у Мейкомбі, може означати від трьох днів до тридцяти років [Kharenko, p. 75].

– Так от, ми з вашим батьком вирішили, що я поживу у вас деякий чар. "Деякий час" у нас в Мейкомі могло означати від трьох днів до тридцяти років [Nekryach: UP, p. 97].

It is no coincidence that M. Mitchell refers to the South as "slow-moving Southern life", which is translated into Ukrainian with the addition of the word "плин" (flow) as "неспішний плин південського життя". This is vividly depicted in the following passage:

Visitors presented no problem, for houses were large, servants numerous and the feeding of several extra mouths a minor matter in that land of plenty. Visitors added excitement and variety to **the slow-moving Southern life** *and they were always welcome* [Mitchell, p. 79].

– Гості нікого не обтяжували, бо будинки були просторі, челядь численна, і кілька зайвих ротів не завдавало ніякого клопоту в цьому краю достатку. Гості пожвавлювали і додавали розмаїття **неспішному плину південського життя**, і їм завжди були раді [Dotsenko: ZV I, p. 164].

At the beginning of the 20th century, calmness and tranquility were associated with a person seeking to find themselves, as a person deprived of a home is incapable of life. In the South, such alienation leads to the search for the thread that connects one to the land, homeland, and family roots. These moments are observed in R. P. Warren, where the image of warmth is represented by silence and the heart:

What they had in common was **a world of wordless silence by the fire**, *a world which could absorb effortlessly and perfectly the movements of their day and their occupations,* *and of all the days they had lived, and of the days that were to come for them to move about in and do the thing which were the life for which they were made* [Warren, p. 20].

*– А в них був спільний **світ глибокої мовчанки біля каміна**, світ, що легко й цілковито вбирав у себе їхні клопоти та справи минулого дня і всіх попередніх днів, і всіх тих днів, що мали ще настати й принести із собою нові клопоти та справи, з яких складалося призначене їм життя* [Mitrofanov: UKB, p. 30].

V. Mitrofanov uses the contextual equivalent "глибока" to convey "wordless" in the phrase "a world of wordless silence by the fire" – "світ глибокої мовчанки біля каміна", because "безмовна мовчанка" would be somewhat absurd in Ukrainian. However, the original employs poetic alliteration, compensating for the semantic dissonance.

The slow pace of life in the South in the 1930s is best captured in the pages of Harper Lee's To Kill a Mockingbird, where the author notes that Southerners never rushed, enjoying every moment and doing everything leisurely:

*People **moved slowly then**. They ambled across the square, shuffled in and out of the stores around it, took time about everything* [Lee: KM, p. 6].

*– Люди в ті часи **жили неквапом**. Ходили собі по площі, заглядали у крамниці, статечно, без поспіху* [Kharenko, p. 4].

*– Люди в ті часи **рухалися повільно**. Вони дріботіли через площу, заглядали з однієї крамниці до іншої і нікуди не поспішали* [Nekryach: UP, p. 3].

At the beginning, the author notes that "people moved slowly". M. Kharenko uses the tactic of semantic development, translating the fragment as "люди жили неквапом", while T. Nekryach translates it literally as "люди рухалися повільно".

The following excerpt from R. P. Warren's All the King's Men: *The boss was a slow mover* [Warren, p. 323] – *З Хазяїна був таки добрячий сидень* [B. Mitrofanov: UKB, p. 35] is translated using the addition of the epithet "добрячий" and semantic development: "a slow mover" – "добрячий сидень".

One of the traits of aristocratic planters was their adherence to the code of honor, a code inherent only to representatives of the higher class, and a well-bred, balanced, and tactful person who follows the rules of conduct. Therefore, the main distinguishing feature of a gentleman (a person of high status) was no longer clothes and a hat but the strict adherence to principles, the so-called "gentleman's code".

*There was much about the South – and the Southerners – that he would never comprehend: but, with the wholeheartedness that was his nature, he adopted his ideas and customs, as he understood them, for his own-poker and horseracing, red-hot politics and the code of duello, **States' Rights** and damnation to all Yankees, slavery and King Cotton, contempt for white trash and exaggerated courtesy to women* [Mitchell, p. 23].

> *– Багато чого на Півдні і південцях лишилось для нього назавжди незбагненним, але з усією щиросердістю своєї натури він сприйняв південські погляди й звичаї такими, як їх розумів: гра в покер і кінні перегони, пристрасть до політики й кодекс честі, **обстоювання "Прав штатів"** і ненависть до янкі, рабство й культ Короля Бавовнику, зневага до "білої голоти" й гіпертрофована гречність до жіноцтва* [Dotsenko: ZV I, p. 50].

To a foreign reader, at first glance, "States' Rights" may mean a document "Права штатів". For someone unaware of the way of life and actions of Southerners, such a translation would seem contradictory. To avoid this and accurately convey the author's intent, the translator uses the tactic of addition "обстоювання "Прав штатів"", which not only preserves the semantic emphasis but also paints a picture of the past life of Southerners.

In truth, in literary works, as in life, there is no final point; instead, there are ellipses as a sign of continuity, a suggestion for the ever-present author-reader to build a speculative perspective based on what has been read or seen. The new Southerners are ready to achieve their goals by ignoble means. They are evil, cruel, and persistent, resembling predators always ready to pounce on new prey. Southerners are hard to break. In the fight for their well-being, they demonstrate determination and indiscriminate use of means.

The following core unit of the concept of **SOCIAL ORDER** is white farmers. The life of an American agrarian worker was difficult, driven by such primary factors as soil depletion, unstable climate, loss of economic self-sufficiency, and lack of adequate protection and assistance from the law. In the South, the fall of the Confederacy led to even more significant changes in agriculture. The most crucial was sharecropping, where tenant farmers had to return up to half of their crop to the landowner in exchange for seed and food.

> *"Yeah", I said to myself, "so that is the tale, for Mason County is **red-neck country** and they don't like niggers, not strange niggers anyway, and they haven't got many of their own"* [Warren, p. 38].

> *– "Егеж", сказав я собі подумки, "то оце так воно. Адже Мейсонська округа – край **дрібного білого фермерства**, і негрів там не люблять, особливо чужих негрів, а своїх у них не багато"* [Mitrofanov: UKB, p. 82–83].

In the novel *All the King's Men* by R. P. Warren, the South is called "red-neck country", where "red-neck" means a poor white farmer (in the Southern USA) – a poor peasant laborer. V. Mitrofanov resorts to a descriptive translation with the preservation of meaning "край дрібного білого фермерства".

In her translation of the sequel to To Kill a Mockingbird, namely Go Set a Watchman, T. Nekryach omits the adjective "rednecked" from the characterization "rednecked white trash" by Alexandra Finch, leaving only "біле бидло", which is evident in the passage:

> We Finches do not marry the children of **rednecked** white trash, which is exactly what Henry's parents were when they were born and were all their lives. You can't call them anything better [Lee: GSW, p. 36].

The "low origin" of white farmers is evident from the description of Walter Cunningham, who "had been raised on fish food", which T. Nekrych translates literally as "не їв нічого крім риби", hinting at the family's diet limited to fishing. M. Kharenko resorts to generalization "завжди недоїдав".

> Walter looked as if he had been raised on fish food: his eyes, as blue as Dill Harris's, were red-rimmed and watery[Lee: KM, p. 26].

> – Він був такий худий і миршавий, ніби завжди недоїдав; очі сині, як у Діла Гарріса, але сльозилися <…> [Kharenko, p. 12].

> – Виглядав Walter так, ніби за все життя не їв нічого крім риби: блакитні, як у Ділла Герріса, очі були водянисті <…> [Nekryach: UP, p. 16].

Harper Lee authentically depicts a life grounded in racism and snobbery from aristocrats towards socially lower-class whites. This is traced in the fragment of Aunt Alexandra and Jean Louise's conversation about the Cunningham family:

> "Jean Louise, there is no doubt in my mind that they're good folks. **But they're not our kind of folks**". Jem says, "She means they're **yappy**, Scout". "What's a yap?" "Aw, tacky. They like fiddling and things like that". "Well, I do too – " "Don't be silly, Jean Louise", said Aunt Alexandra. "The thing is, you can scrub Walter Cunningham till he shines, you can put him in shoes and a new suit, but he'll never be like Jem. Besides, there's a drinking streak in that family a mile wide. Finch women aren't interested in that sort of people" [Lee: KM, p. 253].

> – Джін Луїзо, я не сумніваюся, що вони непогані люди. **Але вони не нашого кола.** – Всевидько, тітонька хоче сказати, що вони **неотесані**, – пояснив Джем.
>
> – Як це – неотесані?
>
> – Ну, грубі. Люблять просту музику і таке інше.
>
> – Ну й що? Я теж люблю…
>
> – Не мели дурниць, Джін Луїзо, – сказала тітка Олександра.
>
> – Річ у тому, що коли навіть вимити Канінгема до блиску, взути в черевики і надіти йому новий костюм, він всеодно ніколи не буде таким, як Джем. Крім того, Канінгеми дуже охочі до спиртного. Жінки з роду Фінчів не цікавляться такими людьми [Kharenko, p. 134–135].

> – Джін-Луїзо, я не маю найменшого сумніву щодо того, що вони хороші люди. **Але це люди не нашого кола.**
>
> – Скаут, вона натякає, що вони неотеси, – втрутився Джемі.

*– Що значить – **неотеси**? – Ну, неуки. Люблять притопувати під просту музику і таке інше.*

– Я теж люблю –

– Не кажи дурниць, Джін-Луїзо, – відтяла тітка Александра.

– Справа в тому, що Волтера Каннінгема можна до блиску відмити, взути його у черевики, одягти в новий костюм, але він ніколи не стане таким, як Джемі. До того ж, у його родині існує нахил до пиятики, глибокий, як колодязь. Жінки з роду Фінчів не можуть цікавитися такими людьми [Nekryach: UP, p. 173].

The low origin of white farmers and the condescending attitude towards them are evident in Aunt Alexandra's words about the Cunningham family: "they're not our kind of folks" – "це люди не нашого кола" (translated by T. Nekryach) / "вони не нашого кола" (translated by M. Kharenko). Confirmation of their low origin and lack of education is that they are "yappy" meaning "an uncouth or stupid person; fool" and "tacky" – "cheaply vulgar; crude person", which the translators render using synonymous equivalents "неотеси" (T. Nekryach) / "неотесані" (M. Kharenko) and "неуки" (T. Nekryach) / "грубі": (M. Kharenko).

"Hard work". In the following fragment from Harper Lee's To Kill a Mockingbird, it is evident that Southerners are industrious workers, as their region is called "farm county" – "фермерський округ" by M. Kharenko and "аграрний округ" by T. Nekryach:

*Atticus said professional people were poor because the farmers were poor. As Maycomb County was **farm country**, nickels and dimes were hard to come by for doctors and dentists and lawyers* [Lee: KM, p. 24].

*– Аттікус пояснив, що серед міських жителів багато бідних через те, що фермери бідні. Мейкомб – **фермерський округ**, ось чому лікарям, дантистам, адвокатам тут важко заробити* [Kharenko, p. 11].

*– Атикус сказав, що правники й лікарі збідніли, оскільки збідніли фермери. **Округ Мейком – аграрний**, тож юристи, дантисти та терапевти тепер рідко бачать живі гроші* [Nekryach: UP, p. 15].

Farmers, who spent most of their time on plantations growing cotton, became poorer after the 1929 crisis due to falling product prices.

The conceptual feature "hard work" of farmers, which actualizes the nomination of white farmers in the concept of **SOCIAL ORDER**, is realized in the description of the Cunningham family, who are willing to live in poverty but work on their land:

*If he held his mouth right, Mr. Cunningham could get **a WPA job**, but his land would go to ruin if he left it, and he was willing to go hungry to keep his land and vote as he pleased* [Lee: KM, p. 24].

> – Якби містер Канінгем умів мовчати, він міг би дістати **роботу на державному підприємстві**, тільки ж тоді йому ніколи було б обробляти свою землю, і вона стала б пустирем; ні, він воліє голодувати, але зберегти землю і голосувати за кого хоче [Kharenko, p. 11].
>
> – Якби містер Каннінгем умів тримати язика за зубами, то міг би **отримати роботу в рамках державної підтримки постраждалих від кризи**, але тоді його земля пропала б зовсім без догляду, а він воліє голодувати, проте залишитися при своїй землі і голосувати за кого схоче [Nekryach: UP, p. 15].

The phrase "a WPA job" means "Works Progress Administration that was the largest and the most ambitious New Deal Agency, employing millions of unemployed people to carry out public works during and after the Great Depression in the United States". M. Kharenko uses a generalized equivalent "робота на державному підприємстві", while T. Nekryach resorts to descriptive translation "робота в рамках державної підтримки постраждалих від кризи", explaining the essence of the socio-political reality of WPA.

The "code of honor", as a set of moral and ethical principles, is represented in texts by superficial human qualities inherent to the inhabitants of the legendary South. Atticus shows a respectful attitude towards the Cunningham family, poor farmers, emphasizing their integrity by noting that they "came from a set breed of men", which both translators render with synonymous equivalents – "порода непохитних" and "тверда людська порода":

> Mr. Cunningham, said Atticus, **came from a set breed of men** [Lee: KM, p. 24].
>
> – Канінгем належить **до породи непохитних**, казав Аттікус [Kharenko, p. 12].
>
> – Містер Каннінгем, пояснив Атикус, належить до **твердої людської породи** [Nekryach: UP, p. 15].

Atticus tries to justify the Cunninghams for their poverty and lack of education. This is evident in the following lines:

> "Mr. Cunningham's basically a good man", he said, "he just has his blind spots along with the rest of us". [Lee: KM, p. 176].
>
> – Містер Канінгем, по суті, непогана людина, але він, як і всі ми, не позбавлений деяких вад [Kharenko, p. 94].
>
> – Містер Каннінгем загалом гарна людина, – промовив він. – Просто він має свої недоліки, як і всі ми [Nekryach: UP, p. 122].

Thus, the study of core units used to realize the way of life and values of Southerners to denote the concept **of SOCIAL ORDER** allows us to draw the following conclusions: as a result of changes at the semantic level in the translation, such emotional features of Southerners as indignation and dissatisfaction with the policies of the northern states are detailed and intensified. By using the domestication strategy and frequently employing the tactic of addition, the original unit retains its semantic load and paints a more detailed picture of the value system of the inhabitants of the Southern USA. In this case, the use of descriptive translation and concretization of meaning enhances and details cultural elements, making their adequate reproduction possible, thus allowing for an appropriate understanding of the literary work and perception of the reality of the American South.

2.2.2 Rendering the Peripheral Components of the SOCIAL STRUCTURE Concept in Primary and Secondary Texts

The periphery of a concept is loosely structured but no less important for representing the entire essence of the concept and its translation. Even slight neglect of some elements can lead to a misinterpretation of the concept and the literary text. The periphery of the concept of **SOCIAL ORDER** includes metaphors and comparisons, the adequate translation of which in literary translation requires significant efforts from the translator, considering the stylistic features of the literary work and the author's idiolect.

Metaphor

The defeat of the South in the Civil War and the subsequent Reconstruction, which effectively meant the imposition of Northern orders, pushed back the internal traditional models of the Southern worldview for a long time. The Southern community indulged in nostalgia and rethought the past, present, and future. R. P. Warren convincingly explains the essence of the processes occurring in the Southern community, which had to rethink and somehow reconnect the interrupted history. The center of this process becomes the individual and their connections in society. Every Southerner is engaged and has a certain sense of home, indicative of a slow-paced, unhurried life:

> *Although Maycomb was ignored during the War Between the States, Reconstruction rule and economic ruin forced the town to grow. It grew inward. New people so rarely settled there; the same families married the same families until the members of the community looked faintly alike. Occasionally, someone would return from Montgomery or Mobile with an outsider, but the result caused only a ripple in the quiet stream of family resemblance. Things were more or less the same during my early years* [Lee: KM, p. 147].

> *– Хоч війна між північними і південними штатами обминула Мейкомб, закон про відбудову та економічна розруха спричинилися до росту міста. Правда, воно росло, не розростаючись вшир. Нові люди з'являлися тут рідко. За традицією, молоді одружувалися в межах певного сімейного кола, а тому жителі Мейкомба ставали*

поступово трохи схожі одне на одного. Траплялося, що хтось повертався з Монтгомері чи Мобіла з жінкою-чужинкою, але це не більше ніж легенька хвилька на спокійній гладіні сімейної схожості. Таким лишалося життя моїх земляків і в роки мого дитинства [Kharenko, p. 77].

– Мейком опинився поза колом активних дій у війні між Півднем та Північчю, але після економічної розрухи і законів про реконструкцію Півдня місто змушено було розростатися. Але то було зростання вглиб. Сюди рідко приїздили оселятися нові люди, родини одружувалися між собою, і через деякий час усі мешканці виглядали більш-менш подібними. Час від часу хтось повертався з Монтгомері чи Мобіла з тамтешньою дружиною, але це викликало ледь помітні брижі на гладкій поверхні родинної схожості. І за часів мого дитинства справи йшли саме так [Nekryach: UP, p. 100].

Atticus said professional people were poor because the farmers were poor. As Maycomb County was farm country, nickels and dimes were hard to come by for doctors and dentists and lawyers [Lee: KM, p. 24].

– Аттікус пояснив, що серед міських жителів багато бідних через те, що фермери бідні. Мейкомб – фермерський округ, ось чому лікарям, дантистам, адвокатам тут важко заробити [Kharenko, p. 11].

– Атикус сказав, що правники й лікарі збідніли, оскільки збідніли фермери. Округ Мейком – аграрний, тож юристи, дантисти та терапевти тепер рідко бачать живі гроші [Nekryach: UP, p. 15].

From the example above, it is evident that the metaphorical expression "nickels and dimes were hard to come by", used by Harper Lee, contains the colloquial term "nickels and dimes", meaning small amounts of money. In M. Kharenko's translation, this metaphor is rendered with a loss of metaphoricality but with the retention of its meaning "важко заробити", while T. Nekryach preserves the expressiveness and metaphoricality – "рідко бачити живі гроші".

The slow pace of life in the Southern USA is vividly represented in the following fragment from R.P. Warren's novel *All the King's Men:*

In a town like Mason City the bench in front of the harness shop is – or was twenty years ago before the concrete slab got laid down – the place where **Time gets tangled in its own feet** *and lies down like an old hound and gives up the struggle* [Warren, p. 37].

– У такому містечку, як Мейсон-Сіті, лава перед лимарнею є – чи принаймні була двадцять років тому, поки туди ще не проклали бетонку, – тим місцем, де **Час підупадає на ноги** *і, мов старий гончак, знеможено лягає долі, вже й не пробуючи звестися* [Mitrofanov: UKB, p. 62].

The metaphor "Time gets tangled in its own feet", which is associated with the factual information – bring time to a stop, is translated as "Час підупадає на ноги", containing the same implied information as the original – stoppage, slowness, and unhurriedness, characterizing the Southern way of life. V. Mitrofanov reproduces it in a way typical of the translation language.

Comparison

Unlike M. Mitchell and Harper Lee, R.P. Warren portrays the South of the USA somewhat differently. In the novel, *All the King's Men*, the social order of the Southern states is characterized by a particular fear of change and a reluctance to move forward, which is seen in the following comparison:

> <…> ***the law is like the pants you bought last year for a growing boy***, but it is always this year and the seams are popped and the shankbone's to the breeze [Warren, p. 88].

> – <…> *закон, наче **штани, куплені хлопчиську торік**, а в нас завжди цей рік, отож штани розлазяться по швах і з-під них стирчать кісточки* [Mitrofanov: UKB, p. 162].

The expression "the law is like the pants you bought last year for a growing boy", in which the law is compared to pants bought "to grow into", is translated by V. Mitrofanov as "закон, наче штани, куплені хлопчиську торік", preserving the connotation of the original – reconciliation with the then social order.

Idioms

The slow pace of life in the South is depicted by Harper Lee in her novel *To Kill a Mockingbird*, where she notes that Southerners never rushed but enjoyed every moment and did everything leisurely, which in the original is actualized by the idiom "took their time about everything", meaning "to act slowly or at one's leisure" [AHDI], which in the translations is rendered descriptively as "статечно, без поспіху" and "нікуди не поспішали":

> People **moved slowly then**. They ambled across the square, shuffled in and out of the stores around it, took their time about everything [Lee: KM, p. 6].

> – *Люди в ті часи **жили неквапом**. Ходили собі по площі, заглядали у крамниці, статечно, без поспіху* [Kharenko, p. 6].

> – *Люди в ті часи **рухалися повільно**. Вони дріботіли через площу, заглядали з однієї крамниці до іншої і нікуди не поспішали* [Nekryach: UP, p. 3].

It is noticeable that the semantic content of the core nomination **aristocrats-planters** in the 19th century changed at the beginning of the 20th century. This is traced in the novel *To Kill a Mockingbird*, where the planter family loses everything except the house. The novel shows how these aristocrats become the intelligentsia by obtaining an education (professional people), which in the Anglo-American context means doctors and lawyers.

English Linguistic Representations (SLAVERY Concept)

> *Well I'm glad he could, or who'd have taught Atticus and them, and if Atticus couldn't read, you and me'd be in a fix* [Lee: KM, p. 256].
>
> *– От і добре, що він умів, бо хто ж би тоді навчив Аттікуса і наших предків? А якби Аттікус не вмів читати, що було б з нами?* [Kharenko, p. 136].
>
> *– А я дуже рада, що він це вмів, бо хто б тоді навчив Атикуса і їх усіх, адже якби Атикус не вмів читати, нам було б непереливки* [Nekryach: UP, p. 175].

This excerpt shows that the family would have lived in poverty if not for Atticus Finch's father's education. Both translators adequately convey the expression, retaining the original's main semantic load.

Humanity, self-sacrifice, and courage are illustrated in the expression "they were for you tooth and nail":

> *He said the Cunninghams hadn't taken anything from or off of anybody since they migrated to the New World. He said the other thing about them was, once you earned their respect they were for you **tooth and nail*** [Lee: KM, p. 251].
>
> *– Відтоді, як Канінгеми переїхали в Новий Світ, вони ні в кого нічого не брали – ніколи. Це такі люди, сказав Аттікус, що заслужиш їхню повагу – і вони за тебе **у вогонь і воду підуть*** [Kharenko, p. 134].
>
> *– Він нагадав нам, що Каннінгеми ніколи нічого ні в кого не брали відтоді, як переселилися у Новий Світ. А іще їм притаманна і така риса: якщо вам вдалося заслужити їхню повагу, вони будуть **стояти за вас тілом і душею*** [Nekryach: UP, p. 171].

The expression "tooth and nail", meaning "with every available means" [AHDI], is rendered in the secondary texts using equivalents – "стояти тілом і душею" and "піти у вогонь і воду".

The periphery of the concept **of SOCIAL ORDER** is represented by metaphors, comparisons, and idioms, which in the secondary texts are mostly rendered literally with a partial loss of imagery and the use of the domestication strategy.

2.3 Rendering of English Linguistic Representations of the SLAVERY Concept of the American South into Ukrainian

The Southern United States gained notoriety in world historiography due to the extreme forms of exploitation of black slaves by the class of white planters. The victims of racism included not only black slaves but also indigenous people – Native Americans. The complete inhumanity of slavery is revealed in Harriet Beecher Stowe's abolitionist novel *Uncle Tom's Cabin* (1852), written before the Civil War, which enjoyed great success both in its own country and abroad. The book's essence lies in its concentrated depiction of the brutal situation faced by black inhabitants of the United States, deprived of civil rights. Beecher Stowe highlights ordinary, everyday phenomena legalized by slavery laws in their proper, horrific, and immoral significance. The fate of the central and episodic characters reflects all the misfortunes and humiliations constantly inflicted upon blacks by the slave-owning system: turning a living person with thoughts and feelings into an object that can be bought and sold; the forced and violent breaking of family ties; crude and cynical treatment of human personality; and the moral degradation of the slave.

Despite the conditionally Christian ending of the novel, where Beecher Stowe attempts to find a compromise reconciliation, the overall idea of the book vividly presents to the reader the entire drama of slavery. The aftermath of the Civil War showed the irrelevance of the political sentiments of the writer. However, *Uncle Tom's Cabin* has long remained in United States literature, almost as the first realistic social novel of the 19th century.

> *This is God's curse on slavery! – a bitter, bitter, most accursed thing! – a curse to the master and a curse to the slave!* [BS, p. 57].
>
> *The most dreadful part of slavery, to my mind, is its outrages on the feelings and affections <…>* [BS, p. 196].
>
> *– Прокляття Господнє тяжіє на рабстві, страшне прокляття! Воно винищує і рабів, і нас, панів* [Kuznetsova, p. 40]. *Але нехтування людськими почуттями <…>. Це обурює мене у рабстві найбільше* [Kuznetsova, p. 129].

White slave owners perceived their slaves in the following manner: *"damn mule-wrestling nigger"* [Faulkner, p. 5] – *"клятий чорношкірий мулопас"* [Dotsenko: K, p. 279]; *"punkin-headed nigger"* [Mark Twain: HF, p. 231] – *"дурноверхий негр"* [Steshenko, p. 148].

After the Civil War, the attitude of white planters towards black slaves began to change gradually, albeit against their will: *"treat them like reasonable creatures"* [BS, p. 281] – *"поводитися, як із розумними людьми"* [Kuznetsova, p. 182]; *"is worth kind treatment"* [BS, p. 274] – *"обходитися з ними треба лагідніше"* [Kuznetsova, p. 176–177].

2.3.1 Rendering the Core Components of the Concept of the SLAVERY Concept

The core of the ethnoculturally marked concept of the American South, **SLAVERY**, in the lexico-semantic context, reflects nationally specific informational elements. These elements present translation challenges as it is crucial to convey not only the form but also the content, the author's intent, and the thoughts and feelings of the characters that mirror the subjugated life in the Southern United States. The core of the concept is represented by the lexemes of "white people" and "negroes", whose translation must reflect the ethnocultural society within which the work was created.

> *But it had always been a struggle to teach Scarlett that most of her natural impulses were unladylike. Mammy's victories over Scarlett were hard-won and represented guile unknown to* **the white mind** [Mitchell, p. 40–41].

> *– А от переконати Скарлет, що майже всі природні дівчачі нахили суперечать приписам добропристойності, щоразу можна було тільки після відчайдушних зусиль. Кожна перемога над Скарлет важко давалася Мамці, бо вимагала таких хитрих викрутів, яких і не знають* ***білі люди*** [Dotsenko: ZV I, p. 81].

The phrase "white mind" requires careful attention in translation, rendered into Ukrainian as "білі люди". However, it raises the question of whether this fully captures what M. Mitchell intended. According to the dictionary, "mind" means "someone knowledgeable, especially in a particular subject or activity" [DCE, p. 1043], suggesting that the author aimed to distinguish whites from blacks, vividly portrayed in George M. Fredrickson's book "The Black Image in the White Mind: The Debate on Afro-American Character and Destiny, 1817–1914": "I advance it therefore as a suspicion only, that the blacks, whether originally a distinct race, or made distinct by time and circumstances, are inferior to whites both in body and mind". The translation "білі люди" may seem somewhat simplified to the Ukrainian reader, extrapolating this concept to all Americans without exception.

It is also pertinent to examine how the terms "white" and "black" are referred to in *Gone with the Wind* and how the proposed translations reflect in the mind of the target reader:

> *Mammy had her own method of letting her owners know exactly where she stood on all matters. She knew it was beneath the dignity of quality white folks to pay the slightest attention to what a darky said when she was grumbling to herself. She knew that to uphold this dignity, they must ignore what she said, even if she stood in the next room and almost shouted* [Mitchell, p. 35].

> *– Мамка виробила своєрідну методу, як доводити до відома господарів власну думку. Вона знала, що гідність не дозволяє білим людям звертати хоч якусь там увагу на буркотню негрів, отож вони вдають, ніби не чують служниці, навіть коли та мало не на весь голос кричить, але в сусідній кімнаті* [Dotsenko: ZV I, p. 74].

In this context, "white folks" is translated literally as "білі люди", which is appropriate since "folks" means "people" and is also "used when talking to a group of people in a friendly way" [DCE, p. 621]. M. Mitchell often refers to blacks with the pejorative term "darky", which R. Dotsenko translates variably into Ukrainian, initially as "чернюки" and in this passage simply as "негри", thus not preserving the stylistic coloration.

The core components of the concept are actualized in literary works through the following conceptual features:

1. **"Near Total Subjugation"**. Striving to depict the horrors of slavery maximally, H. Beecher Stown, from the very first chapters of her book, portrays the ideal relationships between slaves and humane slave owners. The master of the house completely trusts the black man, Tom, who honestly manages the plantation, and the mistress treats the servant girl, Eliza, favorably. However, such relationships also reflect the absolute power of whites over blacks, who understand and acknowledge this:

*"Well", said Eliza, mournfully, "I always thought that **I must obey my master and mistress**, or I couldn't be a Christian"* [BS, p. 30].

*– А я, – сумно мовила Еліза, – я завжди гадала, що як істинна християнка мушу у **всьому коритися своїм господарям** <…>* [Kuznetsova, p. 20]. / *Де ж би то, – сумно мовила Еліза. – Я от завше вважала, що **мушу слухатись своїх пана й пані**, бо так мені належить від Бога* [Mitrofanov: HDT, p. 18].

In the original quadroon, Eliza states, "I must obey my master and mistress". Both translators reproduce this with synonymous equivalents – "мушу у всьому коритися своїм господарям" and "мушу слухати своїх пана й пані".

The significant value of the novel lies in the writer's ability to show the full horror of the lives of blacks on the plantation of the slave owner, Legree, providing a truthful and realistic picture of the country's largest slave markets.

The woman seemed stimulated, for a few moments, to an unnatural strength, and worked with desperate eagerness [BS, p. 556].

– Мулатка зібрала всю свою волю в кулак, підвелася і почала дуже швидко збирати бавовну [Kuznetsova, p. 336]. / *Зробивши над собою надлюдське зусилля, жінка в розпачі підвелась і почала хапливо оббирати бавовну* [Mitrofanov: HDT, p. 328].

*Nevertheless, as this young man was in the eye of the law not a man, but a thing, all these superior qualifications **were subject to the control of a vulgar, narrow-minded, tyrannical master*** [BS, p. 23].

*– Але за законом цей обдарований мулат був не людиною, а лише річчю, **робочою силою**, і **повністю залежав** від свого **деспотичного і обмеженого господаря*** [Kuznetsova, p. 15]. / *Та оскільки перед лицем закону цей молодик вважався не за людину, а лиш за річ, то всі його неординарні здібності **улягали владі** грубого, **дрібноголового й свавільного господаря*** [Mitrofanov: HDT, p. 13].

In this excerpt, the dependence of slaves on slave owners is noted, verbalized in the primary text by the phrase "were subject to the control", which both translators reproduce using synonymous equivalents – "повністю залежав" (L. Kuznetsova) and "улягали владі" (V. Mitrofanov). Through the addition of "робоча сила" (labor force), L. Kuznetsova clarifies the role of the black population for the white people, who were not just things but the labor force that did all the hard work. Such masters are called "a vulgar, narrow-minded, tyrannical master" by H. Beecher Stowe, which L. Kuznetsova translates, omitting the lexeme "vulgar" and using instead the equivalents "деспотичний" and "обмежений господар". V. Mitrofanov uses differentiation of meaning, translating "narrow-minded" as "дрібноголовий" and providing the equivalents "грубий" and "свавільний".

> *If a slave refuses to obey, then "he had to be broken in": "to let any such brangle come up," said Legree; "but, when the boy set up his will, **he had to be broken in**"* [BS, p. 582].

> *Не варто було робити це тепер. Але якщо раб відмовляється коритися, його треба одразу ж **ставити на місце**, інакше – викинуті на вітер гроші* [Kuznetsova, p. 383].

> *<…> я вчинив дурницю, що допустився сутички, – визнав Легрі. – Але ж він затявся на своєму, і треба було його **приборкати*** [Mitrofanov: HDT, p. 376].

In the secondary text, L. Kuznetsova translates the figurative phrase "he had to be broken in" as "поставити на місце кого", meaning "to put someone in their place, sharply correct someone for immodest, arrogant behavior" [SFSUM], using semantic development – "викинуті на вітер гроші", meaning wasted money. V. Mitrofanov uses the equivalent "приборкати", meaning "to subdue, call to order a disobedient, obstinate, or dangerous person" [VTSSUM, p. 1324], thus actualizing the conceptual feature of "near total subjugation".

2. H. Beecher Stowe depicts the actual state of the slave-owning system, the establishment of spiritual and psychological complexes accompanied by the "deprivation of rights" of black people:

> *"Don't you know **a slave can't be married**? There is no law in this country for that; I can't hold you for my wife, if he chooses to part us"* [BS, p. 32].

> *Хіба тобі не відомо, **що раб не має права одружуватися, та й взагалі не має жодних прав**? Закони нашої країни не захищають рабів. Якщо господар чогось захоче, то не питатиме, чи подобається це нам* [Kuznetsova, p. 22].

> *Хіба ти не знаєш, що раб **не правий одружуватись**? Немає на це закону, і, якщо хазяїн надумає нас розлучити, ніхто не визнає тебе за мою дружину* [Mitrofanov: HDT, p. 20].

The lack of rights for black people is highlighted in the statement about the prohibition of marriage, "A slave can't be married", which V. Mitrofanov translates literally as "раб не правий одружуватися", while L. Kuznetsova uses semantic development "раб не має права одружуватися, та й взагалі не має жодних прав".

The conceptual feature of "deprivation of rights" is actualized in the narrative about the prohibition for black people to invent and engage in intellectual activities, vividly depicted through the example of the resourceful mulatto George and his master Harris:

*"**What business** had his slave to be marching round the country, inventing machines, and holding up his head among gentlemen? He'd soon put a stop to it. He'd take him back, and put him to hoeing and digging, and '**see if he'd step about so smart**'"* [BS, p. 23].

*"**Як сміє** якийсь раб щось винаходити та розмовляти із панами, мов з рівнею?! Це необхідно виправити. Негайно забрати його із фабрики, долучити до польових робіт. **Тоді й побачимо, який він герой!**"* [Kuznetsova, p. 15].

*Далебі, **з якої б ото речі** його раб мав роз'їжджати по країні, винаходити машини й не схиляти голови перед панами? Ось він покладе цьому край. Забере його назад і змусить копати й шарувати землю, а відтак, мовляв, "**побачимо, де подінеться його гонор**"* [Mitrofanov: HDT, p. 13].

Mr. Harris, expressing dissatisfaction with his slave's inventions, uses the phrase "what business", which both translators convey with contextual equivalents – "як сміє" (L. Kuznetsova) and "з якої б ото речі" (V. Mitrofanov). As a despotic owner, Harris sends the slave back to the plantations and notes that "see if he'd step about so smart". L. Kuznetsova uses the contextual equivalent "побачимо, який він герой", which adequately conveys the meaning of the original, as "герой" denotes "a person distinguished by their abilities and deeds" [VTSSUM, p. 523], i.e., a "smart person". V. Mitrofanov also uses a contextual equivalent, but a different one – "побачимо, де подінеться його гонор", in which another meaning is actualized: it emphasizes not the slave's cleverness, but his sense of personal dignity.

3. The feature of the "cruel treatment" of wealthy masters towards their slaves is actualized in such fragments:

*The **outrageous treatment** of poor Tom had roused her still more; and she had followed Legree to the house, with no particular intention, but **to upbraid him for his brutality*** [BS, p. 582].

*А коли Легрі наказав так **жорстоко покарати** Тома, вона просто спалахнула від бажання його розчавити, **стерти з лиця землі*** [Kuznetsova, p. 383].

Нелюдська розправа** над бідолашним Томом ще дужче збурила її душу, і вона пішла за Легрі в дім з єдиною метою – **вичитати йому за жорстокість [Mitrofanov: HDT, p. 376].

It is about how the unfortunate black man Tom suffered "outrageous treatment", which is reproduced in the secondary texts with contextual equivalents – "жорстоко покарати" (L. Kuznetsova) and "нелюдська розправа" (V. Mitrofanov).

Then the black woman Lucy, upon hearing about Tom's punishment, is ready "to upbraid him [Legree] for his brutality", that is, to scold the master for such rudeness, which V. Mitrofanov reproduces with the equivalent "вичитати йому за жорстокість". However, in Kuznetsova's translation, the accurate picture is distorted, as it is figuratively translated as "стерти з лиця землі" with a different meaning – "to kill" [SFSUM].

At the first opportunity, the master is ready to "bust him over the head", meaning "to punch him in the head", which is reproduced using contextual translation with derogatory, colloquial vocabulary – "затоплю йому в пику":

*I wouldn' think nuff'n; I'd take en **bust him over de head**. Dat is, if he warn't white. I wouldn' 'low no nigger to call me dat* [Mark Twain: HF, p. 83].

*– Анічогісінько я не подумаю, а тільки **затоплю йому в пику** – звісно, якщо той чолов'яга не білий. **Щоб я дозволив негрові так мене вилаяти!*** [Steshenko, p. 50].

Additionally, mocking, the white man remarks: "I wouldn' 'low no nigger to call me dat", which is translated into Ukrainian with a specification of the meaning of "to call" – "вилаяти": "щоб я дозволив негрові так мене вилаяти".

A cruel overseer sarcastically addresses a black woman who does not manage to fill the basket with the required weight of cotton:

*<…> "you'll know how good it is, **Misse!**"* [BS, p. 554].

*Тепер дізнаєшся, **почім ківш лиха, білоручко!*** [Kuznetsova, p. 363].

*Скуштуйте, **пані**, нашого меду!* [Mitrofanov: HDT, p. 356].

The translators adapt the expression using means inherent to Ukrainian culture, employing contextual equivalents – "по чім ківш лиха" (L. Kuznetsova) and "скуштуйте нашого меду" (V. Mitrofanov). The overseer calls the black woman "Misse". V. Mitrofanov uses the equivalent "пані", while L. Kuznetsova uses semantic development and calls her "білоручкою" – meaning someone who shuns physical, black labor, an idler.

The black population considers their masters "low" – "підлими" (differentiation) and "cruel" – "жорстокими" (equivalent):

They are all of 'em as low and cruel to each other as they can be; there's no use in your suffering to keep from hurting them [BS, p. 566].

Вони підлі та жорстокі, а ти їх оберігаєш, заступаєшся за них, терпиш такі муки! Вони того не варті! [Kuznetsova, p. 371–372].

Вони геть усі підлі й жорстокі один до одного, і ні до чого тобі терпіти муки, аби порятувати їх від побою [Mitrofanov: HDT, p. 362].

Moreover, blacks do not consider themselves an inferior race and oppose the degrading attitude of the white elite and cruel treatment:

<...> *"what right has he to make a **dray-horse** of me?"* [BS, p. 29].

<...> *хто дав йому право мати мене за **худобу**...* [Kuznetsova, p. 19].

*Тож за яким таким правом він обертає мене на **чорну худобу**...*[Mitrofanov: HDT, p. 17].

Undoubtedly, blacks complain that whites consider them "dray-horse" – "a large, powerful horse used to pull heavy loads" [LDELC, p. 563]. L. Kuznetsova offers a hyperonym – "худоба" (cattle), meaning a contemptuous name for the enslaved. V. Mitrofanov resorts to adding the adjective "чорний" – "чорна худоба" (black cattle), emphasizing the slavery of the black population.

*"You ought enter wish that ar to any human crittur." "We wouldn't to anybody but the **soul-drivers**," said Andy; "nobody can help wishing it to them, they's so awful wicked"* [BS, p. 89].

*Вічні муки – це жахливо, **не можна такого бажати навіть ворогам**. – А цим мучителям можна! – уперто гнув свою лінію Енді. – Їм, **кровопивцям**, цього усі зичать* [Kuznetsova, p. 60].

Не можна зичити вічної муки ні одній живій істоті**. А ми й не зичимо нікому, окрім торговців людьми, – озвався Енді. – Таж їм усі цього зичать, отим **проклятущим лиходіям [Mitrofanov: HDT, p. 57].

Aunt Chloe, Mrs. Shelby's servant, clearly expresses her views using the phrase "you ought enter wish that ar to any human crittur" – (lit.: you should not wish that to any human creature) – "не можна такого бажати навіть ворогам". The translation is close to the Ukrainian reader, as the VT speaks of something you wouldn't wish on anyone, and in the PT – you wouldn't wish on even an enemy (Ukrainian expression): V. Mitrofanov reproduces it as "не можна зичити <...> ні одній живій істоті". Aunt Chloe's son Andy calls the white masters "the soul-drivers" and "awful wicked". Reproducing the phrase "the soul-drivers", which means "overseer of slaves, namely blacks; driver" [UAS], since "soul" – "spirit of the black people; self-awareness (of American) blacks; black, Negro" [UAS], both translators use contextual equivalents – "мучителі" and "торговці людьми". The phrase "awful wicked" L. Kuznetsova translates with the derogatory word "кровопивці" meaning oppressors, tyrants, and V. Mitrofanov uses the colloquial and derogatory "проклятущі лиходії".

4. The Conceptual Feature of "Humiliation". This feature is actualized by the contemptuous and offensive attitude of the white population toward the black population, as white masters consider themselves more intelligent and more cunning than blacks:

*Quashy is **ignorant** and weak, and I am intelligent and strong, – because I know how, and can do it, – therefore, I **may steal all he has**, keep it, and give him only such and so much as suits my fancy* [BS, p. 353].

*<…> негр Кваші – істота **темна, неосвічена**, відповідно безпорадна, а я вчений, влада у моїх руках, тож **мені нічого не заважає обібрати його як липку** і з царського плеча виділяти йому лише те, що я вважатиму за потрібне (зазвичай рабовласники дають рабам рівно стільки, щоб вони не померли з голоду і могли працювати)* [Kuznetsova, pp. 229–230].

*Мій **чорний брат** темний і слабкий, а я розумний і сильний – **отож мені вільно привласнювати все, що він має**, а йому давати лиш те, що мені негоже* [Mitrofanov: HDT, p. 214].

Plantation owner Legree calls his black man Quashy "ignorant", which is metaphorically rendered in the translations as "темний" (dark), and L. Kuznetsova also uses semantic development by adding the lexeme "неосвічений" (uneducated), highlighting the lack of education and understanding among blacks, pointing to the absence of basic knowledge. In the Ukrainian translation, the master's attitude towards slaves is depicted with greater expressiveness. If the original text states, "I may steal all he has", in the secondary text, it is rendered with an expressive connotation – "мені нічого не заважає обібрати його як липку" (I can rob him blind). To emphasize the master's ruling role, L. Kuznetsova adds the Russian idiom "з царського плеча" (from the royal shoulder), which is not a suitable decision as it disrupts specific parameters of the original worldview. Additionally, the translator adds a comment that clarifies the attitude of whites toward blacks. On the other hand, V. Mitrofanov's translation is closer to the literal meaning – "мені вільно привласнювати все, що він має" (I am free to take everything he has).

White plantation owners not only despised blacks and oppressed them, but they also did not consider them to be human beings. This is evident in the following excerpt:

"No'm. Killed a nigger." "Well, it's lucky; because sometimes people do get hurt" [BS, p. 215].

– Ні, мем. Убило негра. – Це ще дуже щасливо, бо часом і люди гинуть" [Kuznetsova, p. 137].

The phrase *"a damn mule-wrestling nigger"* [Faulkner, p. 5] is rendered into Ukrainian using a semantic equivalent "цей клятий чорношкірий мулопас" [Dovzhenko: K, p. 279], with the use of a more neutral word "чорношкірий" (black-skinned).

5. The Feature of "Indulgence". In addition to the shameful and cruel treatment of black slaves by white masters, which did not disappear after the Civil War, H. Beecher Stowe depicts rare cases of indulgent relationships. This concerns the slave owner, St. Clare, who was not devoid of humanity. The feature of "indulgence" is exemplified through this character:

> It's abominable, to be sure; but St. Clare will **have high life below-stairs**, and they every one of them live just as they please. The fact is, our servants are over-indulged [BS, p. 271].

> Це, звісно, нікуди не годиться, але Сен-Клер хоче, **щоб слуги були на рівні з господарями**, от вони і живуть собі, як у Бога за пазухою. Певною мірою у цьому винні ми самі, що вони поводяться, як розбещені діти [Kuznetsova, p. 176].

> Це, звісно, нікуди не годиться, але Сен-Клерові, бачте, до вподоби, **щоб його челядь розкошувала**, отож вони й живуть собі, мов пани. Що правда, то правда – наші слуги аж надто розбещені [Mitrofanov: HDT, p. 163].

St. Clare wants to "have high life below-stairs", where "below stairs" means "at or in the basement of a large house, considered as the place where the servants live and work (sometimes used to denote servants in a rich household and the things that are connected with them)" [OGBACLE, p. 695], "high life" refers to high society. L. Kuznetsova translates it descriptively as "слуги були на рівні з господарями" (servants were on par with the masters). At the same time, V. Mitrofanov uses a contextual equivalent, "челядь розкошувала" (servants were living luxuriously).

Moreover, St. Clare's slaves lived "just as they please", meaning "як їм хотілося". This phrase L. Kuznetsova translates with the Ukrainian saying "як у Бога за пазухою" (like in God's bosom), which manifests an entirely different semantics – being in safety. V. Mitrofanov uses a contextual equivalent "живуть собі як пани" (live like masters), meaning to live luxuriously.

St. Clare's daughter Eva did not consider herself superior to the blacks – the phrase "to put oneself on an equality with someone" L. Kuznetsova translates with the omission of the unit and the specification of meaning – replacing the phrase "every creature", which characterizes all people, with the pronoun "ними" (them), which indicates only the blacks. V. Mitrofanov also uses specification in the translation of "creature" – "негри" (blacks):

> But Eva somehow always seems to put herself on an equality with every creature that comes near her [BS, p. 274].

> Але Єва тримається з ними, як із рівними [Kuznetsova, p. 178].

> Але Єва до кожного негра ставиться як до рівні [Mitrofanov: HDT, p. 168].

Ophelia quotes St. Clare, who justifies the actions and behavior of blacks:

> He says **their faults are allowing to us**, and that it would be cruel to make the fault and punish it too [BS, p. 277].

> Він стверджує, що **їхні недоліки – реакція на рабовласницький лад як явище**. Сен-Клер вважає, що саме тому ми не маємо морального права карати їх за їхні ж недоліки [Kuznetsova, p. 180].

> А коли мовляв, **їхні вади йдуть од нас**, то надто жорстоко ще й карати їх за це [Mitrofanov: HDT, p. 171].

Reproducing the phrase "their faults are allowing to us", V. Mitrofanov uses a literal translation "їхні вади йдуть од нас", while L. Kuznetsova resorts to semantic development "їхні недоліки – реакція на рабовласницький лад як явище".

St. Clare's cousin Ophelia calls black people "reasonable creatures", or in Ukrainian equivalents, "розумні люди" (reasonable people) and "immortal creatures", which in translation is rendered descriptively as "наділені безсмертною душею" (endowed with an immortal soul), preserving the meaning:

> You ought to educate your slaves, and treat them like **reasonable creatures**, – like **immortal creatures**, that you've got to stand before the bar of God with [BS, p. 281].

> <…> невільників обов'язково треба вчити; поводитися, як із **розумними людьми, наділеними безсмертною душею**; постійно пам'ятати, що і за них також доведеться відповідати перед Богом [Kuznetsova, p. 182].

In Mark Twain's novel *"Adventures of Huckleberry Finn"*, the main characters are people of noble spirit, Huck and his friend, the runaway slave Jim. Other whites do not approve of the fact that Huck protects a black man. Even Tom Sawyer is not capable of such magnanimity. He tries to free Jim, aware that Jim is already free. For Tom, it is just fun, an adventure, a game, whereas Huck sincerely tries to save Jim, realizing that this makes him a criminal in society. Therefore, the excerpt below is not difficult to translate but is quite essential for understanding how white people (in the form of children) gradually change their view of blacks:

> I couldn't ever understand before, until that minute and that talk, how he could help a body set a nigger free, with his bringing-up [Mark Twain: HF, p. 278].

> – "А я ніяк не міг збагнути, аж до цієї хвилини й до цієї розмови, як він – хлопець, що дістав таке виховання, – міг допомагати мені звільнити негра!" [Steshenko, p. 180].

I. Steshenko resorts to semantic development, rendering the phrase "kind treatment" (good treatment) as "обходитися з ними треба лагідніше" (one should treat them more gently), emphasizing that black people need better treatment. This is evident from the following sentence:

> <…> I tell you, gentlemen, a nigger like that is worth a thousand dollars – and **kind treatment**, too [Twain: HF, p. 274].

*– Запевняю вас, джентльмени, що він вартий і тисячі доларів, та й **обходитися з ними треба лагідніше*** [Steshenko, pp. 176–177].

The change in relations between whites and blacks is characterized by the fact that masters even 1) humble oneself to a nigger [Mark Twain: HF, p. 90] – принижуватися перед негром [Steshenko, p. 54] (antonymic translation) and 2) keep his promise to ole Jim [Mark Twain: HF, p. 93] – єдиний білий джентльмен, що не одурив старого Джіма [Steshenko, p. 56] (semantic development), which follows from the following stories:

It was fifteen minutes before I could work myself up to go and humble myself to a nigger – but I done it, and I warn't ever sorry for it afterwards, neither [Mark Twain: HF, p. 90]

– Минуло хвилин п'ятнадцять, аж поки я переміг себе й пішов принижуватися перед негром; а проте я зробив це і ніколи об тім не шкодував – ніколи! [Steshenko, p. 54];

Dah you goes, de ole true Huck; de on'y white genlman dat ever kep' his promise to ole Jim [Mark Twain: HF, p. 93].

– Щасливо тобі доїхати, чесний, вірний Геку! Ти єдиний білий джентльмен, що не одурив старого Джіма! [Steshenko, p. 56].

Using the example of Huck Finn, Mark Twain depicts the loyal attitude of some whites towards blacks.

The analyzed material allows us to conclude that the core units of the concept SLAVERY are the lexemes "white folks" and "niggers", which are translated using equivalents. The following features characterize the relationships between whites and blacks: 1) almost complete subjugation; 2) deprivation of rights; 3) cruel treatment; 4) humiliation; 5) indulgence, which in Ukrainian translation are rendered using the strategy of domestication to bring the text closer to the Ukrainian reader, and tactics such as a) specification of meaning; b) semantic development; c) omission of lexemes; d) descriptive translation; e) contextual substitution. All these methods allowed translators to fully convey the core components of the analyzed concept for the correct interpretation by the foreign reader, although minor losses in translation occurred.

2.3.2 Rendering the Peripheral Components of the SLAVERY Concept in Primary and Secondary Texts

The periphery of the concept of SLAVERY is represented by elements of the associative field, which includes metaphors, comparisons, and idiomatic expressions. It is appropriate to consider the main features of the concept that are actualized by peripheral elements regarding the relationships between whites and blacks, which are implicitly reflected in literary works, as well as their adequate translation into Ukrainian. It is known that even after the end of the Civil War, slavery in the Southern United States was not abolished, and this area became a "great market for bodies and souls" [BS, p. 116] – "ринок людських тіл і душ" [Kuznetsova, p. 76] – the metaphorical expression is rendered literally with the addition of clarification – "людський".

Using metaphors in the original texts actualizes the feature of **"cruelty"**. Blacks believed that in the South, there continued to exist a

<…> *dread, unhallowed necromancy of evil, that turns things sweetest and holiest to phantoms of horror and affright* [BS, p. 584].

Якась зла чи просто несправедлива сила очорняє все найкраще, перетворюючи його на докори сумління і ще гірше озлоблюючи поганих людей [Kuznetsova, p. 385].

Така вже темна сила зла, що воно, мов лихим чаром, обертає все найкраще та найсвятіше для людини на жаскі, моторошні привиддя [Mitrofanov: HDT, p. 354].

The metaphorical expression is rendered into Ukrainian with neutralization of meaning, as "necromancy of evil" means 1) magic, especially evil magic; 2) the practice of claiming to talk with the dead [DCE, p. 1098], while in the translation, it is rendered as "несправедлива сила" (unjust power). The translator does not fully convey the emotions and sufferings of the blacks.

Aunt Chloe, in H. Beecher Stowe's "Uncle Tom's Cabin," speaking about the abuses by white people who mercilessly sell infants, taking them from their mothers, says:

"Don't nature herself kinder cry out on 'em?" said Aunt Chloe [BS, p. 89].

"Сама мати-природа стане проти них", said Aunt Chloe [Kuznetsova, p. 60].

"Чи не волає проти них сама природа!" exclaimed Aunt Chloe [Mitrofanov: HDT, p. 52].

L. Kuznetsova renders the metaphorical expression "Don't nature herself kinder cry out on 'em?" using a partial Ukrainian equivalent with slight changes in imagery – "сама мати-природа стане проти них" – adding the lexeme "мати-природа" (Mother Nature), which is typical and understandable to Ukrainians. V. Mitrofanov resorts to a literal translation – "волає проти них сама природа" (Nature herself cries out against them).

However, despite the inhumane treatment of blacks, whites are aware of their actions:

We are breaking all humanizing ties, and making them brute beasts <…> [BS, p. 424].

Ми самі винні, що негри втрачають людську подобу і стають тваринами [Kuznetsova, p. 277].

Ми зневажаємо всі людські почуття й робимо з них грубих звірів [Mitrofanov: HDT, p. 260].

Translators use functional substitution in rendering the metaphorical phrase "we are breaking all humanizing ties" – "ми самі винні, що негри втрачають людську подобу" (L. Kuznetsova) and "ми зневажаємо всі людські почуття" (V. Mitrofanov). The metaphorical phrase "making them brute beasts" is narrowed by omitting the adjective "brute," whose translation would not add additional information – "стають тваринами" (become animals). V. Mitrofanov uses a literal translation – "робимо з них грубих звірів" (make them brutish beasts).

A metaphor is based on internal, rather than external, manifestations of life, as confirmed by the thoughts of one of the main characters in "Uncle Tom's Cabin" – the black man Tom:

<...> *that this kind o' trade is hardening to the feelings; but I never found it so* [BS, p. 13].

<...> *що на нашій роботі черствієш душею. Але це не про мене* [Kuznetsova, p. 8].

<...> *нібито така комерція робить людину бездушною, а я не згоден* [Mitrofanov: HDT, p. 6].

The metaphorical expression "this kind o' trade is hardening to the feelings" contains two metaphors, the first of which in L. Kuznetsova's translation is rendered with a neutralization of imagery, but with retention of meaning – "trade is hardening" (work makes us callous) – "на роботі черствієш" (you become callous at work). The following metaphor "harden to the feelings" the translator appropriately renders with a phraseological analog – "черствіти душею" (become callous at heart). V. Mitrofanov resorts to demetaphorization with retention of the original meaning – "така комерція робить людину бездушною" (this kind of commerce makes a person heartless).

Blacks understand the root of the evil. This is brilliantly conveyed through a metaphor that evokes vivid, eerie associations and shapes the concept of SLAVERY:

<...> *but now **you've got his ill will upon you**, to follow you day in, day out, **hanging like a dog on your throat**, – sucking your blood, bleeding away your life, drop by drop* [BS, p. 598].

*Тепер же тобі **не позаздриш, він мстивий**. Буде щодня **заганяти тебе під землю**, повільно питиме твою кров* [Kuznetsova, p. 395].

*Але тепер він на тебе **лютим чортом дихатиме**. Він **не дасть тобі спокою ні на мить, мов той собака**, пильнуватиме, як би вчепитися в горлянку! Всю кров із тебе виточить по краплі!* [Mitrofanov: HDT, p. 384].

In this fragment from "Uncle Tom's Cabin," Tom and Cassy, who were in slavery under the ruthless white master Legree, discuss their punishment for disobedience. The metaphorical expression "you've got his ill will upon you" means "unfriendly or unkind feelings towards someone" [DCE, p. 809], and in L. Kuznetsova's translation is rendered descriptively with the addition of some features – "не позаздриш, він мстивий" (you wouldn't envy him, he's vindictive) – and with a loss of imagery. In contrast, V. Mitrofanov uses the Ukrainian idiom "лютим чортом дихати" (breathe like an angry devil).

Rendering the comparison "hanging like a dog on your throat", L. Kuznetsova uses the Ukrainian idiom "заганяти під землю" (drive into the ground), meaning to torment, drive to death. The translation retains the original meaning. V. Mitrofanov translates the comparison literally – "не дасть тобі спокою ні на мить, мов той собака" (won't give you a moment's peace, like that dog). To avoid repetition in the secondary text, the phrase "bleeding away your life" is omitted, as it refers to the master "sucking your blood", equivalent to "питиме твою кров" (drink your blood) in L. Kuznetsova's translation. V. Mitrofanov uses a phraseological analog – "вчепитися в горлянку" (grab the throat), meaning to engage in a fierce argument, quarrel, or irreconcilable conflict, persistently demanding something [SFSUM].

The feature of **"humiliation"** is represented by metaphors and comparisons that convey the negative, offensive behavior of the white population towards the black population. This is driven by the belief that whites are more innovative and superior to blacks:

This is simply saying that the negro mind has been more crushed and debased than the white [BS, p. 544].

Та це лише тому, що негри нетямущі, затуркані люди [Kuznetsova, p. 355].

<…> і, відбувши ту науку, вони стали мало чим різнитися від лютих собак [Mitrofanov: HDT, p. 340].

The cruel oppressor, Legree, in "Uncle Tom's Cabin", metaphorically speaks about the unintelligence of blacks. In L. Kuznetsova's translation, this is rendered neutrally with a loss of imagery – "нетямущі, затуркані люди" (ignorant, driven people), leading to demetaphorization. V. Mitrofanov resorts to a trope shift, replacing the metaphor with a phraseological unit – "мало чим різнитися від собак" (little different from dogs).

In G. Beecher Stowe's novel, superiority is also observed:

"Wash my dishes!" said Dinah, in a high key, as her wrath began to rise over her habitual respect of manner <…> [BS, p. 333].

"Мити одразу?" – зойкнула тітонька Ді, забувши про правила спілкування із панами [Kuznetsova, p. 215].

"Щоб я мила посуд!" – аж скрикнула Діна, в якої гнів починав брати гору над позірною штивістю [Mitrofanov: HDT, p. 321].

In the described situation, the black servant Dinah addresses her masters "in a high key", i. e., in an authoritative tone, which in the secondary text is rendered as "зойкнула" (exclaimed), meaning to shout frantically (out of horror, despair, pleading for help). Saying this, "wrath began to rise over her habitual respect of manner", where "wrath" means "extreme anger" [DCE, p. 1910]. L. Kuznetsova resorts to demetaphorization – "забувши про правила спілкування із панами" (forgetting the rules of communication with the masters), losing expressiveness. V. Mitrofanov translates with a metaphor, using a contextual equivalent – "гнів починав брати гору над позірною штивістю" (anger began to take over her outward stiffness).

W. Faulkner depicts the arrogance of whites towards blacks, using colloquial language, which R. Dotsenko domesticates, using an analog that preserves the meaning: "a damn mule-wrestling nigger either criticize my private tail" [Faulkner, p. 5] – "як цей клятий чорношкірий мулопас ганить мій зад" [Dotsenko: K, p. 279].

The analyzed material shows that the peripheral elements of the concept of SLAVERY, represented by metaphors, comparisons, and idiomatic expressions, are translated using various strategies to convey the emotional and cultural nuances to the Ukrainian reader. These strategies include functional substitution, demetaphorization, descriptive translation, and contextual equivalents, which help preserve the original meaning and expressiveness of the text.

Furthermore, whites *considered the negro, through all possible gradations of color, as* **an intermediate link between man and animals** <…> [BS, p. 544]. – *Але негри усіх відтінків – від квартеронів до найчорніших – він вважав* **перехідною ланкою від тварин до людей** <…> [Kuznetsova, p. 232] – rendered literally in the translation. Additionally, masters treated them like dogs: *They treat them worse than dogs* [BS, p. 171]. – *Поводитьсягірше, ніж з собакою* [Kuznetsova, p. 107] – a literal translation.

Apart from the cruel treatment of the dark-skinned population by the white elite, H. Beecher Stowe, along with W. Faulkner, for whom the patriarchal South was the only ideal of a society where every person was not separated from the social fabric but instead connected to it by even a criminal but blood tie, where there was the sin of slavery, try to show in their works a change in relations as whites begin to feel guilt towards blacks:

At last, one day, John's **great heart had swelled altogether too big to wear his bonds any longer** <…> [BS, p. 148]. – *Іодного дня* **чоловік вирішив скинути з душі цей камінь**<…> [Kuznetsova, p. 96]. / *Нарешті його* **велике серце переповнилось і не витримало** [Mitrofanov: HDT, p. 82]. H. Beecher Stowe metaphorically conveys the state of one of the whites, John – "*great heart had swelled altogether too big to wear his bonds any longer*". The translator deforms this expression by rendering it with a Ukrainian idiom – "*скинути з душі цей камінь*" (to shed this weight from his soul), which means *"to free oneself from something that oppresses, torments"* [SFSUM]. V. Mitrofanov's translation is close to the original – *"велике серце переповнилось і не витримало"* (his great heart overflowed and could not bear it any longer).

L. Kuznetsova uses the tactic of addition to precisely mirror the relationships between whites and blacks in the Southern United States: *"aiding"* – *"helping runaway negroes"* and *"abetting"* – *"assisting their escape,"* which is easily perceived in the sentence, while V. Mitrofanov resorts to a literal translation: *"Why, yes, my dear; that would be **aiding and abetting**, you know"* [BS, p. 128]. – *Не можна, моя люба. Бо саме це і означає **"допомагати неграм-утікачам"** і **"сприяти їхній втечі"*** [Kuznetsova, p. 84]. / *Саме так, голубонько. Це ж, бач, і є **допомога й сприяння*** [Mitrofanov: HDT, p. 69]. However, *"aid and abet"* is a fixed expression that should not be translated into parts. Excessive translation distorts the message.

St. Clare firmly believes in the disappearance of slavery and states: <…> *for, just begin and thoroughly educate one generation, and **the whole thing** would be blown sky high* [BS, p. 368]. – *Досить буде навчити грамоті одне покоління негрів – і рабовласницька система лусне, як мильна бульбашка* [Kuznetsova, p. 239]. To bring the source text closer to the target intercultural audience, the translator uses semantic development in rendering the phrase "рабовласницька система", which *"would be blown sky high"*. This idiom means *"to destroy something completely"* [AHDI], which in the Anglo-Ukrainian idiomatic dictionary means *"to tear apart, criticize, leave no stone unturned"* [AUFS, p. 147], L. Kuznetsova conveys with the Ukrainian analog – *"лусне, як мильна бульбашка"* (burst like a soap bubble).

The negro George in the novel "Uncle Tom's Cabin" understands and openly says that <…> *for slavery always ends in misery* [BS, p. 185]. – *Рабство нічого, крім гірких сліз, нам не принесе* [Kuznetsova, p. 121]. / <…> *бо рабство завжди несе біду* [Mitrofanov: HDT, p. 108]. In the Ukrainian text, L. Kuznetsova uses the tactic of semantic development: *"misery"* – "гіркі сльози".

Thus, the difficulties in reproducing the means of imagery to denote the relations between the white and black populations in the Southern United States arise due to the associative mismatch between the elements of the metaphor in the source and target languages. Furthermore, translators manage, with minor losses, to reproduce the Ukrainian linguistic peripheral representations of the concept of SLAVERY and create an overall picture of the relationships between whites and blacks based on subjugation and disdain for the Ukrainian reader. In this regard, the peripheral elements – metaphors, comparisons, and idioms – are translated primarily using the strategy of domestication and, to a lesser extent, foreignization. The translated texts are rendered literally using tactics of omission and addition, semantic development, trope shift, and demetaphorization. Cases of excessive translation – distortion – are also observed.

Conclusions to Chapter 2

The implementation of linguistic representations of the historical-social concepts of the American South – CIVIL WAR, SOCIAL STRUCTURE, SLAVERY – in the material of literary works by Southern authors such as M. Twain, W. Faulkner, H. Beecher Stowe, R. P. Warren, M. Mitchell, and H. Lee mostly corresponds to the semantic load of the original.

The study identified the core and peripheral components of the concepts, their nature and application, and their adequate reproduction in translation. The concept of CIVIL WAR is objectified in the original texts by nominative units *Civil War* and *Yankee*. The core of this concept includes features such as "ideological opponents", "Yankee treachery", "Yankee humiliation of Southerners", "Southern patriotism", and "land". The core elements of the concept are actualized in secondary texts through descriptive translation, semantic development, and intratextual explanation.

The periphery of the concept of CIVIL WAR consists of value-imagery components expressed through metaphors, comparisons, and idiomatic expressions. Descriptive translation of metaphors, demetaphorization, and simplification of semantics leads to a loss of imagery in translation. Semantic development, on the contrary, contributes to a more adequate reproduction of the patriotism and bravery of Southern soldiers. Translation comparisons are lost due to cultural differences and usage peculiarities in the source and target languages.

Behavioral models and lifestyles of Southerners, representing the concept of SOCIAL STRUCTURE, are extremely important to consider when translating a literary text, as they reflect ethnospecific fragments of the nation's mentality, social, historical, and cultural uniqueness. The strategy of domestication, descriptive translation, addition, and specification enhance and clarify some cultural elements, leading to an adequate understanding of the original by the intercultural reader.

The core of the concept of SLAVERY includes the lexemes *white folks* and *nigger*, whose translation into Ukrainian does not pose difficulties. The relationships between masters and blacks are mainly characterized as follows: absolute subjugation, deprivation of rights, cruel treatment, and humiliation. The inhumane treatment of slave owners towards their slaves is conveyed by translators using semantic equivalents, clarifications, semantic developments, and omissions, although certain losses are noticeable in translation. However, after the Civil War, an attitude of indulgence towards blacks begins to prevail, leading to an incomplete reproduction of conceptual features.

The periphery of the concept is represented by metaphors and comparisons, which in Ukrainian translation partially lose the embedded meaning due to the conceptual asymmetry of the two cultures. What is insignificant for a Ukrainian may be essential and integral for a resident of the Southern United States.

A comparative analysis of the originals and their corresponding Ukrainian versions demonstrates the adequacy of reproducing the main elements of meaning-making in Ukrainian, revealing the conceptual content of the American South's historical, social, and cultural phenomena.

Chapter 3.
Rendering of English Linguistic Representations of Ethically Marked Concepts of the American South into Ukrainian

Artistic exploration of the spiritual and emotional sphere of human life expresses and complements the worldview of any society. Socio-historical information alone cannot provide a comprehensive understanding of the unique world of Southerners. The concept sphere of the American South will only be panoramic with the ethical, socio-psychological, and individual-psychological dimensions. To comprehend and grasp these dimensions, it is necessary to understand the foundational elements of the so-called "Southern myth". M. Mitchell, in the spirit of the "plantation tradition", portrays aristocrats as true gentlemen, devoid of mercantile interests and known for their chivalrous attitude towards women. An essential element of the "Southern myth" was the ideal embodied in the image of the Southern lady – a woman of impeccable behavior and origin, accustomed to seeing not what is but what should be. These images appear throughout almost all works dedicated to the Southern United States; thus, their adequate reproduction in translation requires excellent attention from the translator and the division of concepts into core and peripheral elements.

The concept of social stratification implies the structure of society and, secondly, the system of signs of social stratification and inequality. Describing such key cultural concepts from the perspective of translation studies, such as SOUTHERN LADY and SOUTHERN GENTLEMAN, WHITE TRASH, and BLACKS, will help to approach an understanding of the peculiarities of this mentality and, therefore, to find adequate equivalents in translation. To achieve this, it is advisable to study the verbalization of the system of relations and behavior of various strata of society in the Southern United States in both original and translated texts.

3.1 Rendering of English Linguistic Representations of the SOUTHERN LADY and SOUTHERN GENTLEMAN Concepts of the American South into Ukrainian

First of all, it is necessary to identify the linguistic units representing the core of the studied concepts SOUTHERN LADY and SOUTHERN GENTLEMAN, used by Southern writers such as M. Mitchell, H. Lee, W. Faulkner, M. Twain, R. P. Warren, H. Beecher Stowe, to create images of ladies and gentlemen according to the main traits of their character and behavior before and after the Civil War in the Southern United States; how these concepts are verbally reflected in different authors and how these aspects are realized in the translation into Ukrainian. To do this, it is worth examining the development of stereotypical perceptions of ladies and gentlemen in dynamics as history, political situation, and their environment change.

3.1.1 Rendering the Core Components of the Concept SOUTHERN LADY and SOUTHERN GENTLEMAN Concepts

All the qualities of representatives of both sexes that constitute the core of the concepts of SOUTHERN LADY and SOUTHERN GENTLEMAN, vividly depicted in the novels of M. Mitchell, H. Lee, R. P. Warren, and M. Twain, are expressed by the linguistic units "lady" and "gentleman". According to the semantic content, a lady is 1) a woman who is polite and behaves very well; 2) a woman of a good family or superior social position, and a gentleman is 1) a man of a high social class, especially one whose family owns much property; 2) a man who is always polite, has good manners, and treats other people well.

In the original works, the concept of SOUTHERN LADY is actualized through the following main conceptual features: 1) noble origin, 2) impeccable behavior, 3) higher social status, and 4) etiquette designation. Depending on the feature depicted in the primary works, the core lexeme-nomination "lady" is reproduced by translators using the strategy of foreignization or domestication. For example:

Noble origin: *A gentleman always appeared to believe **a lady** even when he knew she was lying. That was Southern chivalry. A gentleman always obeyed the rules and said the correct things and made life easier for **a lady*** [Mitchell, p. 95]. – *Джентльмен завжди вдає, ніби вірить **дамі**, навіть знаючи, що вона каже неправду. Це в крові у вихованих південців. Джентльмен завжди дотримується усталених приписів, каже те, чого вимагають правила доброго тону, чим і полегшує життя **дамі*** [Dotsenko: ZV I, p. 197]. When reproducing the lexeme "lady", R. Dotsenko uses the Ukrainian analogy "дама", which has the same meaning as a lady – a woman from an aristocratic, intelligent environment.

Impeccable behavior: *You want to grow up to be **a lady**, don't you?* [Lee: KM, p. 47]. – *Ти ж напевно хочеш вирости **справжньою леді?*** [Kharenko, p. 90]. / *Ти ж хочеш вирости **справжньою леді**, хіба ні?* [Nekryach: UP, p. 61]. In translations, transcoding "леді" is often observed, which contains the connotative meaning of elegance, politeness, and decency. In the secondary text, both translators reinforce the feature of impeccable behavior by adding the adjective "справжня". M. Kharenko, in the following fragment, adapts the lexeme with a corresponding phrase with the meaning of decency – "порядна дівчинка", thus creating the image of a polite, modest girl incapable of brazen acts, while T. Nekryach transcribes and uses a direct translation "young" – "юна", bringing the original closer to the secondary text reader: *You should be in a dress and camisole, **young lady!*** [Lee: KM, p. 116]. – ***Порядній дівчинці*** *належить ходити в платті і корсажі* [Kharenko, p. 60]. – *Тобі слід вдягатися у сукню з корсажем, **юна леді!*** [Nekryach: UP, p. 63]. However, in another passage of the novel, "young lady" is translated as "міледі". Since it refers to a twelve-year-old girl, the translation variant "міледі" seems inappropriate because "міледі" is a term used for a married woman in aristocratic circles of England. *I could not possibly hope to be **a lady** if I wore breeches <…>* [Lee: KM, p. 48] – *Я ніколи не стану **леді**, якщо ходитиму в штанях <…>* [Kharenko, p. 93] – *Нема чого й сподіватися стати **справжньою леді**, якщо я носитиму штани* [Nekryach: UP, p. 96]. In this case, both translators use transcoding "леді", and T. Nekryach adds the adjective "справжня".

Higher social status: ***The lady*** *was leading a child* [Mark Twain: TS, p. 32]. – ***Пані*** *тримала за руку дівчинку* [Koretskyi, p. 25]. The passage describes the wife of a nobleman, so the lexeme "пані" in the secondary text is appropriate, as "пані" means: 1) a woman who had a privileged status in pre-revolutionary society; 2) a woman who, by external signs, belongs to the privileged strata of society; 3) someone's wife [VTSSUM]. *She's **an old lady** and she's ill* [Lee: KM, p. 114]. – *Вона **стара жінка**, до того ж хвора* [Kharenko, p. 60]. / *Вона **стара дама**, та ще й хвора* [Nekryach: UP, p. 63]. The Ukrainian translation variant "жінка" is neutral and general about the lexeme "lady", as the word "жінка" denotes any female person. Transcoding would cause misinterpretation by a foreign reader. However, for an American reader, these signs are an additional characteristic of social relations among Southerners, who verbalize not simply "woman" but "lady", indicating the speaker's upbringing and the character's status. Therefore, T. Nekryach domesticates with "дама", reflecting respect and high social status. *Who goaded you into admitting that you thought men were fools to die for high-sounding principles? Who has aided you in giving **the old ladies** plenty to gossip about?* [Mitchell, p. 233]. – *Хто витяг з вас зізнання, що* *тільки дурні можуть іти на смерть заради високодумних слів? Хто допоміг вам дати поживу для пліток **старим матронам?*** [Dotsenko: ZV I, p. 263]. In this fragment, "old ladies" is evaluated negatively and thus loses the component of nobility. R. Dotsenko translates this phrase contextually as "старі матрони" (in ancient Rome, "матрона" meant a noble, respected married woman) since, in Ukrainian usage, the word "матрона" is used ironically to denote a stout, authoritative woman.

Etiquette designation: *And now you wouldn't mind telling me and this **lady** some of the things you've learned...* [Mark Twain: TS, p. 36]. – *А тепер, чи не скажеш ти мені і цій **пані** дещо з вивченого тобою* [Koretskyi, p. 28–29]. Domesticating "lady" to "пані" does not contradict the general tone of the narrative, implying Southern etiquette and suggesting that these "ladies" do not belong to the highest social stratum. In the following examples, R. Dotsenko and M. Kharenko generalize "ladies", meaning respectful treatment, using the neutral word "жінки": *In fact, men willingly gave the **ladies** everything in the world except credit for having intelligence* [Mitchell, p. 81]. – *Чоловіки, коли на те пішло, залюбки обдаровували **жінок** усім на світі, за єдиним винятком розуму* [Dotsenko: ZV I, p. 168]. *No, just **the lady**. There was **a lady** in the moon in Maycomb* [Lee: KM, p. 57]. – *Ні, просто **жінка**. Коли в Мейкомбі дивишся на місяць, то бачиш **жінку*** [Kharenko, p. 29]. However, ***ladies** have seldom held any charms for me* [Mitchell, p. 64]. – *Хоча **справжні дами**, як на мене, рідко коли бувають привабливі* [Dotsenko: ZV I, p. 132]. When translating the word "lady", R. Dotsenko uses the Ukrainian equivalent "дама", which has the same meaning as a lady – a woman from an aristocratic, intelligent environment. R. Dotsenko also uses the variant "жінка" when referring to women in general: *In fact, men willingly gave the **ladies** everything in the world except credit for having intelligence* [Mitchell, p. 81]. – *Чоловіки, коли на те пішло, залюбки обдаровували **жінок** усім на світі, за єдиним винятком розуму* [Dotsenko: ZV I, p. 168]. While the translator of "To Kill a Mockingbird", M. Kharenko, translates "old lady" as the neutral variant "стара жінка", R. Dotsenko in his translation of "Gone with the Wind" selects a more refined variant: *With **old ladies** you were sweet and guileless and appeared as simple-minded as possible, for **old ladies** were sharp and they watched girls as jealously as cats, ready to pounce on any indiscretion of tongue or eye* [Mitchell, p. 91]. – *У товаристві **літніх паній** треба бути лагідною, наївною і по змозі недалекою, оскільки **літні пані** ревниві до дівчат і зірки, мов кішки: досить одного необачного слова чи погляду, як вони так і вчепляться пазурами* [Dotsenko: ZV I, p. 188]. R. Dotsenko's variant "літні панії" in this context is more appropriate as it conveys both respect, politeness, and the marital status of older women. In contrast, the translator of Mark Twain's "The Adventures of Tom Sawyer", Yu. Koretsky domesticates "old lady" with the Ukrainian diminutive affectionate word "старенька" or avoids translation: *The* *old lady sank down into a chair and laughed a little, then cried a little, then did both together* [Mark Twain: TS, p. 44]. – *Старенька впала на стілець і заплакала* [Koretskyi, p. 35]. *The old lady made one end of the silk threat <...>* [Mark Twain: TS, p. 45]. – *Тітка Поллі зробила зашморг на кінці нитки* [Koretskyi, p. 36]. Yu. Koretsky tries to avoid transcoding the lexeme "lady", domesticating it with the Ukrainian equivalent "пані": *And now you wouldn't mind telling me and this **lady** some of the things you've learned <...>* [Mark Twain: TS, p. 36]. – *А тепер, чи не скажеш ти мені і цій **пані** дещо з вивченого тобою* [Koretskyi, p. 28–29]. Such a translation, despite domestication, does not contradict the general tone of the narrative and implies Southern etiquette.

The concept of the **Southern Gentleman** is realized in the primary texts of fiction through several fundamental conceptual features, which influence the translator's choice of specific translation strategies:

Noble origin: *With **old gentlemen**, a girl was pert and saucy and almost, but not quite, flirtatious, so that the old fools' vanities would be tickled* [Mitchell, p. 91]. – *У товаристві **літніх добродіїв** дівчина має бути загониста, грайлива і навіть у міру кокетлива, аби влестити марнославству старих дурнів* [Dotsenko: ZV I, p. 188]. The Ukrainian translator conveys "gentlemen" as "добродії" since a "gentleman" is not only "a man who is always polite, has good manners, and treats other people well" but also "a man of a high social class" [DCE, p. 672]. *If a man's not **a gentleman**, he's no business on a horse. The infantry is the place for him* [Mitchell, p. 49]. – *Коли ти **не з порядної родини**, до коней не рипайся. Твоє місце в піхоті* [Dotsenko: ZV I, p. 102].

The Ukrainian descriptive translation "порядна родина" is a generalization, highlighting one of the features of the concept **of Southern Gentleman**, bringing the worldviews of the two cultural areas closer and showing the translation reader that not only men with good manners can ride horses but also those who have a high social status. In Ukraine, a respectable family does not necessarily belong to the privileged classes. It is more of an ethical category, and the translator's choice, which favors domestication, does not convey the figurative or value component of the concept **of Southern Gentleman**, changing the perspective of the foreign reader on the world of the American South. A vivid example of the complete reproduction of the semantic content of the lexeme *gentleman* is an excerpt from Mark Twain's "The Adventures of Huckleberry Finn": *Col. Grangerford was **a gentleman**, you see. He was **a gentleman**, and so was his family* [Mark Twain: HF, p. 107]. – *Полковник Гренджерфорд був **джентльмен, справжній джентльмен** з голови до п'ят; така ж і сім'я його вдалася* [Steshenko, p. 66].

Impeccable behavior: *A **gentleman** always obeyed the rules and said the correct things and made life easier for a lady* [Mitchell, p. 95]. – *Джентльмен завжди дотримується усталених приписів, каже те, чого від нього вимагають правила доброго тону, чим і полегшує життя дамі* [Dotsenko: ZV I,

p. 197]. Translators reproduce the lexeme "gentleman" to denote impeccable behavior, resorting to foreignization. *A gentleman always appeared to believe a lady even when he knew she was lying. That was Southern chivalry* [Mitchell, p. 95]. – *Джентльмен завжди вдає, ніби вірить дамі, навіть знаючи, що вона каже неправду. Це в крові у вихованих південців* [Dotsenko: ZV I, p. 197].

Integrity: *He listened quietly until Stuart Tarleton, his red hair tousled and his eyes gleaming, repeated: "Why, we could lick them in a month!* ***Gentlemen*** *always fight better than rabble. A month – why, one battle –"* [Mitchell, p. 58]. – *Він мовчки прислухався до їхньої розмови, аж поки Стюарт Тарлтон – руде волосся розкуйовджене, очі палають вогнем – почав вигукувати: – Та ми розтрощимо їх за один місяць!* ***Люди благородні*** *завжди краще воюють, ніж усякий набрід. Та що там місяць! Нам і однієї битви вистачить* [Dotsenko: ZV I, p. 121]. Here, the translator uses the contextual equivalent "люди благородні". The translator of Faulkner's "Intruder in the Dust", R. Dotsenko, often renders the linguistic unit "gentleman" with a single semantic meaning – a person incapable of bad, dishonest, or immoral acts, using descriptive translation – "порядна людина": *<…> that no* ***gentleman*** *ever referred to anyone by his race or religion* [Faulkner, p. 41]. – *<…> що* ***порядна людина****, звертаючись до будь-кого, ніколи не згадує його раси чи віри* [Dotsenko: K, p. 374]. *<…> something he would never have failed to do in the hearing of any white man he considered his equal, because John was* ***a gentleman*** [Faulkner, p. 4]. – *<…> чогось такого він би ніколи не допустивсь раніше в присутності білого, якого вважав собі рівнею, бо він був* ***порядною людиною*** [Dotsenko: K, p. 275]. *If I had been* ***a gentleman****, of course, I would have let him kill me and that would have wiped the blot from the Butler escutcheon* [Mitchell, p. 227]. – *Звісно, якби я був* ***джентльменом****, то мусив би підставити себе під його кулю і таким чином змити ганебну пляму з герба Батлерів* [Dotsenko: ZV I, p. 256–257]. L. Kuznetsova follows this tactic in her translation of H. Beecher Stowe's "Uncle Tom's Cabin": *His companion, Mr. Shelby, had the appearance of* ***a gentleman*** [BS, p. 7]. – *Його співрозмовник (а це був господар маєтку, в якому проходила зустріч) – містер Шелбі – справляв враження справжнього* ***джентльмена*** [Kuznetsova, p. 4]. However, the transcription used by M. Kharenko and T. Nekryach in their translation of H. Lee's "To Kill a Mockingbird" reflects identical connotations in the meaning of the word "gentleman". The foreign reader faces the task of understanding the meaning of this lexeme – good manners or social status: *Little Chuck Little was another member of the population who didn't know where his next meal was coming from, but he was* ***a born gentleman*** [Lee: KM, p. 29]. – *Коротун, як і чимало інших його земляків, снідаючи, не знав, де йому пощастить пообідати, але він* ***мав удачу справжнього джентльмена*** [Kharenko, p. 14]. – *Маленький Чак Літл походив з того прошарку, який не знає, звідки узяти харчі, але він* ***був уроджений джентльмен*** [Nekryach: UP, p. 16]. From the given Ukrainian translations, it is evident that in the first variant, "мати удачу справжнього джентльмена", and in T. Nekryach's translation, "уроджений джентльмен", it is about upbringing. The translator of R. P. Warren's "All the King's Men", V. Mitrofanov, often adheres to the foreignization strategy: *"Yeah", the Boss was saying, "you're **a gent**, and so you don't ever get impatient"* [Warren, p. 32]. - *Еге ж, - провадив Хазяїн, - а ви **джентльмен**, суддя, і ніколи не дозволяєте собі нетерпеливитись* [Mitrofanov: К, p. 53].

Thus, all translators resort to foreignization and domestication strategies when reproducing the lexemes *lady* and *gentleman* – however, the translator of Mark Twain's "The Adventures of Tom Sawyer", Yu. Koretsky and the translator of H. Lee's "To Kill a Mockingbird", T. Nekryach, lean towards domestication (*пані, дама, жінка*), bringing the text closer to the Ukrainian reader.

To characterize Southern society in the United States, authors use a wide range of adjectives that actualize the qualities that ladies and gentlemen should possess: **perfect, great, nice, fine, well-bred, worthy lady, real lady, devout lady, respectable, chaste, decent, honest, fair, smart, sweet, good, good-hearted, simple-hearted, generous, innocent**, as well as **perfect, great gentleman, nice, fine, honorable, reasonable, deliberate, brave, sincere, honest, soft-hearted, good, proper, easy man.** Among the adjectives used by Southern authors – M. Mitchell, M. Twain, H. Lee, H. Beecher Stowe, R. P. Warren, W. Faulkner – to describe both sexes, the most general variants are "perfect" and "great". In contrast, others specify these concepts: "nice", "fine", and "good". To understand the peculiarities of the author's use of these lexemes in literary texts, how well the translators have preserved the authors' intent, and whether there are differences in the portrayal of both sexes to denote the concepts **of Southern Lady** and **Southern Gentleman**, it is advisable to analyze the semantic content of these linguistic units and their variants in Ukrainian translation.

The core components of the **Southern Lady** concept show that the semantic content of women's characteristics almost entirely coincides with the works of M. Mitchell, M. Twain, H. Lee, H. Beecher Stowe, R. P. Warren, and W. Faulkner, namely the conceptual features of **noble origin, impeccable behavior, higher social status, etiquette designation.** In the post-war period, less attention was paid to women's intellectual qualities; instead, the beauty of Southern women was emphasized, which is successfully depicted by writers with the addition of specific features.

The conceptual features of the core elements of the **Gentleman** concept – **noble origin, impeccable behavior, higher social status** – used to portray a gentleman, are consistent across all the considered works.

Even though the concepts of **Southern Lady** and **Southern Gentleman** may lose or, conversely, gain specific characteristics, their behavioral models and relationships remain unchanged.

3.1.2 Rendering the Peripheral Components of the SOUTHERN LADY and SOUTHERN GENTLEMAN Concepts in Primary and Secondary Texts

To fully reveal the essence of the ethnoculturally marked concepts **SOUTHERN LADY** and **GENTLEMAN**, it is necessary to reproduce in the translation not only the core components of the concepts but also the peripheral elements – figurative means such as metaphors, idioms, and comparisons that represent the society's perception of men and women and what they can be compared to. Moreover, conveying these images requires the translator to correctly interpret the actualized part of the connotative meaning and adequately express it in another language. The figurative meaning may have barely noticeable shades that acquire high significance in the author's worldview. Therefore, even slight neglect of the semantic nuances of figurative means in translation can lead to significant semantic losses. This is seen in the character of Miss Ophelia in H. Beecher Stowe's "Uncle Tom's Cabin", who, like the main character of M. Mitchell's "Gone with the Wind", Scarlett O'Hara, through her actions and beliefs, sharply contrasts with the ideal Southern woman with her declared innocence, honesty, and moderation:

*In punctuality, she was **as inevitable as a clock**, and **as inexorable as a railroad engine**; and she held in most decided contempt and abomination anything of a contrary character* [BS, p. 252]. – *Вона **настільки пунктуальна, що по ній годинники можна звіряти**. Ця жінка **до своєї мети йде наполегливо**. Найстарша Огюстенова кузина вкрай категорична до всього, що не підпадає під її розуміння правильності й суперечить її переконанням* [Kuznetsova, p. 164]. The author uses metaphorical comparisons to depict a strong and determined woman – "as inevitable as a clock" and "as inexorable as a railroad engine". In L. Kuznetsova's translation, the metaphoricity and imagery are partially lost as the translator renders the expressions descriptively – "настільки пунктуальна, що по ній годинники можна звіряти" and "до своєї мети йде наполегливо". The strategy of domestication is applied. As we see, the Ukrainian translation does not convey the image of a strong woman inherent in the original, which blurs the foreign reader's perception. Additionally, L. Kuznetsova uses the neutral expression "вкрай категорична до всього", rendering "hold in contempt and abomination", which means "despised and abhorred".

Striking examples of the archetypal Southern lady are the characters of Melanie from "Gone with the Wind" and Mrs. Shelby from "Uncle Tom's Cabin". M. Mitchell and H. Beecher Stowe portray their heroines quite vividly, so reproducing their characteristics in Ukrainian requires additional translators' effort. Through epithets, metaphors, and comparisons, the authors convey not only the external but also the internal beauty of Southern women, which is translated into Ukrainian a) literally, b) with semantic development, c) by adding a linguistic unit with a change in the figurative basis: a) the heart shape of her face [Mitchell, p. 53] – обличчя схоже на серце [Dotsenko: ZV I, p. 111–112], inner grace [Mitchell, p. 64] – внутрішня порядність [Dotsenko: ZV I, p. 123]; b) a woman of high class, both intellectually and morally [BS, p. 56] – була жінкою зі світлим розумом і великим серцем [Kuznetsova, p. 12]; c) with her face afire like sunset [Mark Twain: HF, p. 184] – як спалахне на обличчі, мов небо на заході сонця [Steshenko, p. 116].

It is appropriate to consider such descriptions of heroines and their translation: *There was only one thing that was capable of arousing her, and that provocation came in on the side of her **unusually gentle and sympathetic nature**; – anything in the shape of cruelty would throw her into a passion, which was the more alarming and inexplicable in proportion to **the general softness of her nature*** [BS, p. 128–129]. – *Тільки одне могло її вибити із рівноваги – навіть найменший вияв жорстокості викликав у жінки **праведний** гнів, що надзвичайно контрастував із її **неконфліктним характером*** [Kuznetsova, p. 84–85]. Senator's wife, Mrs. Bird, is depicted with the epithets "gentle and sympathetic nature", which L. Kuznetsova omits in the Ukrainian translation but immediately compensates with a lexical-semantic substitution of the general meaning "праведний" – "shape of cruelty would throw her into a passion". However, the metaphor "general softness of her nature" is rendered descriptively by the translator as "неконфліктний характер", which in the secondary text results in the loss of the depiction of the woman's internal state.

The following fragment is an example of Melanie's femininity: *She thought of Melanie and saw her **quiet brown eyes** suddenly with their far-off look, her placid little hands in their black lace mitts, her **gentle silences*** [Mitchell, p. 62]. – *Скарлет побачила раптом перед собою Мелані – її **лагідні карі очі**, втуплений у далечінь погляд, тендітні малі руки в чорних мереживних рукавичках, її **чемну мовчазність*** [Dotsenko: ZV I, p. 129]. The epithet "quiet eyes" is translated by R. Dotsenko using a lexico-grammatical transformation – differentiation – "лагідні очі". The word "gentle" means "having or showing a mild, kind, or tender temperament or character" [NWDTEL, p. 723], while "чемний" (courteous) means 1) respectfully polite to people; 2) in which courtesy, attentiveness, and kindness are shown [VTSSUM, p. 1459] and has a more specific meaning, so the translation of the epithet "gentle silences" – "чемна мовчазність" reflects a different shade.

To depict feminine virtue and kindness, M. Mitchell uses multifaceted metaphors, which the translator successfully reproduces in Ukrainian: *As Melanie looked at Ashley, her **plain face lit up as with an inner fire**, for if ever a loving heart showed itself upon a face, it was showing now on Melanie Hamilton's* [Mitchell, p. 54]. – *Коли Мелані дивилась на Ешлі, її **простацьке лице світилося внутрішнім світлом**, і якщо коли-небудь любляче серце можна було* *розпізнати по очах, то це саме у випадку з Мелані Гамільтон* [Dotsenko: ZV I, p. 112]. The phrase "plain face lit up as with an inner fire, for if ever a loving heart showed itself upon a face" is metaphorical, which causes difficulties for adequate reproduction. However, despite some transformations, the author's intent is preserved in the secondary text – "простацьке лице світилося внутрішнім світлом". The phrase "plain face" meaning 'not distinguished by any particular beauty, ordinary looking' is rendered by R. Dotsenko with the colloquial word "простацький", which means a) belonging to a non-privileged class; b) a simple, uneducated person [VTSSUM, p. 1134], which contradicts the traits of Melanie from "Gone with the Wind", who exemplifies what a true lady should be. The translator replaces the metaphorical basis of the metaphor "inner fire" with "внутрішнє світло", thus applying the tactic of metaphorical differentiation. The following metaphor, "a loving heart showed itself upon a face", is also reproduced by R. Dotsenko using metaphorical differentiation, changing the figurative basis – "любляче серце можна було розпізнати по очах".

<…> *she was most awful beautiful, and her face and her eyes was **all lit up like glory*** <…> [Mark Twain: HF, p. 161]. – <…> *вона справжня красуня, а обличчя та очі в неї аж **сяяли з радощів*** <…> [Steshenko, p. 101]. The translator of Mark Twain's "The Adventures of Huckleberry Finn", I. Steshenko, translates the metaphor "her face and her eyes was all lit up" literally as "обличчя та очі в неї аж сяяли", and replaces the comparison "like glory" with the metaphor "обличчя та очі в неї аж сяяли з радощів". Such a transformation does not distort the meaning and conveys the author's intent.

She was gentle and sweet, like a dove [Mark Twain: HF, p. 108]. – <…> *вдача в неї була ніжна й лагідна, наче у голубки* [Steshenko, p. 66]. In I. Steshenko's Ukrainian translation, the imagery is preserved, though with the addition of the lexeme "вдача" (temper), which does not change the overall meaning, as it refers to the sum of mental characteristics that constitute a person's personality, that is, what is implied in the source text.

In the following description of a woman's inner beauty and kindness, realized in the source text through comparisons, the translator resorts to a literal translation: *She looked – and was – as simple as earth, as good as bread, as transparent as spring water* [Mitchell, pp. 53–54]. – *Вона здавалася – та, власне, й була – простою, як земля, доброю, як хліб, чистою, як джерельна вода* [Dotsenko: ZV I, p. 112]. This approach is entirely justified as it harmoniously fits into the figurative system of the translation language.

While men, unlike women, are less vividly depicted in literary works, there are fragments in which the inner qualities of gentlemen are clearly realized: *sincere and honest at heart* [Mark Twain: TS, p. 31] – *серце – щире й чисте*[Koretskyi, p. 25]; *decent body* [Mark Twain: HF, p. 70] – *порядна людина* [Steshenko, p. 41] (metaphorical differentiation is applied: *honest* – *чистий*, *body* – colloquial *person*).

A true gentleman is one whose company is easy and pleasant: *Everybody loved to have him around, too;* **he was sunshine** *most always – I mean it seemed* **like good weather** [Mark Twain: HF, p. 108] – *Кожен щиро тішився з його товариства; він був для всіх* **наче сонячний промінь** *– здавалося, немов* **усе навколо яснішає**, *тільки-но він з'являється* [Steshenko, p. 66]. In the Ukrainian text, the metaphor "he was sunshine" is rendered as a comparison, enhancing imagery and specifying the meaning – "наче сонячний промінь". The comparison "like good weather" is descriptively translated by I. Steshenko as "усе навколо яснішає", resulting in a loss of imagery.

The sophistication of a gentleman is vividly portrayed in the following excerpt from Mark Twain's *The Adventures of Tom Sawyer:* <…> *began to feel a sensible elevation and* **enlargement of his moral faculties**, – *a phenomenon not unusual with gentlemen of a serious and reflective turn, under similar circumstances* [Mark Twain: TS, p. 108]. – <…> *і задоволений,* **піднісся аж до вершини своєї великодушності**, *як це нерідко трапляється при подібних обставинах* [Koretskyi, p. 71]. In the translated text, Y. Koretsky enhances the imagery in the portrayal of a man by reproducing the "enlargement of his moral faculties" through semantic development – "піднісся аж до вершини своєї великодушності".

In the texts of the novels by M. Mitchell, H. Lee, W. Faulkner, M. Twain, R. P. Warren, and H. Beecher Stowe, a significant number of metaphors, comparisons, and epithets is noted, often involving the words "cat", "bird", and "horse" to describe certain groups of images.

The metaphorical component, expressed by the lexeme "cat", is most frequently used in the original texts. However, the concept's connotations are ethnically specific (a feline animal → treachery, fickleness, unpredictability). Associative connections are acquired individually, according to personal experience, such as loyalty or domestic comfort. Considering this, it is worth examining the connotative meanings embedded in the works to depict gentlemen and how they are rendered in translation:

1. <…> *his voice could be as silky as cat's fur* [Mitchell, p. 793] – *шовковистий як котяча шерсть* [Dotsenko: ZV I, p. 384]. In this context, the *cat* correlates with the implied subtextual information of warmth, softness, and gentleness.
2. *like a cat at a mouse hole* [Mitchell, p. 794] – *немов кіт на мишачу нору* [Dotsenko: ZV I, p. 385]; *with his cat-at-a-mouse-hole look* [Mitchell, p. 904] – *як ото кіт пасе мишу* [Dotsenko: ZV I, p. 521]. The translator uses the direct equivalent "cat" – "кіт" with the implied meaning of agile, focused, collected, and predatory.

3. *That old wild cat* [Mitchell, p. 715] – *старий суціга* [Dotsenko: ZV I, p. 289]. The translator domesticates and renders "wildcat" (wildcat) with the Ukrainian derogatory word "суціга", meaning a cunning, sly, skillful person, a rogue. Here, R. Dotsenko explicates the negative connotations of the lexeme "cat".

Another lexeme used to realize the figurative part of the concept **of GENTLEMAN** is a "bird". According to conceptual features, a "bird" signifies a person distinguished by something unusual or unique (regarding social status and significance). However, analyzing the usage of this word, we can highlight such characteristics of men: <...> *like a tropical bird* [Mitchell, p. 174] – *схожий чи то на мавпочку, чи то на тропічну рослину* [Dotsenko: ZV I, p. 194]. The translator compares the representatives of the more vigorous sex to a tropical plant, depicting specific bright appearances yet losing the imagery. In the second instance, the translator uses an equivalent – *bird*: <...> *free lak ze bird* [Mitchell, p. 621] – <...> *тепер я вільний, мов птах* [Dotsenko: ZV I, p. 171].

Since "the horse" is a large and robust animal, comparing a man to a horse indicates his strength and bravery:
1. *He was well born, as the saying is, and that's worth as much in a man as it is in a horse* <...> [Mark Twain: HF, p. 107]. – *Він був, сказати б, доброї породи, а для людини це так само важливо, як і для коня* <...> [Steshenko, p. 66].
2. *the boys as mettlesome as the horses they rode* <...> [Mitchell, p. 26]. – <...> *юнаки не менш запальні, ніж їхні коні* <...> [Dotsenko: ZV I, p. 6]. Both translators use the equivalent – "кінь".

The analyzed material allows us to conclude that the periphery of the concepts **SOUTHERN LADY** and **SOUTHERN GENTLEMAN** consists of epithets, metaphors, and comparisons, which clearly outline the main traits of men and women in the South of the USA. To render these figurative means into Ukrainian, translators resort to the strategy of domestication, which is implemented through the following tactics:
(a) **equivalence:** *the boys as mettlesome as the **horses** they rode* <...> [Mitchell, p. 26]. – <...> *юнаки не менш запальні, ніж їхні **коні*** <...> [Dotsenko: ZV I, p. 6];
(b) **literal translation** (comparisons): *She looked – and was – as simple as earth, as good as bread, as transparent as spring water* [Mitchell, pp. 53–54]. – *Вона здавалася – та, власне, й була – простою, як земля, доброю, як хліб, чистою, як джерельна вода* [Dotsenko: ZV I, p. 112];
(c) **addition:** *with her face afire like sunset* [Mark Twain: HF, p. 184] – *як спалахне на обличчі, мов небо на заході сонця* [Steshenko, p. 116]; *She was*

gentle and sweet, like a dove [Mark Twain: HF, p. 108]. – <...> вдача в неї була ніжна й лагідна, наче у голубки [Steshenko, p. 66];

(d) **semantic development:** *a woman of high class, both intellectually and morally* [BS, p. 56] – *була жінкою зі світлим розумом і великим серцем* [Kuznetsova, p. 12]; *enlargement of his moral faculties* [Mark Twain: TS, p. 108] – *піднісся аж до вершини своєї великодушності* [Koretskyi, p. 71];

(e) **metaphorical differentiation:** *plain face lit up as with an inner fire* [Mitchell, p. 54] – *простацьке лице світилося внутрішнім світлом* [Dotsenko: ZV I, p. 112]; *a loving heart showed itself upon a face* [Mitchell, p. 54] – *любляче серце можна було розпізнати по очах* [Dotsenko: ZV I, p. 112]; *sincere and honest at heart* [Mark Twain: TS, p. 31]. – *серце – щире й чисте* [Koretskyi, p. 25]; *decent body* [Mark Twain: HF, p. 70] – *порядна людина* [Steshenko, p. 41];

(f) **tropical shift** (replacing metaphor with comparison and vice versa): *Everybody loved to have him around, too; he was sunshine* <...> [Mark Twain: HF, p. 108] – *Кожен щиро тішився з його товариства; він був для всіх наче сонячний промінь* <...> [Steshenko, p. 66]. *Her face and her eyes were all lit up like glory* <...> [Mark Twain: HF, p. 161]. – <...> *а обличчя та очі в неї аж сяяли з радощів* <...> [Steshenko, p. 101];

(g) **descriptive translation:** *as inevitable as a clock* [BS, p. 252] – *настільки пунктуальна, що по ній годинники можна звіряти* [Kuznetsova, p. 164]; *it seem like good weather* [Mark Twain: HF, p. 108] – *немов усе навколо яснішає* [Steshenko, p. 66].

Difficulties in rendering figurative means to denote the main traits of ladies and gentlemen arise from the mismatch of connotative meanings, as they are oriented towards conveying the imagery of the source culture rather than the target culture. Overall, translators quickly minimize losses by reproducing the Ukrainian linguistic peripheral representations of the concepts **SOUTHERN LADY** and **SOUTHERN GENTLEMAN**, creating a general picture of the main traits of gentlemen and ladies for the Ukrainian reader and creating an adequate understanding of their defining traits in the translation text.

3.2 Rendering of English Linguistic Representations of the WHITE TRASH Concept of the American South into Ukrainian

In the general consciousness, the Southern United States is depicted as a "paradise for whites, hell for blacks". However, alongside the aristocratic caste, an entire stratum of pioneer farmers worked hard on the land, sometimes alongside a few slaves. Additionally, there were those disdainfully referred to as "white trash" – landless and unfortunate whites. This declassed stratum differed from planters in their low social status and level of knowledge. These people occupied a lower social rung than even the blacks, as every black person belonged to some owner, thus having a "place in the sun" (in the social structure), whereas the "white trash" did not. They lived entirely off the produce of their lands and the game in the swamp, conducting their business generally by the barter system and seldom seeing five dollars in cash a year, and horses and uniforms were out of their reach [Mitchell, p. 10]. – *Вони жили тільки з того, що виростять на своїх клаптях землі та що вполюють, часто-густо задовольняючись простою міновою торгівлею; п'ятидоларова банкнота потрапляла їм до рук хіба раз на рік, і вони й думати не могли, щоб самим забезпечити себе кіньми та формою* [Dotsenko: ZV I, p. 24].

3.2.1 Rendering the Core Components of the WHITE TRASH Concept

The incompatibility of conceptual and linguistic worldviews of representatives of different cultures causes significant difficulties in adapting the original author's information to perceive a foreign cultural recipient. This results in asymmetry when translating ethnospecific concepts of a particular culture. O. I. Bykova rightly notes that the degree of adequacy in conveying the connotative content of a translation variant is directly proportional to the ethnocultural markedness of the original text units. A high level of ethnocultural markedness limits the equivalence of meaning transfer in the translation [18, p. 162]. Since there is no equivalent phenomenon in Ukrainian culture as "біла голота", and hence no corresponding term, translators rely on context and stylistic coloring in their choice:

There was much about the South – and the Southerners – that he would never comprehend, but, with the whole-heartedness that was his nature, he adopted his ideas and customs, as he understood them, for his own – poker and horse racing, red-hot politics and the code of duello, States' Rights and damnation to all Yankees, slavery and King Cotton, contempt for **white trash** *and exaggerated courtesy to women* [Mitchell, p. 23]. – *Багато чого на Півдні і південцях лишилось для нього назавжди незбагненним, але з усією щиросердістю своєї натури він сприйняв південські погляди й звичаї такими, як їх розумів: гра в покер і кінні перегони, пристрасть до політики й кодекс честі, обстоювання "Прав штатів" і ненависть до янкі, рабство й культ Короля Бавовнику, зневага до* ***"білої голоти"*** *й гіпертрофована ґречність до жіноцтва* [Dotsenko: ZV I, p. 50]. To depict the image of landless poor whites in the Southern USA, referred to as "white trash", R. Dotsenko uses the archaic term "біла голота", thus adequately reflecting the Southerners' attitude towards this social stratum.

The following example shows that the translator cannot settle on one variant and chooses synonymous equivalents that are not always precise: *The house negroes of the County considered themselves superior to **white trash**, and their unconcealed scorn stung him. At the same time, their more secure position in life stirred his envy. By contrast with his own miserable existence, they were well-fed, well-clothed and looked after in sickness and old age* [Mitchell, p. 26]. – *Хатні челядники багатих плантаторів дивилися згорда вниз на **білих злидарів**, і їхнє неприховане презирство допікало його до живого, а те, що вони були забезпечені шматком хліба, викликало у нього заздрість. Як порівняти з тим, що у них і харчі повсякдень, і одежа, і дах над головою, і догляд у хворобі чи в старості, то його існування виглядало зовсім жебрацьким* [Dotsenko: ZV I, p. 56]. Translating the phrase "white trash" as "білі злидарі", R. Dotsenko opts for a less emotional and derogatory coloring than "біла голота", rendering it through lexical-semantic replacement – generalization, striving to preserve the connotation of "trash", which implies "someone from a low social class who you do not respect because you think they are lazy or immoral" [DCE, p. 1769], meaning scum, worthless people; "злидар" merely denotes a person living in poverty.

Consider other ways Ukrainian translators render the phrase "white trash": *An' Ah tole her an' tole her ter let dem **w'ite trash** alone, but she din' pay me no mine* [Mitchell, p. 394]. – *І скі'ки я вже казала їй і приказувала, аби махнула рукою на цих **білих голодранців**, а вона все не слухала* [Dotsenko: ZV I, p. 437]. Here, the translator aptly uses the term "білий голодранець", which denotes not just a poorly dressed person but also someone of low social status.

R. Dotsenko selects contextual equivalents for the term "white trash", which appears to be a sound strategy given the absence of a similar lexical phrase in Ukrainian. Other translators, including M. Kharenko and T. Nekryach, who translated Harper Lee's *To Kill a Mockingbird* at different times, follow the same path, highlighting different facets of this polysemantic concept. When addressing moral qualities (or, more often, their absence), translators use the lexeme "покидьки". When moral aspects are downplayed, and behavioral patterns, lack of refined manners, and subjective evaluations by certain characters are emphasized, the phrase "біле бидло" is suggested.

The slang term "crackers also referred to landless whites in the Southern USA". Accurately rendering this lexeme to denote the poor in the Southern States results in an adequate understanding and interpretation of the worldview of this unique area. In Ukrainian translations, the rendering methods vary <...> ***Crackers** and, in very few cases, even **poor whites**, if they were above the average of their class* [Mitchell, p. 10]. – *<...> **бідняків** і навіть уже зовсім **злиденних*** *білих*, коли ті бодай чимось вирізнялися серед свого стану [Dotsenko: ZV I, p. 23]. The pejorative term "crackers", also known as "poor white" – a free European-descended American living in poverty in the Southern USA mainly before the Civil War, supposedly characterized by boastfulness. The Ukrainian equivalent "бідняк" reflects the main content of the term "crackers" but does not carry the stylistic load of the original, thus losing those connotations.

Since there is no concept of "crackers" in Ukrainian, as with "white trash", which is unique to the Southern USA, R. Dotsenko renders them in translation with partial equivalents, choosing the variant from the synonymous row that, in his opinion, most accurately reflects the linguoculture of the American South: *She looked **Cracker**, even worse. She looked **poor white**, shiftless, slovenly, trifling* [Mitchell, p. 673]. – *Вона виглядала на **останню злидарку**, а той ще гірше. Чисто як **біла голодранка**, зачухана й недбала* [Dotsenko: ZV I, p. 220]. R. Dotsenko clarifies the slang lexeme "cracker" by adding the evaluative adjective "останній", which intensifies emotionality and appropriately highlights the contextual translation "остання злидарка".

The main task facing a translator of a literary work is to convey all dimensions of the original so that the reader understands the spirit and mood of the society within which the work was written. Systematic omission of specific units can deprive an ethnoculturally marked concept of its imagery and value: *He was not of the planter class, though he was not poor white. He was just plain **Cracker**, a small farmer, half-educated, prone to grammatical errors, and ignorant of some of the finer manners the O'Haras were accustomed to in gentlemen* [Mitchell, p. 485]. – *Він же не належав до стану плантаторів, хоч його не можна було залічити й до білої голоти. Просто він був собі **звичайний незаможний фермер**, малоосвічений, не дуже підкутий у граматиці, не обізнаний з деякими добрими манерами, що їх, на думку родини О'Гар, повинен мати кожен джентльмен* [Dotsenko: ZV I, p. 536]. It is evident that in the translation, the word "cracker", which is fundamental and contains the primary semantic information in the sentence, is rendered descriptively.

In addition to the lexical units "white trash" and "cracker", which are dominant components of the concept "WHITE TRASH", several other linguistic units are also noted, complementing and more clearly defining the meaning of "біле бидло". Therefore, the core nominations represent such conceptual features:

The term **"low origin"** indicates a lack of money and a declassed status. These people need an established system of values, norms, and standards of relations and behavior. Such traits are characterized in the Ewell family from the novel *To Kill a Mockingbird*, where it is mentioned that they are "another member of the population", which T. Nekryach translates literally as "належав до того прошарку", and M. Kharenko uses semantic development, translating as "як і чимало інших його земляків":

*Little Chuck Little was **another member of the population** who didn't know where his next meal was coming from, but he was a born gentleman* [Lee: KM, p. 251].

– *Коротун, як і чимало інших його земляків, снідаючи, не знав, де йому пощастить пообідати, але він мав удачу справжнього джентльмена* [Kharenko, p. 14]. / *Коротулька Чак Литл також **належав до того прошарку**, який не знає, коли й чим обідатиме наступного разу, але він був природжений джентльмен* [Nekryach: UP, p. 18].

Atticus said the Ewells had been the disgrace of Maycomb for three generations. None of them had done an honest day's work in his recollection [Lee: KM, p. 35].

– *І Аттікус розповів мені, що Юели ось уже протягом трьох поколінь – ганьба Мейкомба. Скільки він пам'ятав, жоден з них і дня не прожив чесною працею* [Kharenko, p. 17]. / *Атікус пояснив, що Юели – ганьба для Мейкома вже протягом цілих трьох поколінь. Жоден з них не пропрацював чесно й одного дня, скільки він пам'ятає* [Nekryach: UP, p. 22].

Harper Lee uses the word "society" to depict the collective group of "white trash", meaning: a) the community of people living in a particular country or region and having shared customs, laws, and organizations; b) [with adj.] a specified section of such a community [WTNIDELU, p. 1987], which translates to "суспільство, громада, громадськість". In the target text, M. Kharenko specifies this meaning by using the word "каста", implying a closed social group maintaining its separateness and privileges, equivalent to "caste" in English – any class or group of people who inherit exclusive privileges or are perceived as socially distinct [WTNIDELU, p. 748]. T. Nekryach uses the term "товариство", meaning a circle or group of people connected by a certain commonality (origin, social status, interests). *He said that the Ewells were members of an **exclusive society** made up of Ewells. In certain circumstances, the common folk judiciously allowed them certain privileges by becoming blind to some of the Ewells' activities. They didn't have to go to school, for one thing. Another thing, Mr. Bob Ewell, Burris's father, was permitted to hunt and trap out of season* [Lee: KM, p. 35]. – *Аттікус сказав, що Юели – це **своєрідна каста**. За певних умов звичайні люди розважливо надають їм деякі переваги; іншими словами, намагаються не помічати деякі їхні вчинки. Не помічають, наприклад, що Юели не ходять до школи. Що містер Боб Юел, батько Барріса, стріляє і ловить капканами дичину в той час, коли це заборонено* [Kharenko, p. 17]. / *Він додав, що Юели становлять **виняткове товариство**, яке складається з самих Юелів. За певних обставин звичайні люди розважливо надають Юелам певні привілеї, просто закриваючи очі на деякі їхні вчинки. По-перше, їх не примушують ходити до школи. По-друге, містеру Бобу Юелу, батьку Барріса, дозволяється полювати не в сезон* [Nekryach: UP, p. 23].

The low status of white trash is explained by their place of residence, which is even worse than the housing of the black population, as they "lived behind the town garbage dump", which both translators reproduce literally: *Maycomb's Ewells* **lived behind the town garbage dump** *in what was once a Negro cabin* [Lee: KM, p. 191]. – *Мейкомбські Юели* **жили за міським звалищем**, *в колишній негритянській халупі* [Kharenko, p. 101]. / *Мейкомські Юели селилися* **за міським звалищем** *у колишній негритянській хижі* [Nekryach: UP, p. 132].

Over time, the concept of "white trash" has lost some of its latent meanings. By the 1950s, material status was practically removed, and only low origin and lack (real or perceived) of good manners remained. Henry Clinton from Harper Lee's *Go Set a Watchman* (a sequel to *To Kill a Mockingbird*) has higher education, a law practice, sufficient funds, his own house, and a car, and he dresses well. However, in the eyes of Alexandra Finch, a descendant of planters, he is just "trash". Since "голота", "голодранці", and "покидьки" are not suitable here, the translator T. Nekryach chooses the term "бидло", which predominantly evaluates the character's origin: *The only reason Henry's like he is now is because your father took him in hand when he was a boy and because the war came along and paid for his education. Fine a boy as he is,* **the trash** *won't wash out of him. "Have you ever noticed how he licks his fingers when he eats cake?* **Trash**. *Have you ever seen him cough without covering his mouth?* **Trash**. *Did you know he got a girl in trouble at the University?* **Trash**. *Have you ever watched him pick at his nose when he didn't think anybody was looking?* **Trash** *– "* [Lee: GSW, p. 37]. – *Єдина причина, чому Генрі став тепер таким, як він є, полягає в тому, що Атикус опікувався ним, коли він ще був хлопчиком, а участь у війні дала йому можливість платити за освіту. Він прекрасний хлопець, але* **бидло** *залишається бидлом. Ти помічала, як він облизує пальці, коли їсть торт?* **Бидло**. *Ти бачила, як він кашляє, не прикриваючи рота?* **Бидло**. *Ти знаєш, що він занапастив одну дівчину, коли вчився в університеті?* **Бидло**. *Ти звертала увагу, що він колупається в носі, коли думає, що ніхто не дивиться?* **Бидло** [Nekryach: ІВП].

The "lack of education" characteristic highlights insufficient cultural and intellectual development caused by low origin, poverty, and unwillingness to learn and work. An example of an undeveloped and uncultured person is Huck Finn's father, who does not want education for his son, noting that no one in their family has ever learned: ***You lemme catch you fooling around that school again, you hear?*** *Your mother couldn't read, and she couldn't write, nuther, before she died. None of the family couldn't before they died* [Mark Twain: HF, p. 28]. – *Насмілишся мені тільки швендяти ще коло тієї школи, –* ***я тобі покажу, де раки зимують!*** *Твоя мати не вміла ні читати, ні писати, так і померла. Ніхто з твоїх родичів грамоти не вчився – всі неписьменні померли* [Steshenko, p. 28]. In this fragment, Huck's father scolds his son for attending school, saying, "You lemme catch you fooling around that school again, you hear?". In the translation, I. Steshenko adds the idiom "я тобі покажу, де раки зимують" to intensify the father's emotional state.

It was kind of lazy and jolly, laying off comfortable all day, smoking and fishing, and no books nor study [Mark Twain: HF, p. 32].

– Жилося мені й справді непогано. Вилежуйся собі цілісінькі дні, попихкуючи люлькою, та лови рибу; ніяких тобі книжок, ніякого навчання [Steshenko, p. 28].

<...> and the rest of his speech was all the hottest kind of language – mostly hove at the nigger and the government [Mark Twain: HF, p. 35].

– <...> й закінчив промову нескінченним потоком найдобірнішої лайки; найбільше перепало тоді негрові й урядові [Steshenko, p. 18].

The low, unworthy actions of this social stratum actualize the conceptual characteristic of "immorality" of some representatives of white trash.

*Why, Atticus said they were **absolute trash** <...>* [Lee: KM, p. 139].

*– І ще Аттікус сказав, що це **справжні покидьки*** [Kharenko, p. 73]. / *Але ж Атикус казав мені, що вони – **суцільні покидьки*** [Nekryach: UP, p. 95].

In another passage, M. Kharenko also renders "trash" with the derogatory term "покидьок", which means morally corrupt, declassed people; scum, filth: *Because – he – is – **trash**, that's why you can't play with him* [Lee: KM, p. 254]. *– А тому, – сказала вона, – що він – **покидьок**. Саме тому ти з ним не гратимешся* [Kharenko, p. 135]. The translation "покидьок" reflects the social status of white trash.

Thus, having studied the essence and main features of white trash, we can conclude that the core of the concept of WHITE TRASH comprises the lexical units "white trash" and "cracker", which undergo variations in Ukrainian translation – білі голодранці, біла голота, біле бидло, білі злидарі, біла шантрапа, покидьок, бідняки, остання злидарка. The core of the concept contains conceptual characteristics: 1) low origin; 2) lack of education; 3) immorality, which are rendered into Ukrainian using a) contextual equivalents, b) concretization of meaning, c) differentiation, d) descriptive translation, e) literal translation.

3.2.2 Rendering the Peripheral Components of the WHITE TRASH Concept in Primary and Secondary Texts

The periphery of the "White Trash" concept consists of figurative means that depict this concept. To confirm that "white trash" or "poor whites" are a declassed segment of society, Harper Lee uses figurative comparisons that do not pose excessive difficulties in Ukrainian translation.

Aristocrats did not consider poor whites as human beings, so the authors compare this population to animals: *They were people, but they **lived like animals*** [Lee: KM, p. 35] – *Ці люди **живуть, як тварини*** [Kharenko, p. 17]. The translator does not change the figurative system, as the image is entirely understandable to the intercultural reader without additional explanations. However, T. Nekryach uses concretization – *Вони люди, але **живуть, як свині*** [Nekrych: UP, p. 22].

Furthermore, people like the Ewells "live as guests of the county", which both translators render literally: *No economic fluctuations changed their status – people like the Ewells **lived as guests of the county** in prosperity as well as in the depths of a depression* [Lee: KM, p. 191]. – *У кожному невеликому місті на зразок Мейкомба є свої юели. Ніякі економічні коливання не здатні вплинути на їхнє становище. Люди, подібні до Юелів, **живуть як гості в своєму окрузі**, незалежно від того, процвітає він чи переживає занепад* [Kharenko, p. 101]. / *Кожне невелике місто на кшталт Мейкома має родини, схожі на Юелів. Жодні економічні коливання не впливають на їхній статус – люди типу Юелів **живуть, ніби гості у своєму окрузі**, як у часи процвітання, так і у період глибокої депресії* [Nekryach: UP, p. 131].

For the idiom "drunk as a fiddler" [Mark Twain: HF, p. 30], I. Steshenko chooses the Ukrainian equivalent "п'яний як хлющ" [Steshenko, p. 15], meaning very drunk. The translator wisely opts for a semantic equivalent, as in both languages, the worn-out comparisons have lost their imagery and have practically become intensifiers. Preserving the image in translation would be unnatural and divert the reader's attention (drunk as a fiddler is too unusual for the target culture).

Mark Twain depicts poor whites as unfortunate beings using metaphors: with a broken spirit [Mark Twain: HF, p. 132] – *хто духом занепав* [Steshenko, p. 82]; with a contrite heart [Mark Twain: HF, p. 132] – *у кого розбите серце* [Steshenko, p. 82]; breaking heart [Mark Twain: HF, p. 134] – *недуже серце* [Steshenko, p. 83]; luck didn't run my way [Mark Twain: HF, p. 36] – *мені все-таки не поталанило* [Steshenko, p. 19].

Mark Twain also depicts poor whites as intelligent people using metaphors: *your head's level agin* [Mark Twain: HF, p. 175] – *світлу ж голову маєте ви* [Steshenko, p. 110]; *astonishing head* [Mark Twain: HF, p. 165] – *світла голова*

[Steshenko, p. 102]; *nothing that smacked of charity* [Mitchell, p. 10] – *не пристали б ні на яке доброчинство*[Dotsenko: ZV I, p. 24]: *But they were as fiercely proud in their poverty as the planters were in their wealth, and they would accept nothing that smacked of charity from their rich neighbors* [Mitchell, p. 10]. – *Але у своїх злиднях вони були так само горді, як плантатори у своєму багатстві, і повік-віку не пристали б ні на яке доброчинство з боку заможних своїх сусідів* [Dotsenko: ZV I, p. 24].

In translating metaphors, translators use a denotative approach, which consists of three stages: 1) the stage of perceiving the message in the source language; 2) the stage of forming a mental image of this message; 3) the stage of interpreting this image using the means of the target language. This approach allows for the free choice of translation, which means conveying the original message's content. The task of such a translation is to convey the content and create adequate images that evoke appropriate associations and emotions in the reader.

Thus, the periphery of the concept "White Trash" consists of comparisons and metaphors, which translators render through literal translation and a denotative approach to translating the literary text's figurative means.

3.3 Rendering of English Linguistic Representations of the BLACKS Concept of the American South into Ukrainian

In the Southern United States during the 18th and early 19th centuries, a plantation economy prevailed, which relied on the labor of enslaved Black people. In this section, it is necessary to identify which linguistic units represent the core of the concept of BLACK PEOPLE and how they are rendered into Ukrainian. It is advisable to consider the dynamic development of this concept, particularly before and after the American Civil War, using examples from the works of M. Mitchell, H. Lee, W. Faulkner, M. Twain, R. P. Warren, and H. Beecher Stowe. This examination is essential and inevitable in research, as both the original and its translations can only be fully understood within the context of their cultural existence. As M. O. Zurabyan notes, a literary text "engages in a dialogue with the reader: the perception of a literary text is communication with it. Understanding reveals the objective layer of cultural traditions, embodied on one side in the text and on the other in the spiritual world and cultural preparation of the interpreter, i. e., the reader. They rely not only on the individual baggage of what is perceived but also on the collective experience and tradition, i.e., culture" [75, pp. 126–127]. Thus, one of the most critical and challenging criteria of adequacy is the accurate transmission of linguistic representations of ethnoculturally marked concepts.

3.3.1 Rendering the Core Components of the BLACKS Concept

In M. Mitchell's descriptions of the pre-Civil War period, as well as in H. Beecher Stowe's depictions of the deeper Southern states, and M. Twain's works, the central linguistic units representing the core of the concept of BLACK PEOPLE are *negro, nigger,* and *darky.* Additional terms include *servants, slaves, field hands, house negroes, homecoming hands, valet, black wench,* and *wench.* It is necessary to examine their representation in the secondary text and analyze how the translations of these linguistic units reflect the concept and how intercultural readers perceive them.

The lexeme "a nigger" is rendered differently by I. Steshenko and L. Kuznetsova in the target text, either amplifying or softening the meaning. For example:

*I see it warn't no use wasting words – you can't learn **a nigger** to argue* [Mark Twain: HF, p. 84]. – *Я побачив, що даремно сперечатися з **негром**. Свого розуму йому не вкладеш* [Steshenko, p. 50]. In this context, the word "nigger", considered impolite, politically incorrect, and derogatory in the United States today, retains its neutral meaning in Ukrainian, without the connotations of slavery or humiliation.

In *Uncle Tom's Cabin*, the lexeme "nigger" is translated into Ukrainian as "чорнопикий" (dark-faced) and the general term "раб" (slave): *"Here, Andy, you **nigger**, be alive!" called Sam* [BS, p. 118]. – *Енді! Рухайся, **чорнопикий**! – прикрикнув Сем* [Kuznetsova, p. 77]. *Yes, I consider religion a valuable thing in **nigger**, when it's the genuine article, and no mistake* [BS, p. 80]. – *Що й казати, побожність (якщо вона справжня, звісно) додає ціни **рабам**!* [Kuznetsova, p. 5].

Translators of *To Kill a Mockingbird* M. Kharenko and T. Nekryach also neutrally render the linguistic unit "nigger" as "чорномаза", which denotes both black skin color and the lower echelons of society: *"Stop right there, **nigger**"* [Lee: KM, p. 133]. – *Не підходь, **чорномаза**!* [Kharenko, p. 70]. / *Стій де стоїш, **чорномаза*** [Nekryach: UP, p. 73].

H. Beecher Stowe also uses the lexeme "low nigger", emphasizing the low social status of Black people: "ranking below other people or things in importance or class" [WTNIDELU, p. 1124], which L. Kuznetsova renders as "червонопика" (lit. *red-faced*), a colloquial and vulgar term. The translator seems to have neglected the author's intent to highlight the enslaved status and low social class, focusing instead on the color of the face: *Low nigger* [BS, p. 381] – *червонопика* [Kuznetsova, p. 247].

M. Mitchell presents a panoramic view of the American South. She vividly depicts what deeply troubles W. Faulkner: the South's guilt towards Black people.

However, Mitchell's narrative strongly emphasizes the apologetic portrayal of Southern life before the Civil War.

"<...> I swear, **darkies** are more trouble. Sometimes I think the Abolitionists have got the right idea" [Mitchell, p. 11]. – *Їй-бо, з цими **чернюками** сама морока. Деколи мені здається, аболіціоністи таки мають слушність* [Dotsenko: ZV I, pp. 25–26]. One of the characters, Stuart, acknowledges the correctness of abolitionists – fighters for the liberation of Black people – but uses the derogatory term "darkies", which is rendered into Ukrainian as "чернюки", meaning common people or the lower classes. This deeply characterizes the conflict between white and Black people. This intent is carefully preserved in the translation. However, in the following passage, R. Dotsenko employs a different translation strategy: *She knew it was beneath the dignity of quality white folks to pay the slightest attention to what **a darky** said when she was just grumbling to herself. She knew that to uphold this dignity, they must ignore what she said, even if she stood in the next room and almost shouted* [Mitchell, p. 35]. – *Вона знала, що гідність не дозволяє білим людям звертати хоч якусь там увагу на буркотню **негрів**, отож вони вдають, ніби не чують служниці, навіть коли та мало не на весь голос кричить, але в сусідній кімнаті* [Dotsenko: ZV I, p. 74]. The author repeatedly uses the derogatory term "darky". At the same time, the translator chooses a variety of translations, initially using "чернюки" and later the neutral term "негри," which denotes the Indigenous population of Tropical Africa, having dark skin and belonging to the Negro race. This approach avoids preserving the stylistic connotation, thus opting for a foreignizing strategy.

For a long time, patriarchal relations persisted in the Southern United States. The importation of slaves provided cheap labor, and patriarchalism, combined with slavery, acquired its peculiarities: *To the ears of the three on the porch came the sounds of hooves, the jingling of harness chains, and the shrill careless laughter of **negro voices, as the field hands** and mules came in from the fields* [Mitchell, p. 4]. – *До слуху їх трьох на веранді долинув цокіт копит, побрязкування упряжі й лункий безтурботний сміх **негрів**, що із мулами поверталися з поля* [Dotsenko: ZV I, p. 12]. Mitchell's descriptions are so vivid that readers can easily imagine the lifestyle dominated by slavery and violence. The translator's task is to ensure that the target readers also see this picture of life. The author uses the phrase "careless laughter of negro voices, as the field hands", emphasizing that some slave owners treated their slaves well, feeding them adequately, and not all slave owners oppressed them. The translator renders the phrase "negro voices, as the field hands" simply as "негри", omitting the specification "as the field hands", which is already clear to Ukrainian readers, as this omission does not distort the intercultural reader's understanding.

Mitchell refers to the Black people working on the plantation as "homecoming hands". The adjective "homecoming" confirms that these people work in the cotton fields and return home late in the evening to rest. At the same time, "hands" means "a person who engages in manual labor, especially in a factory, on a farm, or board a ship" [DCE, p. 731]. R. Dotsenko omits the adjective and renders "hands" by applying the strategy of concretizing the meaning as "негри": *The high-pitched, childish voice answered "Yas'm", and there were sounds of footsteps going out the back way toward the smokehouse where Ellen would ration out the food to **the homecoming hands*** [Mitchell, p. 4]. – *Тоненький дитячий голосок відповів: "Добре, мем", і стало чутно, як хода з тильного ганку подаленіла в напрямку коптильні, де Еллен щовечора роздавала харчі **неграм*** [Dotsenko: ZV I, p. 12].

Some Black people, also referred to as house negroes, valets, slaves, and servants, worked in the house for their masters. Their depiction in the secondary text is not always justified: ***The house negroes*** *of the County considered themselves superior to white trash, and their unconcealed scorn stung him, while their more secure position in life stirred his envy* [Mitchell, p. 26]. – ***Хатні челядники*** *багатих плантаторів дивилися згори вниз на білих злидарів, і їхнє неприховане презирство допікало його до живого, а те, що вони були забезпечені шматком хліба, викликало у нього заздрощі* [Dotsenko: ZV I, p. 56]. Since plantation owners perceived Black people as domestic animals and their property, R. Dotsenko, seeking the best translation option, concretizes the meaning to preserve the visual concreteness and connotation in rendering the word "negroes". He uses the historical term "челядники", indicating a serf status, as these were household people who lived and worked in the manor. This translation strategy bridges the worldviews of the two cultures, favoring contextual meaning.

House servants were also called "valet". The translator managed to convey the original meaning: *<...> that brought to Gerald two of his three most prized possessions, his **valet** and his plantation* [Mitchell, p.24]. – *<...> Джералд і завдячував два з трьох своїх найкоштовніших набутків – **служника-негра** й плантацію* [Dochenko: ZV I, p. 51]. By using the translation "служник-негр" for "valet", the translator adds a lexeme and creates an adequate image since a literal translation as "лакей" or "служник" from the dictionary could evoke a different image in the target reader's mind, not necessarily of a Black person. For Southerners, the word "servant" is almost always associated with Black people, especially in a chronologically distant text.

A similar approach is observed in another minimal context: *the wagons of their **slaves*** [Mitchell, p. 23] – *фургонами з **чорною челяддю*** [Dochenko: ZV I, p. 50]. If M. Mitchell used the word "valet" in the previous sentence, meaning a servant who attends to the master, here she uses "slaves", a word with a slightly different connotation, and Dochenko translates it as "чорною челяддю", adding an explanation. However, the word "челядь" (archaic) means servants in general, while "slave" means "someone who is owned by another person and works for them for no money" [DCE, p. 1224]. We see that in the translation, using a lexico-semantic substitution, the general term "slave" (any bondservant) is rendered as "челядь" – house servants. However, this approach unjustifiably softens the dichotomy of "slave owners" – and "slaves"; thus, excessive domestication distorts the concept of BLACK PEOPLE itself.

The same word "челядь", devoid of connotations of serfdom for the Ukrainian reader, is used by the translator for the neutral lexeme "servants": *Visitors presented no problem, for houses were large, **servants** numerous and the feeding of several extra mouths a minor matter in that land of plenty* [Mitchell, p.79]. – *Гості нікого не обтяжували, бо будинки були просторі, **челядь** численна, і кілька зайвих ротів не завдавало ніякого клопоту в цьому краю достатку* [Dochenko: ZV I, p. 164]. In this context, the translation "челядь" seems correct, as the translator accurately captures the speech style and mood since servants play an essential role in the Southern way of life, and the author depicts them respectfully, which Dochenko certainly noticed.

Since "servant" means "a person who performs duties for others, especially a person employed in a house on domestic duties or as a personal attendant" [WTNIDELU], Dotsenko's choice of "челядь" conveys both the speech style and mood accurately. However, L. Kuznetsova, the translator of "Uncle Tom's Cabin", specifies this term with the lexeme "негри", clarifying that both house and field work were performed by Black people: *Now, you know these **servants** are nothing but grown-up children* [BS, p. 276]. – *Адже **негри** – це хоч і дорослі, та все одно діти* [Kuznetsova, p. 179].

In "Gone with the Wind", there are words that do not have direct equivalents in Ukrainian, so Dochenko resorts to contextual equivalents: *They promised all **the black wenches** silk dresses and gold earbobs – that's what they did* [Mitchell, p.424]. – *Наобіцяли **чорнюкам** шовкових суконь та золотих сережок – ось що вони зробили* [Dotsenko: ZV I, p. 470]. In the Ukrainian dictionary, there is no variant for the archaic term "wench", which means "a girl or young woman, especially a servant" [DCE, p. 1875]. Dochenko translates it as "чорнюки", which refers to both genders, so "чорнючки" could have been used, but from the context, it is clear that it refers to Black women. In this case, the translator's choice is entirely justified.

M. Twain and H. Beecher Stowe often refer to slaves as "things" and "creatures" in their novels. Using the lexemes "thing" and "creature," meaning a being, living creature, or human, in the original texts is evidence of a neutral attitude towards Black people. However, in the translated text, these words are specified with the meaning of slavery: *wicked creature* [BS, p. 279] – *негри* [Kuznetsova, p. 181]; *poor thing* [Mark Twain: HF, p. 100] – *бідна дитина* [Steshenko, p. 61].

All the above linguistic units characterizing the core of the concept of the following conceptual features actualize BLACK PEOPLE:

- slaves: slaves, drudge
1) **lower race:** low nigger [BS, p. 364; Mark Twain: TS] – нижча маса, червонопика [Kuznetsova, p. 236; Koretsky]; to crush [BS, p. 178] – пригнічувати [Kuznetsova, p. 116]; to deep down [BS, p. 178] – утвердити наше безправ'я [Kuznetsova, p. 117]; forlorn [BS, p. 28] – безправний [Kuznetsova, p. 19].
2) **oppression:** to oppress [BS] – гнобити, пригнічувати [Kuznetsova]; oppressed [Mitchell; BS] – пригнічені, невільник [Dochenko; Kuznetsova]; mental anguish [BS, p. 567] – душевні муки [Kuznetsova, p. 372]; grow loathsome [BS, p. 569] – стаємо ненависні [Kuznetsova, p. 374]; we loathe ourselves [BS, p. 569] – гидкі самим собі [Kuznetsova, p. 374]; nothing but whipping, scolding, starving [BS, p. 180] – пригощали лише лайкою та канчуками [Kuznetsova, p. 118]; tyrannized her [BS, p. 629] – знущався над нею [Kuznetsova, p. 417]; gave a groan of utter despair [BS, p. 560] – застогнавши від відчаю і втоми [Kuznetsova, p. 366].
3) **capacity for deceit:** represented guile unknown to the white mind [Mitchell, p. 40-41] – вимагала таких хитрих викрутів, яких і не знають білі люди [Dochenko: ZV I, p. 81]; underhand ways open to it [BS, p. 338] – усе треба здобувати хитрощами [Kuznetsova, p. 219].
4) **intellectual limitation:** dull [Mitchell, p. 96] – тупий [Dochenko: ZV I, p. 134]; stupid [Mitchell, p. 118; BS, p. 160] – нерозумна [Dochenko: ZV I, p. 149], дурень [Kuznetsova, p. 105]; slow-witted [Mitchell, p. 127] – тупа [Dochenko: ZV I, p. 158]; poor [BS, p. 28] – нікчемний [Kuznetsova, p. 19]; punkin-headed nigger [Mark Twain: HF, p. 231] – дурноверхий негр [Steshenko, p. 148]; ignorant [Mitchell, p. 245; Warren, p. 61] – неуцький, темні [Dochenko: ZV I, p. 278; Mitrofanov: UKV, p. 107]; simple-minded [Mitchell, p. 359] – недотепне [Dochenko: ZV I, p. 398]. I see it warn't no use wasting words – you can't learn a nigger to argue [Mark Twain: HF, p. 84]. – Я побачив, що даремно сперечатися з негром. Свого розуму йому не вкладеш [Steshenko, p. 50].
- **honesty:** honest [BS; Mitchell; Mark Twain: HF] – чесний [Kuznetsova; Dochenko: ZV I; Steshenko]; good [Mitchell; Mark Twain: HF] – добрий [Dochenko: ZV I; Steshenko]; code of conduct [Mitchell, p. 12] – добропристойність [Dochenko: ZV I, p. 27]; sense of pride [Mitchell, p. 12] – почуття власної гідності [Dochenko: ZV I, p. 27]: Mammy was black, but her **code of conduct** and her sense of pride were as high as or higher than those of her owners [Mitchell, p. 12]. – Так, шкіру Мамка мала чорну, але коли йшлося про **добропристойність** і почуття власної гідності, то тут вона нічим не поступалася перед своїми господарями, а то ще й перевищувала їх [Dochenko: ZV I, p. 27]. At the semantic level, the translator selects an accurate contextual equivalent in Ukrainian for the lexical phrase "code of

conduct" – "добропристойність", which has the same meaning: a code (rules) of behavior in a specific environment. Planters were distinguished by their manners and knowledge of etiquette in various situations. Where necessary, they restrained themselves, showing themselves as polite people. However, when they wanted to gain something or win in poker, they could resort to tricks and immediately forget about politeness. However, some Black people, despite their status as slaves and bondservants, were no different from their masters.

The Civil War of 1861–1865 eradicated slavery in the South and eliminated the remaining remnants of pre-capitalist social structures. However, Black people did not receive land after the Civil War. Moreover, to ensure a labor force for the plantations, the parliaments of the southern states issued decrees known as "black codes". Black people were forbidden from engaging in crafts and trade, and those under eighteen were forcibly apprenticed to white owners.

Despite the abolition of slavery in the southern states, African Americans continued to work in the cotton fields and remained the property of plantation owners. However, Southern authors in the literary works under consideration refer to them with less offensive and more neutral linguistic units, indicating a specific change in the status of Black people: colored people, black, lower class, low fellow, black fellow, degraded race, housefull, black man-of-all-work. Nonetheless, derogatory terms such as Negro and niggers were still recorded.

Among the authors considered, only H. Beecher Stowe employs a wide range of stylistically neutral vocabulary to denote Black people. She does not describe them as free but notes a change in the white population's attitude toward them. She is the first to refer to them as fellow [BS, p. 176] – людина [Kuznetsova, p. 115]; black fellow [BS, p. 182] – слуга [Kuznetsova, p. 119]; and also: the black man-of-all-work [BS, p. 132] – чорний слуга [Kuznetsova, p. 86]; housefull [BS, p. 221; p. 274] – слуги, негри [Kuznetsova, pp. 119, 178]; their only colored domestic [BS, p. 132] – єдина їхня чорна служниця [Kuznetsova, p. 87]; colored child [BS, p. 338] – негритянські діти [Kuznetsova, p. 219]; degraded race [BS, p. 277] – нижча раса [Kuznetsova, p. 180]; lower class [BS, p. 364] – нижчі маси [Kuznetsova, p. 236].

H. Lee selects three lexical units from the entire synonymic range to denote the concept of BLACK PEOPLE, two of which are neutral – black, colored people, field hands. However, in Ukrainian, "colored people" is translated by the translators in two ways: 1) through calquing – "кольорові": *Colored folks don't show their ages so fast", she said* [Lee: KM, p. 140]. – *Це тому, що **кольорові** не так швидко старіють, як білі, – відповіла Келпурнія* [Kharenko, p. 73]; 2) *with the derogatory term "негри"*: *In her place was a solid mass of colored people* [Lee: KM, p. 134]. – *На тому місці стіною стояли **негри*** [Kharenko, p. 70].

The descriptive translation of "field hands" [Lee: KM] – "робітники на плантаціях" [Kharenko], as well as the combination of calquing and descriptive translation "field Negroes" [Lee: KM] – "негритянки, що працювали на бавовникових полях" [Kharenko], is concise and accurate.

Additionally, in H. Lee's "To Kill a Mockingbird", the term Negro is often used but with a capital letter, indicating respect for Black people: *He seemed to be a respectable Negro, and a **respectable Negro** would never go up into somebody's yard of his own volition* [Lee: KM, p. 217]. – *З усього видно, він **порядний негр**, а порядний негр ніколи не зайде на чуже подвір'я, якщо його не запросять* [Kharenko, p. 115]. / *Здавалося, він **поважний негр**, а поважний негр ніколи не зайшов би на чуже подвір'я з власної волі* [Nekryach: UP, p. 118]; *a Negro girl* [Lee: KM, p. 113] – *прислуга* [Kharenko, p. 59]. The novel depicts politeness toward Black people from genuinely intelligent Southerners: "*Atticus says cheating **a colored man** is ten times worse than cheating a white man", I muttered* [Lee: KM, p. 227]. – *Аттікус каже: обманути білого – погано, але обманути **кольорового** – в десять разів гірше, – промимрила я* [Kharenko, p. 121]. / "*Аттікус каже, що обманути **негра** вдесятеро гірше, ніж обманути білого", – пробубоніла я* [Nekryach: UP, p. 124].

The "Southern guilt" – the longstanding injustice of whites towards Blacks – is emphasized: *As you grow older, you'll see white men cheat black men every day of your life* [Lee: KM, p. 249]. – *Коли ти виростеш, то побачиш, як білі на кожному кроці ошукують чорних* [Kharenko, p. 132]. / *Коли ти підростеш, ти побачиш, як білі щоденно обдурюють чорних* [Nekryach: UP, p. 170].

W. Faulkner, whose works depict the unique atmosphere of the American South and its tragedy, rooted in the destructive power of money and the flawed ideology of racial superiority of whites and inferiority of Blacks, feels the South's guilt and depicts a relatively respectful attitude of the white population towards Black people, using colored boy and black, which R. Dochenko reproduces in the secondary text without significant losses, preserving the author's intent in the VT: colored boy [Faulkner] – кольоровий парубок [Dochenko: K]; they were all there, black and white [Faulkner] – повно їх зібралося, чорних і білих [Dochenko: K, p. 278]. Faulkner does not mention slavery.

However, R. P. Warren and M. Twain accept stereotypes and frequently use the term nigger. I. Steshenko conveys M. Twain's intent in the target text, showing that even after the abolition of slavery, Black people still belonged to wealthy planters: nigger [Mark Twain: HF] – негр [Steshenko]: *He was the most down on Solomon of any **nigger** I ever see* [Twain: HF, p. 83]. – *І ще такого не бувало, щоб якийсь **негр** отак на того Соломона нападався* [Steshenko, p. 49]; nigger woman [Mark Twain: HF, p. 78; p. 100] – негритянка, служниця-негритянка [Steshenko, pp. 46, 61] – in the first variant, the translator calques – "Black woman", and in the second – adds the lexeme "servant", emphasizing the persistence of slavery in the southern USA even after the Civil War.

The phrase "acorn-field nigger", used by R. P. Warren negatively, is translated by V. Mitrofanov as "any Black person from the plantation", removing this negative connotation, although it cannot be stated that it is absent in the analyzed context; it is known that Black people call each other "nigger" without the intention of insulting.

The words and phrases "colored people, black, lower class, low fellow, black fellow, degraded race, housefull, black man-of-all-work, Negro, and niggers", which are the core components of the concept of BLACK PEOPLE after the Civil War, are mainly actualized by the following conceptual features:

1. **integrity:** honest [Mark Twain: TS, p. 78] – порядний [Koretsky, p. 83]; respectable Negro [Lee: KM, p. 217] – порядний Негр, поважний негр [Kharenko, p. 115; Nekryach: UP, p. 108]; decent [BS, p. 231] – порядний [Kuznetsova, p. 129]; an impregnable simplicity of nature [BS, p. 323] – вроджена порядність [Kuznetsova, p. 210]; had the unmitigated temerity to "feel sorry" for a white woman [Lee: KM, p. 231] – мав необережність пожаліти білу жінку [Kharenko, p. 123]; affable [BS, p. 108] – люб'язність [Kuznetsova, p. 71]; noble-hearted [BS, p. 55] – благородний [Kuznetsova, p. 39].

2. **honesty:** honest [BS; Lee: KM; Mark Twain: TS] – чесний [Kuznetsova; Kharenko; Nekryach: UP; Koretsky]; a good nigger [Mark Twain: HF, p. 115] – добрий негр [I. Steshenko, p. 70]; kindly race [BS, p. 233] – вразливі і добрі [Kuznetsova, p. 152]. a) innocence: childlike simplicity of affection [BS, p. 286] – по-дитячому наївний [Kuznetsova, p. 185]; facility of forgiveness [BS, p. 286] – незлобливий [Kuznetsova, p. 185]; grown-up children [BS, p. 276] – дорослі, та все одно діти [Kuznetsova, p. 179]; spoiled children [BS, p. 391] – розбещені діти [Kuznetsova, p. 254]; made his trembly and feverish [Mark Twain: HF, p. 91] – то циганський піт пройма, то морозом всипає [Steshenko, p. 55].

3. **loyalty:** his loyalty [Faulkner, p. 4] – вірність [Dochenko: K, p. 276]; faithful [BS, p. 55] – вірний [Kuznetsova, p. 39]; faithful member of this family [Lee: KM, p. 153] – відданий член нашої сім'ї [Kharenko, p. 80]; steady [BS, p. 7] – надійний [Kuznetsova, p. 4]; faithful [Twain: HF, p. 274] – дбайлива [Steshenko, p. 176].

4. **presence of intellect:** bright nigger [BS, p. 172] – мудрий негр [Kuznetsova, p. 113]; smart [Mark Twain: HF, p. 115] – спритний [Steshenko, p. 70]; capable [BS, p. 7] – меткий і працьовитий [Kuznetsova, p. 4].

5. **worthy of condemnation:** low fellows [BS, p. 8] – нікчемні людці [Kuznetsova, p. 5]; she is selfish – dreadfully selfish [BS, p. 269] – жахлива егоїстка, жахлива [Kuznetsova, p. 175]; so bad, so deceitful, so lazy [BS, p. 279] – негідники і ледарі [Kuznetsova, p. 181].

6. **unfortunate:** po' niggers [Mark Twain: HF, p. 96] – бідолашні негри [Steshenko, p. 58]; poor girls [Mark Twain: HF, p. 180] – сердешні дівчата [Steshenko, p. 113].

The analyzed material shows that although slavery in the South was abolished and Black people were de jure freed after the Civil War in the USA, they continued to de facto belong to wealthy farmers and planters and performed various jobs. However, the attitude of white people towards Blacks became more lenient, evidenced by the use of neutral and less offensive vocabulary to denote Black people and slavery – colored people, black, lower class, black fellow, degraded race, housefull, black man-of-all-work, and less frequently Negro and niggers, which translators translate through direct translation and explication.

Before the Civil War, the core concept of BLACK PEOPLE – negro, nigger, darky, servants, slaves, field hands, house negroes, homecoming hands, valet, black wench, wench – was supplemented with such conceptual features as 1) lower race; 2) oppression; 3) cunning; 4) lack of common sense; 5) lack of knowledge; 6) decency. After the war, the prevailing features are: 1) integrity, 2) honesty, 3) loyalty, 4) presence of intellect, 5) unfortunate, and 6) worthy of condemnation. The authors depict the South's guilt towards Black people.

3.3.2 Rendering the Peripheral Components of the BLACKS Concept in Primary and Secondary Texts

The periphery of the BLACK PEOPLE concept is represented by figurative components – metaphorical expressions and comparisons, the translation of which is a multi-level process aimed at finding equivalent elements in the target language, whose content and emotional value should be equivalent to the metaphors and comparisons of the original. Establishing criteria for the equivalence of figurative means is a challenging task, requiring the improvement of the formal representation of equivalence in the original and translation.

Therefore, it is appropriate to consider the figurative and expressive elements that constitute the periphery of the BLACK PEOPLE concept and their reproduction in Ukrainian and to analyze how the translation affects understanding the entire concept.

1. Metaphorical Expressions. Metaphors actualize people's image-emotional characteristics, behavior, and cultural experiences fixed in consciousness. The evaluative component of a metaphorical expression provides expressive-emotional coloring. An essential condition for adequately conveying a metaphor is reproducing the meaning rather than the literal sense. This avoids false connections and erroneous associations arising from subjective interpretations of the conceptual picture. The translation should elicit the same reaction in the recipients as the original text does in its audience.

The most frequently observed metaphorical component in the source texts is expressed by the lexeme "dog". However, the concept's connotations are ethnically specific (animal of the dog family → loyalty, devotion). The lexeme "dog" in a figurative and pejorative sense means "an unpleasant, contemptible, or wicked person" [NWDTEL, p. 947]; that is, it can be used to refer to a mean, cruel, or unkind person. H. Beecher Stowe uses "dog" with various connotative meanings, which the translator cannot overlook: with his doggish nature [BS, p. 108] – із псячим норовом [Kuznetsova, p. 71] – L. Kuznetsova uses a semantic equivalent; poor dog [BS, p. 280] – бідолашний [Kuznetsova, p. 182]. In this case, the adjective "poor" gives "dog" positive qualities, specifically those that elicit pity; thus, "dog" is omitted in the target text.

The syntactic transformation of the metaphorical phrase "poor, shiftless dogs" [BS, p. 366] – "негри" [Kuznetsova, p. 238], i.e., the use of functional replacement and narrowing, is due to differences in emotional-evaluative associations. In American society, the image of "poor, shiftless dogs" – "poor, helpless, and miserable people" – is associated with unfortunate, unprotected slaves – Black people. In contrast, in Ukrainian culture, it is associated with poor, unrealized people.

Additionally, Black people are also referred to as "pups", meaning small, defenseless, and inexperienced creatures: "<…> they is raised as easy as any kind of critter there is going; they an't a bit more trouble than **pups**" [BS, p. 204] – Які там клопоти? Ростуть, як **цуценята**, самі по собі [Kuznetsova, p. 134].

Another lexeme used to realize the figurative part of the BLACK PEOPLE concept is the word "bird". According to conceptual features, a bird is distinguished by something unusual or unique (regarding social status and significance). H. Beecher Stowe calls the Black man Tom "old bird" – (jocular) a wary and astute person, i.e., a cautious and shrewd person. L. Kuznetsova translates this meaning with the semantic equivalent "experienced".

The most vividly expressive conceptual feature of "oppression of Black people", which confirms the mistreatment of Black people by white slave owners in the Southern USA, is depicted metaphorically: *He's in pretty hard luck* [Mark Twain: HF, p. 236]. – *Йому зараз, мабуть, не з медом* [Steshenko, p. 57]. Since there is no analogous metaphor in the target language, the translator domesticates the conventional metaphor "pretty hard luck" by using a phraseological equivalent – "не з медом".

The following metaphorical expression, *"and my poor broken heart will be at rest"* [Mark Twain: HF, p. 123] – *"і моє бідне, розбите серце матиме нарешті спокій"* [Steshenko, p. 76], contains the conventional metaphor "poor broken heart", which is translated in the target language without changing the imagery "бідне, розбите серце". The second part of the expression, "will be at rest", is also literally translated with the addition of the lexeme "нарешті" – "will finally be at rest", used to express joy, delight, and satisfaction. The translation enhances the sense of the slaves' oppression and their long wait for freedom.

In the following fragment, the feelings of Black people in captivity are metaphorically depicted: "<…> *waited till my head is dizzy and my heart sick*" [BS, p. 621] – "<…> *я від цього чекання вже поволі втрачаю розум, а серце моє розривається на шматки*" [Kuznetsova, p. 412]. The phrase "head is dizzy" is translated by equivalence with the concretization of meaning, namely the addition of the adverb "поволі" – "slowly losing my mind". For the metaphor "heart sick", the translator finds an equivalent in Ukrainian, "серце розривається на шматки" with a change of imagery since the original language does not have the corresponding image in the target language.

The suffering of a Black woman in bondage is metaphorically described as: "<…> but **the ear was deaf with anguish**, and the palsied heart could not feel" [BS, p. 209]. – "<…> та **горе настільки заглушило нещасну**, що скам'яніла душа не могла сприйняти жодних слів, навіть цих" [Kuznetsova, p. 137]. In reproducing the metaphor "ear was deaf with anguish", the translator succeeds in preserving and conveying the message content through a slight change in the object of metaphorization, i. e., the content is conveyed with a more appropriate metaphor – "горе заглушило нещасну" – with the addition of the lexeme "нещасна", which clarifies and complements the content.

However, adding certain words to clarify meaning is not always appropriate: *But, as time, and **debasing influences**, and despair, hardened womanhood within her, and waked the fires of fiercer passions* <…> [BS, p. 629]. – *Довгі роки підневільного життя, розлука з дітьми, приниження і відчай висушили її колись благородну, тонку душу, і в ній розгорілися темні загрозливі пристрасті* [Kuznetsova, p. 417]. Reproducing the metaphorical expression "debasing influences, and despair, hardened womanhood within her", L. Kuznetsova in the target text uses functional replacement with an explication of the concept "womanhood" – "humiliation and despair dried up her once noble, delicate soul", as there is no metaphor "harden womanhood" in Ukrainian, which means to make femininity cruel, to petrify. At the structural level, the translated phrase "dark threatening passions flared up in her" does not correspond to the original "debasing influences, and despair waked the fires of fiercer passions". The original is about how humiliation and despair ignited threatening passions in her, while the translation indicates a connection to the previous metaphor. Such changes, however, do not distort the imagery and expressiveness, but adding the lexeme "темні загрозливі пристарсті" seems redundant as it does not carry additional information.

The part of the sentence "<...> ***peace and trust, which had upborne him hitherto***, *should give way to tossings of soul and despondent darkness*" [BS, p. 610-611]. – "<...> ***віра і спокій почали слабшати***, *що їм на зміну прийшли* ***пригніченість і сум'яття***" [Kuznetsova, p. 405], which describes Tom's disbelief in becoming free and independent, is metaphorical. The original phrase "peace and trust, which had upborne him hitherto" does not match the target phrase "віра і спокій почали слабшати" at either the structural or functional levels. However, the subsequent phrase "їм на зміну прийшли пригніченість і сум'яття" compensates for the message content.

H. Beecher Stowe, depicting the misery and fatigue of the Black slave Lucy in the bondage of the wealthy southerner Legree, uses the metaphor: *"flesh and blood can't bear it any longer"* [BS, p. 29], meaning a living person can no longer endure it. The translator replaces this metaphor with a Ukrainian phraseological analog – *"терпець мій урвався"* [Kuznetsova, p. 20], maintaining the imagery and expressiveness.

The use of semantic development in the reproduction of metaphors is appropriate with a slight change in the object of the image: *"past its fluctuations of hope, and fear, and desire"* [BS, p. 615] – *"серце більше не тремтіло від мрій, надій чи страху"* [Kuznetsova, p. 408].

In the following fragment of Uncle Tom's thoughts about his life and longing for home, the translator appropriately uses the method of semantic development by the context: **The world may go on just as it's always done**, *and take everything from me – loved ones, property, everything –* **but it can't take that** [BS, p. 123]. – *Хай світ поводиться зі мною й надалі так само жорстоко, хай позбавляє мене всього – моїх близьких, моїх достатків, всього-всього,* **але моєї домовини він не відбере!** [Kuznetsova, p. 76]. In the Ukrainian translation, the author's metaphor "the world may go on just as it's always done" is rendered with greater specificity – "хай світ поводиться зі мною й надалі так само жорстоко". The phrase "but it can't take" is also rendered using modulation – "але моєї домовини він не відбере".

Moreover, H. Beecher Stowe highlights the idea that not only Black people but also their entire land belongs to white aristocrats: *"the land groans under it"* [BS, p. 368] – *"але наша країна страждає від цього іга"* [Kuznetsova, p. 239]. The translator renders the metaphor literally with the concretization of the meaning "the land" – "наша країна" and explication according to the context – "it" – with the archaic "іга", meaning oppression, burden.

The character Tom in "Uncle Tom's Cabin", who was sold into slavery in the South, embodies courage and bravery. The author uses a series of metaphors to depict these traits of his character: strong in heart [BS, p. 85] – сповнений рішучості [Kuznetsova, p. 58]; the placid, sunny temper [BS, p. 610] – душевний спокій і оптимізм [Kuznetsova, p. 405]. However, in L. Kuznetsova's translation, the technique of stylistic neutralization is applied with the loss of the image.

Interestingly, Tom cared for himself and the other Black people who had lost their faith and will to live. He was a Black man worthy of respect, so it is worth examining this eloquent fragment: *The poor, worn-down, brutalized creatures, at first, could scarce comprehend this; but, when it was continued week after week and month after month, it began **to awaken long-silent chords in their benumbed hearts*** [BS, p. 618] – *Спочатку ці жалюгідні істоти, які майже втратили людську подобу, не розуміли Тома. Але минали дні, тижні і місяці, і ця людина **завоювала повагу і любов у своєму оточенні. Чи не диво, до них повернулися людські почуття!*** [Kuznetsova, p. 410]. The translation of the metaphorical expression "to awaken long-silent chords in their benumbed hearts" – "завоювала повагу і любов; до них повернулися людські почуття" differs from the original at the syntactic level: for better visualization of Tom's actions, the structure is expanded, leading to the neutralization of the stylistic meaning "benumbed hearts" – "людські почуття". Overall, this translation preserves the content and imagery, thus retaining the peripheral component of the concept.

Likewise, L. Kuznetsova manages to fully convey the content and imagery of the metaphorical expression depicting Tom's courage: *When Tom stood face to face with his prosecutor and heard his threats, and thought in his very soul that his hour was come, his heart swelled bravely in him <…>* [BS, p. 609]. – *Коли Том стояв напроти свого мучителя, слухаючи його страшних погроз, мужнє серце його не зрадило* [Kuznetsova, p. 405].

The only force that sustained the Black people and strengthened their oppressed hearts was the desire to become independent citizens. Some of them, despite the laws, became free. The following excerpts depict their feelings: *<…> but it seems as if I smell the free air <…>* [BS, p. 297]. – *<…> але мені здається, що вітер свободи вже обдуває моє **обличчя*** [Kuznetsova, p. 193]. L. Kuznetsova preserves the content and imagery of the message in the target language, adding the lexeme "обличчя" and changing the agent of the action.

The metaphorical expression *"an inviolable sphere of peace encompassed the lowly heart of the oppressed one <…>"* [BS, p. 368] – *"спокій надійно оселився в душі знедоленого невільника"* [Kuznetsova, p. 408] is translated with a generalization of meaning and the omission of the word "the lowly heart" – "душа", but this is immediately compensated for: "the oppressed one" – "знедолений невільник", as "low" means a depressed, humiliated person.

2. Comparisons. Authors use comparisons to clarify and specify the image, and adequate reproduction ensures the correct understanding of the concept. H. Beecher Stowe most frequently compares Black people to animals – *dogs, pigs, crows,* and *eels*.

I shall be kicked out and buried like a dog <...> [BS, p. 185]. – *Закопають у землю, як дохлого пса* <...> [Kuznetsova, p. 121]. In the target language, the analyzed comparison is rendered using the strategy of concretization with the addition of lexemes – "у землю" and "дохлий", which are made for clear visualization of the situation.

Black people are compared to a domesticated animal – pig, which in both linguocultures is associated with "a greedy, dirty, or unpleasant person" [DCE, p. 1534]: <...> *they don't understand a word of the sermon, more than so many pigs* <...> [BS, p. 282]. – <...> *бо читати їм проповідь – що* ***сипати бісер перед свиньми*** [Kuznetsova, p. 183]. In describing the ignorance of Black people who cannot understand a word of the sermon, the author compares them to pigs. In the Ukrainian translation, the comparison is not reproduced; the translator resorts to a trope shift – replacing the comparison with an idiom: "сипати бісер перед свиньми".

The comparison of Black children to crows is translated literally: *Very soon, about a dozen young imps were roosting, like so many crows, on the verandah railings* <...> [BS, p. 68]. – *На ґанку вже повсідали рядочком, мов гайвороння на гілці, з десяток чорномазих бісенят* [Kuznetsova, p. 47].

To reproduce the comparison "slippery as eels", the translator uses functional replacement (eel – snake, not eel) and explication for clear visualization and better understanding: *If he'd hear to me, he wouldn't trust any on ye –* ***slippery as eels!*** [BS, p. 91]. – *Кажу йому: не довіряйте неграм, бо негр,* ***як вуж: мить – і вислизне з рук***. *Та він мене не слухає* [Kuznetsova, p. 61]. The eel (a marine fish with a snake-like body) is a geographically specific lexeme without clear emotional-evaluative associations for an average Ukrainian. The translation equivalent "вуж" is apt, as this reptile is widespread throughout Ukraine and thus understandable to Ukrainians.

The author compares the hope of Black people for freedom to a spider's web. In the Ukrainian text, the comparison is reproduced metaphorically with the addition of a word: <...> *such parting as those may make whose hope to meet again is as the spider's web* <...> [BS, p. 34]. – *Так прощаються люди, коли їхня надія на нову зустріч тонша за павутинку* [Kuznetsova, p. 23].

The following comparison is rendered with an idiom based on a metaphor: <...> *her heart lay as if a great stone had fallen on it* [BS, p. 202]. – <...> *безвихідь каменем залягла їй на серце* [Kuznetsova, p. 133].

H. Beecher Stowe, depicting Tom's reliability and diligence, compares him to a clock. In the secondary text, this comparison is rendered metaphorically: *Why, the fact is, Haley, Tom is an uncommon fellow, he is certainly worth that sum anywhere, – steady, honest, capable, manages my whole farm like a clock* [BS, p. 7]. – *Але Гейлі! Том сторицею відпрацює ці гроші. Він незвичайний негр –*

надійний, чесний, меткий і працьовитий. Під його наглядом моє господарство працює безперебійно [Kuznetsova, p. 4].

Thus, it can be argued that the periphery of the BLACK PEOPLE concept is predominantly composed of metaphors and comparisons, the adequate reproduction of which requires significant effort from the translator, as some translation losses impoverish the concept's richness and complicate its understanding. The peripheral elements of the concept are rendered in Ukrainian using such strategies as trope shift, addition, compensation, and concretization of meaning.

Conclusions for Chapter 3

Adequate reproduction of the linguistic representations of the fundamental ethical concepts of the American South – SOUTHERN LADY and SOUTHERN GENTLEMAN, WHITE TRASH, BLACK PEOPLE – is not always achieved without artistic losses.

The research revealed that reproducing the core components of the SOUTHERN LADY and SOUTHERN GENTLEMAN concepts – lady and gentleman – depends on the essential conceptual feature actualized by these linguistic units in a specific context.

The periphery of the SOUTHERN LADY and SOUTHERN GENTLEMAN concepts consists of metaphors and comparisons, the adequate reproduction of which is a challenging task due to the mismatch of connotative meanings. Using such translation methods as equivalence, literal translation, addition, semantic development, metaphorical differentiation, descriptive translation, and trope shift ensures the adequate reproduction of the peripheral components of the concepts. It allows foreign readers to correctly interpret the SOUTHERN LADY and SOUTHERN GENTLEMAN concepts.

The core of the WHITE TRASH concept includes the phrase white trash and the word cracker, which undergo variability in translation into Ukrainian. The concept contains such conceptual features as 1) low origin, 2) lack of education, and 3) dishonesty, and its periphery consists of comparisons and metaphors. Adequate reproduction of the linguistic representations of the concept is mainly achieved through a) contextual equivalents, b) concretization of meaning, c) differentiation, d) descriptive translation, and e) literal translation. This concept is dynamic, and with changing socio-cultural and historical-political conditions, it loses some meanings and acquires others, requiring the search for an adequate equivalent considering these significant changes.

It was found that before the Civil War, the core of the BLACK PEOPLE concept included such words and phrases as negro, nigger, darky, servants, slaves, field hands, house negroes, home-coming hands, valet, black wench, wench. Translators do not always succeed in adequately rendering them into Ukrainian. Using meaning concretization in specific contexts helps the foreign reader correctly interpret the concept. A syncretic image of Black people is created through the methods of omission, addition, and semantic development. After the war, the attitude of white people towards Black people became more lenient, evidenced by the use of neutral and less offensive vocabulary by writers to characterize Black people and slavery, which Ukrainian translators render through direct translation and explication.

The periphery of the BLACK PEOPLE concept is represented by metaphorical expressions and comparisons with expressive-emotional coloring, misinterpretation of which leads to subjective interpretation of the conceptual picture. As a result of changes at the semantic level, translators clarify or generalize some conceptual features. Through functional replacement and narrowing, omission, addition, and stylistic neutralization with the loss of the image, translators enhance or weaken the depicted image.

The study of the verbalization of the system of relationships and behavior of various Southern United States social strata in primary and secondary texts revealed that reproducing the core components of the analyzed concepts presents manageable difficulties, although minor losses are observed here. The peripheral features conveyed through metaphors, comparisons, and idioms pose a real challenge for the translator, as conveying the content and implied culturally conditioned information is necessary.

Conclusions

Adequate reproduction of linguistic representations of ethnoculturally marked concepts encompasses the full range of translation strategies and tactics, as well as elements of conceptual analysis. A translation strategy is the translator's general action plan within the given task. In contrast, translation tactics are the specific steps to implement the chosen strategy. It is only sometimes possible to fully convey all aspects of the original, leading to inevitable translation losses. Therefore, the translator must establish a hierarchy of priorities in advance, highlighting the key features of the original and minimizing inevitable losses.

Key Findings of the Monograph

An ethnoculturally marked concept has been further developed as a set of people's personal, historical-cultural, social, and traditional values influenced by ethnocultural content. It denotes phenomena that possess a specific lexical code of an ethnic group and society.

To adequately render linguistic representations of the cultural concept sphere, it is necessary to clarify pre-textual presuppositions, such as the time and place of the original creation, the source culture, and information about the author. Keywords representing the core concepts should be identified, their place in the linguistic picture of the world established through encyclopedic dictionaries, and the synonymous series highlighted. This helps to isolate the concept's core, which bears the main semantic load and must be reproduced in translation. To fully model the structure of a concept, its periphery, including figurative and value components like metaphors, comparisons, epithets, and phraseological units, must also be defined.

The study of linguistic representations in original and translated texts of ethnoculturally marked concepts of the American South – such as CIVIL WAR, SOCIAL ORDER, SLAVERY, SOUTHERN LADY and SOUTHERN GENTLEMAN, WHITE TRASH, and BLACKS – confirms complete translation on one hand, and variability in reproducing the core units of some concepts on the other. For example, linguistic units like "lady" (леді, пані, дама, міледі, жінка) and "gentleman" (джентльмен, добродій, люди благородні, з порядної родини) reveal only one shade of meaning.

In rendering the conceptual features that constitute the core of a concept, minor shifts at the semantic level are observed in secondary texts, slightly distorting the original's vision. These changes result in adding or omitting certain features present in the original or clarifying some conceptual features. To accurately reflect the linguistic representations of the concept, translators employ tactics such as a) selecting semantic equivalents, b) direct translation, c) meaning specification, d) differentiation, e) descriptive translation, and f) replacing a stylistically neutral word with a stylistically marked one.

The figurative conceptualization of the concepts of CIVIL WAR, SOCIAL ORDER, SLAVERY, SOUTHERN LADY and SOUTHERN GENTLEMAN, WHITE TRASH, and BLACKS forming the periphery comprises metaphors, comparisons, epithets, and phraseologisms. These tools actualize people's entrenched figurative-emotional characteristics, behavior, and cultural experience. Adequate reproduction requires deep background knowledge and broad erudition from the translator. Using literal translation, addition, semantic development, metaphorical differentiation, descriptive translation, and trope shifts enables the adequate reproduction of peripheral concept components, preserving the author's pragmatic intent and ensuring the correct interpretation of ethnoculturally marked concepts of the American South.

The following strategies are identified in the reproduction of linguistic representations of ethnoculturally marked concepts:
- Foreignization (32%): Aiming to preserve the ethnospecific characteristics of the original text.
- Domestication (40%): Adapting the expression to the target language.
- Translational dispersion (18%): A unique "dispersal of the original", manifesting as "clusters of equivalents" based on the universal law of linguistic and interlinguistic synonymy.
- Translational convergence (10%): The merging, convergence, or combination of elements. Applying the principle of translational convergence leads to creating a hyperonym, which accumulates several meanings. This simplifies the translator's task and eases the target culture recipient's perception of foreign reality. However, this approach can sometimes distort the original text.

The adequate reproduction of linguistic representations of ethnoculturally marked concepts of the American South in the analyzed works is achieved through a comprehensive analysis of the concept sphere, its place in American culture, and appropriate translation strategies and tactics. In translation, linguistic representations of concepts are reproduced fully (71%) when there is a match in the cognitive bases of the original and target audience, partially (22%) when the adequate conveyance of linguistic expression does not ensure the contextual meaning, and deformatively (7%) when excessive exploitation of the original content leads to the inclusion of information absent in the original text.

References

Avtonomna, N. S. (2006). O filosofskom perevode [On Philosophical Translation]. *Voprosy filosofii*, (2), 89–101.

Adonina, I. V. (2005). Kontsept USPEKH v sovremennoy amerikanskoy rechevoy kulture: Diss. kand. filol. nauk: spets. 10.02.04 "Germanskie yazyki" [The Concept of SUCCESS in Modern American Speech Culture] (Doctoral monograph, Khabarovsk). 199 pages.

Alekseeva, I. S. (2004). *Vvedenie v perevodovedenie: ucheb. posobie dlya stud. filol. i lingv. fak. vyssh. ucheb. zavedeniy* [Introduction to Translation Studies: Textbook for Students of Philology and Linguistics Faculties of Higher Educational Institutions]. SPb.: Izdatelskiy tsentr Akademiya.

Alefirenko, N. F. (2005). Sinergetika kulturnogo kontsepta i znaka v sisteme yazyka i tekste [Synergetics of Cultural Concept and Sign in the System of Language and Text]. *Kulturologiya*, 11–12.

Apresyan, Yu. D. (1995). Obraz cheloveka po dannym yazyka: popytka sistemnogo opisaniya [The Image of a Person According to Language Data: An Attempt at Systematic Description]. *Izbrannye trudy. Integralnoe opisanie yazyka i sistemnaya leksikografiya*, 2, 348–388.

Arutyunova, N. D. (2000). Naivnye razmyshleniya o naivnoy kartine yazyka. Vvedenie [Naive Reflections on a Naive Picture of Language. Introduction]. *Yazyk o yazyke*, 7–19.

Arutyunova, N. D. (1988). *Tipy yazykovykh znacheniy: Otsenka. Sobytie. Fakt* [Types of Linguistic Meanings: Evaluation. Event. Fact]. Moscow: Nauka.

Babenko, L. G. (2004). *Lingvisticheskiy analiz khudozhestvennogo teksta. Teoriya i praktika: uchebnik i praktikum* [Linguistic Analysis of Literary Text. Theory and Practice: Textbook and Practical Guide]. 2nd ed. Moscow: Flinta; Nauka.

Babina, L. V. (2000). O vtorichnoy reprezentatsii kontseptov v tekstakh literaturnoy prozy [On the Secondary Representation of Concepts in Literary Prose Texts]. *Kognitivnaya semantika. Materialy vtoroy mezhdunarodnoy shkoly-seminara*, 2, 131–132.

Babushkin, A. P., & Zhukova, M. T. (2001). Perevod khudozhestvennogo proizvedeniya kak kulturnaya adaptatsiya kartiny mira [Translation of a Literary Work as Cultural Adaptation of the Worldview]. *Yazyk, kommunikatsiya i sotsialnaya sreda*, (1). Retrieved from http://tpl1999.narod.ru.

Bazylev, V. N., & Sorokin, Yu. A. (2001). Interpretativnoe perevodovedenie. Propedevticheskiy kurs [Interpretative Translation Studies. Propaedeutic Course]. *Vestnik VGU. Seriya lingvistika i mezhkulturnaya kommunikatsiya*, (2), 12–14.

Barkhudarov, L. S. (1975). Yazyk i perevod [Language and Translation]. *Voprosy obshchey i chastnoy teorii perevoda*. Moscow: Mezhdunarodnye otnosheniya.

Bauman, Z. (2002). *Glokalizatsiya, ili komu globalizatsiya, a komu lokalizatsiya* [Glocalization, or for Whom Globalization, and for Whom Localization]. Globalizatsiya: Kontury XXI veka. Ref. sb., edited by Yu. I. Igritskiy, P. V. Malinovskiy, 134.

Belaya, E. N. (2000). *Idiomatika i naivnaya kartina mira* [Idiomaticity and Naive Picture of the World]. Yazyk. Chelovek. Kartina mira. Materialy Vseross. konf., 2, 6-11.

Belyaevskaya, E. G. (2000). Printsipy kognitivnykh issledovaniy: problema modelirovaniya semantiki yazykovykh edinits [Principles of Cognitive Research: The Problem of Modeling the Semantics of Language Units]. *Kognitivnaya semantika. Materialy vtoroy mezhdunarodnoy shkoly-seminara*, 1, 8-10.

Bielekhova, L. I. (2002). *Slovesnyy poeticheskiy obraz v istoriko-tipologicheskoy perspektive: lingvokognitivnyy aspekt (na materiale amerikanskoy poezii)* [Verbal Poetic Image in Historical and Typological Perspective: Linguocognitive Aspect (based on American Poetry)]. Kyiv: Ailant.

Biessonova, O. L. (2002). *Otsinnyy tezaurus anhliyskoyi movy: kohnityvno-henderni aspekty* [Evaluative Thesaurus of the English Language: Cognitive and Gender Aspects]. Donetsk: DonNU.

Bykova, O. I. (2008). Kriterii peredachi kulturnosti edinits teksta-originala pri perevode [Criteria for Conveying the Culturality of Original Text Units in Translation]. *Sotsiokulturnye problemy perevoda*, 161-167.

Bogin, G. I. (1989). *Skhemy deystviya chitatel'ya pri ponimanii teksta* [Reader's Action Schemes in Understanding the Text]. Kalinin: KGU.

Boduen de Kurtene, I. A. (1963). *Izbrannye trudy po obshchemu yazykoznaniyu* [Selected Works on General Linguistics]. Moscow.

Boldyrev, N. N. (2000). Znachenie i smysl s kognitivnoy tochki zreniya i problema mnogoznachnosti [Meaning and Sense from a Cognitive Perspective and the Problem of Polysemy]. *Kognitivnaya semantika. Materialy II mezhdunarodnoy shkoly-seminara*, 1, 11-17.

Bolshakova, N. I. (2004). Natsionalnaya kartina mira i problema lakunarnosti igry slov v khudozhestvennom perevode [National Picture of the World and the Problem of Lacunarity of Wordplay in Literary Translation]. *Visnyk ZhDU imeni I. Ya. Franka*, (17), 87-88.

Bondarenko, E. V. (1999). Kontseptualnaya metamorfoza "teploy" kartiny vremeni v sovremennoy poezii [Conceptual Metamorphosis of the "Warm" Picture of Time in Modern Poetry]. *Visnyk Kharkivs'koho derzhavnoho universytetu. Seriya romano-hermans'ka filolohiya*, (461), 33-39.

Borukhov, B. L. (1991). "Zerkalnaya" metafora v istorii kultury ["Mirror" Metaphor in the History of Culture]. *Logicheskiy analiz yazyka: Kulturnye kontsepty*, 109-116.

Brutyants, G. A. (1971). Yazyk i kartina mira [Language and Worldview]. *Filosofskie nauki: nauchnyy zhurnal*, (1), 6-8.

Bialyk, V. D. (2004). Problema kategorizatsii neologicheskoy kartiny mira [The Problem of Categorizing the Neological Worldview]. *Naukovyy visnyk Chernivetskoho universytetu: zbirnyk naukovykh prats*, 188, 189: Hermanska filolohiya, 62-72.

Weisgerber, J. L. (1993). *Rodnoy yazyk i formirovanie Dukha* [Native Language and the Formation of the Spirit]. Moscow: MGU.

Valeeva, N. G. *Perevod – yazykovoe posrednichestvo, sposob mezhkulturnoy i mezhyazykovoy kommunikatsii* [Translation as Language Mediation, a Means of Intercultural and Interlingual Communication]. Retrieved from www.trpub.ru/valeeva-perevod-kommunik.html.

Valchuk, G. V. (2000). Do pytannya pro kartynu svitu ta pro zv'yazok movy y myslennya [On the Issue of the Worldview and the Relationship Between Language and Thought]. *Mova i kultura: zbirnyk naukovykh prats*, 1(2), 34–37.

Valchuk, G. V. (2003). Movne vtilennya kontseptu "yevropeyska intehratsiya": semantyko-kohnityvnyy aspekt (na materiali dokumentiv Yevrosoyuzu ta publikatsiy hazety The Times): dys. kand. filol. nauk: 10.02.04 [Linguistic Representation of the Concept "European Integration": Semantic-Cognitive Aspect (Based on the Documents of the European Union and Publications of The Times)] (Doctoral monograph). Kyiv.

Vannikov, Yu. V. (1988). Problemy adekvatnosti perevoda: tipy adekvatnosti, vidy perevoda i perevodcheskoy deyatelnosti [Problems of Translation Adequacy: Types of Adequacy, Types of Translation and Translation Activity]. *Tekst i perevod*, 34–37.

Vezhbitskaya, A. (2001). *Ponimanie kultur cherez posredstvo klyuchevykh slov* [Understanding Cultures Through Key Words]. (A. D. Shmeleva, Trans.). Moscow: Yazyki slavyanskoy kultury.

Vezhbitskaya, A. (1999). *Semanticheskie universal'ii v opisanii yazykov* [Semantic Universals in the Description of Languages]. (A. D. Shmeleva, Trans.; T. V. Bulygina, Ed.). Moscow: Yazyki russkoy kultury.

Vishnyatskiy, L. B. (2002). Proiskhozhdenie yazyka: sovremennoe sostoyanie problemy [The Origin of Language: The Current State of the Problem]. *Voprosy yazykoznaniya*, (2), 48–63.

Vlahov, S., & Florin, S. (1986). *Neperovodimoe v perevode* [Untranslatable in Translation]. Moscow: Vysshaya shkola.

Vorkachev, S. G. (2001). Kontsept schastya: ponyatiynyy i obraznyy komponenty [The Concept of Happiness: Conceptual and Imaginary Components]. *Izvestiya RAN. Seriya literatury i yazyka*, 60(6), 47–58.

Vorkachev, S. G. (2003). Kulturnye kontsepty i perevod: makarizmy v tekste Evangelii [Cultural Concepts and Translation: Makarisms in the Text of the Gospel]. *Vestnik MGOU*, (4), 88–93.

Vorkachev, S. G. *Lingvokul'turologiya, yazykovaya lichnost', kontsept: stanovlenie antropotsentricheskoy paradigmy v yazykoznanii* [Linguoculturology, Language Personality, Concept: Formation of the Anthropocentric Paradigm in Linguistics]. Retrieved from http://kubstu.ru/docs/lingvoconcept/lingvocult.htm.

Vorobyova, O. P., & van Peer, Willie. (n.d.). *Z pohlyadom u maybutnye = Greeting the Future*. 222–225.

Gabunia, Z., & Tirado, R. G. (2003). Kulturologicheskiy aspekt perevoda khudozhestvennogo istoricheskogo teksta [Cultural Aspect of Translation of a Literary Historical Text]. *Sopostavitelnaya filologiya i polilingvizm*, 67–70.

Gak, V. G. (1971). Asimmetriya lingvisticheskogo znaka i nekotorye obshchie problemy terminologii [Asymmetry of the Linguistic Sign and Some General Problems of Terminology]. *Semioticheskie problemy yazykovoy nauki, terminologii i informatiki*, 68–71.

Guleeva, N. L. (1997). *Osnovy deyatelnostnoy teorii perevoda* [Foundations of the Activity Theory of Translation]. Tver: TGU.

Guleeva, N. L. (1999). *Parametry tipologii khudozhestvennykh tekstov v deyatelnostnoy teorii perevoda:* avtoref. dis. kand. filol. nauk: 10.02.20 [Parameters of the Typology of Literary Texts in the Activity Theory of Translation: Author's Abstract of Candidate of Philological Sciences Monograph]. Yekaterinburg.

Garbovskiy, N. K. (2004). *Teoriya perevoda* [Translation Theory]. Moscow: Izdatelstvo MGU.

Gachev, G. D. (1995). *Natsionalnye obrazy mira: Kosmo-Psykho-Logos* [National Images of the World: Cosmo-Psycho-Logos]. Moscow: Progress; Kultura.

Gachechiladze, G. (1967). O realizme v iskusstve perevoda [On Realism in the Art of Translation]. *Aktualnye problemy teorii khudozhestvennogo perevoda: sbornik statey,* 39–51.

Hertz, H. (1973). Printsipy mekhaniki, izlozhennye v novoy svyazi [Principles of Mechanics Presented in a New Connection]. *Zhizn nauki: antropologiya vstupitelnykh k klassike estestvoznaniya,* 206–210.

Glossariy: Adekvanty perevod. Polnotsennyy perevod [Glossary: Adequate Translation. Full Translation]. Retrieved from http://www.glossary.ru/.

Gnatyuk, L. P. (2003). Movni kartyny svitu dvo- i kilkamovnoyi osobystosti [Language Pictures of the World of Bilingual and Multilingual Individuals]. *Movni i kontseptualni kartyny svitu, 9,* 71–75.

Holubenko, N. I. (2015). Adyekvatnist' vidtvorennya u khudozhn'omu perekladi movnykh reprezentatsiy kontseptiv [Adequacy of Reproduction in Literary Translation of Language Representations of Concepts]. *Ukraina i svit: Dialoh mov ta kul'tur: Materialy Mizhnarodnoi naukovo-praktychnoi konferentsii* (Kyiv, 01–03 April 2015), 76–78.

Holubenko, N. I. (2013). Bazovi skladnyky kontseptosfery "amerykanskoho Pivdnya" v perekladoznavchomu rakursi [Basic Components of the Conceptual Sphere "American South" in Translation Studies Perspective]. *Naukovy zapysky. Seriya: Filolohichni nauky (movoznavstvo),* 274–278.

Holubenko, N. I. (2015). Vidtvorennya ukrayins'koyu movoyu movnykh reprezentatsiy etnokul'turno markovanoho kontseptu amerykanskoho Pivdnya RABSTVO [Reproduction of the Linguistic Representations of the Ethnoculturally Marked Concept of the American South SLAVERY in Ukrainian]. *Visnyk KNLU. Seriya Filolohiya, 18*(2), 30–36.

Holubenko, N. I. (2014). Vplyv kontseptual'noyi ta movnoyi asymetriyi na pereklad [The Influence of Conceptual and Linguistic Asymmetry on Translation]. *Naukovy zapysky Natsional'noho universytetu "Ostroh Academy". Seriya "Filolohichna", 45,* 214–216.

Holubenko, N. I. (2015). Zasady kontseptual'noho analizu v perekladoznavstvi [Principles of Conceptual Analysis in Translation Studies]. *Naukovyy visnyk Drohobyts'koho derzhavnoho pedahohichnoho universytetu imeni Ivana Franka. Seriya: "Filolohichni nauky" (movoznavstvo), 3,* 67–71.

Holubenko, N. I. (2013). Kontsept u suchasniy perekladoznavchiy paradyhmi [Concept in the Modern Paradigm of Translation Studies]. *Ukraina i svit: Dialoh mov ta kul'tur: Materialy Mizhnarodnoi naukovo-praktychnoi konferentsii* (Kyiv, 03–05 April 2013), 67–69.

Holubenko, N. I. (2015). Osoblyvosti vidtvorennya u perekladi movnykh reprezentatsiy kontseptiv amerykanskoho Pivdnya PIVDENNA LEDI i PIVDENNYY DZHENTL'MEN [Peculiarities of Reproducing in Translation the Linguistic Representations of the

Concepts of the American South SOUTHERN LADY and SOUTHERN GENTLEMAN]. *Problemy zistavnoyi semantyky*, 328–333.

Holubenko, N. I. (2014). Perekladats'ki stratehiyi vidtvorennya etnokul'turnoho kontseptu [Translation Strategies for Reproducing the Ethnocultural Concept]. *Naukovyy visnyk Mizhnarodnoho humanitarnoho universytetu. Seriya: Filolohiya, 10*(2), 126–128.

Holubenko, N. I. (2014). Problema perekladnosti etnokul'turnoho kontseptu [The Problem of Translating the Ethnocultural Concept]. *Naukovy zapysky. Seriya: Filolohichni nauky (movoznavstvo), 126*, 322–325.

Holubenko, N. I. (2014). Trudnoshchi vidtvorennya peryferiynykh oznak kontseptu [Difficulties of Reproducing Peripheral Features of the Concept]. *Filolohichni nauky v umovakh suchasnykh transformatsiynykh protsesiv: Materialy Mizhnarodnoi naukovo-praktychnoi konferentsii* (Lviv, 26–27 September 2014), 40–41.

Holubovskaya, I. A. (2002). *Etnicheskie osobennosti yazykovykh kartin mira* [Ethnic Features of Language Pictures of the World]. Kyiv: Kyivskyi natsionalnyi universytet imeni T. H. Shevchenka.

Gudkov, D. B. (2003). *Teoriya i praktika mezhkulturnoy kommunikatsii* [Theory and Practice of Intercultural Communication]. Moscow: Gnozis.

Guketlova, F. N. (2009). *Zoomorfnyy kod kultury v yazykovoy kartine mira (na materiale frantsuzskogo, kabardino-cherkesskogo i russkogo yazykov):* avtoref. dis. d-ra filol. nauk: 10.02.02 [Zoomorphic Code of Culture in the Linguistic Picture of the World (Based on French, Kabardian-Circassian, and Russian Languages): Author's Abstract of Doctor of Philological Sciences Monograph]. Moscow.

Humboldt, W. von. (2000). *Izbrannye trudy po yazykoznaniyu* [Selected Works on Linguistics]. Moscow: Progress.

Humboldt, W. von. (1985). *Yazyk i filosofiya kultury* [Language and Philosophy of Culture]. Moscow: Progress.

Dijk, T. A. van (1989). *Yazyk. Poznanie. Kommunikatsiya* [Language. Cognition. Communication]. (V. I. Gerasimov, Trans.; Ed. V. I. Gerasimov). Moscow: Progress.

Denysova, T. N. (2012). *Istoriya amerykanskoyi literatury* [History of American Literature]. NAN Ukrayiny, Instytut literatury im. T. H. Shevchenka. Kyiv: Vyd. dim "Kyyevo-Mohylyanska akademiya".

Dymytrenko, L. V. (1999). Kontseptualna kartyna svitu v poetychnykh tvorakh (na materiali poetychnykh obraziv amerykanskoyi poeziyi XX st.) [Conceptual Picture of the World in Poetic Works (Based on Poetic Images of American Poetry of the 20th Century)]. *Movni i kontseptualni kartyny svitu*, 37–44.

Dolinin, K. A. (1985). *Interpretatsiya teksta* [Text Interpretation]. Moscow: Prosveshchenie.

Einstein, A. (1967). Vliyanie Maksvella na razvitie predstavleniy o fizicheskoy realnosti [Maxwell's Influence on the Development of Concepts of Physical Reality]. *Sobraniye nauchnykh trudov, 4*, 599.

Yesin, A. B., Dolinina, S. Y., & Averina, E. V. (2003). *Literaturovedenie; Kulturologiya: izbrannye trudy* [Literary Criticism; Cultural Studies: Selected Works]. Moscow: Flinta.

Zhabotinskaya, S. A. (2000). Kontseptualnyy analiz: tipy freymov [Conceptual Analysis: Types of Frames]. *Kognitivnaya semantika. Materialy II mezhdunarodnoy shkoly-seminara, 2*, 10–13.

Zhayvoronok, V. V. (2002). Problema kontseptualnoyi kartyny svitu ta yiyi movnoho vidobrazhennya [The Problem of the Conceptual Picture of the World and Its Linguistic Representation]. *Kultura narodov Prichernomorya, 31*, 51-53.

Zalevskaya, A. A. (2002). Natsionalno-kulturnaya spetsifika kartiny mira i razlichnye podkhody k yeye issledovaniyu [National-Cultural Specificity of the Worldview and Various Approaches to Its Study]. *Yazykovoe soznanie i obraz mira*, 39-54.

Zorivchak, R. P. (1989). *Realia i perevod (na materiale anhlomovnykh perevodiv ukrayinskoyi prozy)* [Realities and Translation (Based on English Translations of Ukrainian Prose)]. Lviv: Vyd-vo pry Lvivskomu un-ti.

Zurabyan, M. O. (2008). Original i perevod: Vzaimodeystvie dvukh kultur (problema natsionalnogo i istoricheskogo koloryta) [Original and Translation: Interaction of Two Cultures (Problem of National and Historical Color)]. *Aktualnye problemy literatury i kultury (Voprosy filologii)*, (3), 126-127.

Kahanovska, O. M. (2001). Semiotychnyy aspekt kontseptualnoyi orhanizatsiyi khudozhnoho tekstu [Semiotic Aspect of the Conceptual Organization of a Literary Text]. *Movni i kontseptualni kartyny svitu, 5*, 82-87.

Kahanovska, O. M. (2002). *Tekstovi kontsepty khudozhnoyi prozy* [Text Concepts of Literary Prose]. Kyiv: Vyd. tsentr KNLU.

Kade, O. (1979). K voprosu o predmete lingvisticheskoy teorii perevoda [On the Subject of the Linguistic Theory of Translation]. *Tetradi perevodchika, 16*, 3-11.

Kazakova, T. A. (1988). Strategii resheniya zadach v khudozhestvennom perevode [Strategies for Solving Problems in Literary Translation]. *Perevod i interpretatsiya teksta*, 215.

Karasik, V. I. (1988). *Kategorialnye priznaki v znachenii slova* [Categorical Features in the Meaning of the Word]. Moscow: MOPI im. N. K. Krupskoy.

Karasik, V. I., & Slyshkin, G. G. (2001). Lingvokulturnyy kontsept kak yedinitsa issledovaniya [Linguocultural Concept as a Unit of Study]. *Metodologicheskie problemy kognitivnoy lingvistiki*, 75-80.

Karasik, V. I. (2004). *Yazykovoy krug: lichnost, kontsepty, diskurs* [Linguistic Circle: Personality, Concepts, Discourse]. Moscow: Gnozis.

Karaulov, Yu. N. (1976). *Obshchaya i russkaya ideografiya* [General and Russian Ideography]. Moscow: Nauka.

Kaioa, R. (2003). *Viyna i sakralne* [War and the Sacred]. Kyiv: Vakler.

Kedrov, B. M. (1986). Sverkhsadacha kompleksnogo izucheniya tvorchestva [The Super Task of Comprehensive Study of Creativity]. *Khudozhestvennoe tvorchestvo. Voprosy kompleksnogo izucheniya*, 15-28.

Kyyak, T. R., Naumenko, A. M., & Ohuy, O. D. (2006). *Teoriya i praktyka perekladu* [Theory and Practice of Translation]. Vinnytsya: Nova knyha.

Kovaleva, L. V. (2004). Natsionalnoe svoeobrazie yazykovoy ob'ektivizatsii kontseptov, vyrazhennykh frazeosochetaniyami, oboznachayushchimi realii okruzhayushchey sredy [National Peculiarities of Linguistic Objectification of Concepts Expressed by Phrases Indicating Environmental Realities]. *Vestnik Voronezhskogo gosudarstvennogo universiteta. Seriya Lingvistika i mezhkulturnaya kommunikatsiya*, (1), 54-60.

Kovhanyuk, S. P. (1968). *Praktyka perekladu (z dosvidu perekladacha)* [Translation Practice (From the Experience of a Translator)]. Kyiv: Dnipro.

Kolesov, I. Yu. (2009). *Aktualizatsiya zritelnogo vospriyatiya v yazyke: kognitivnyy aspekt (na materiale angliyskogo i russkogo yazykov): avtoref. dis. d-ra filol. nauk: 10.02.19*

"Teoriya yazyka" [Actualization of Visual Perception in Language: Cognitive Aspect (Based on English and Russian Languages): Author's Abstract of Doctor of Philological Sciences Monograph]. Barnaul, 12–13.

Kolomiiets, L. V. (2011). *Perekladoznavchi seminari: aktualni teoretychni kontseptsii ta modeli analizu poetychnoho perekladu* [Translation Studies Seminars: Current Theoretical Concepts and Models for the Analysis of Poetic Translation]. Kyiv: Vydavnycho-polihrafichnyy tsentr "Kyivskyy universytet".

Kolshansky, G. V. (1990). *Ob'yektivnaya kartina mira v poznanii yazyka* [The Objective Picture of the World in Language Cognition]. Moscow: Nauka.

Komissarov, V. N. (2001). *Sovremennoe perevodovedenie* [Modern Translation Studies]. Moscow: ETS.

Koptilov, V. V. (2003). *Teoriya i praktyka perekladu* [Theory and Practice of Translation]. Kyiv: Yunivers.

Koptilov, V. V. (1971). *Aktualni pytannya ukrayinskoho khudozhn'oho perekladu* [Current Issues of Ukrainian Literary Translation]. Kyiv: Dnipro.

Kornilov, O. A. (2003). *Yazykovye kartiny mira kak proizvodnye natsionalnykh mentalitetov* [Linguistic Pictures of the World as Derivatives of National Mentalities]. Moscow: CheRo.

Korunets, I. V. (2000). *Teoriya i praktyka perekladu (aspektnyy pereklad)* [Theory and Practice of Translation (Aspect Translation)]. Vinnytsya: Nova Knyha.

Kravchenko, A. V. (2004). *Yazyk i vospriyatie: Kognitivnye aspekty yazykovoy kategorizatsii* [Language and Perception: Cognitive Aspects of Linguistic Categorization]. Irkutsk: Izdatelstvo Irkutskogo universiteta.

Krasnykh, V. V. (2003). *"Svoy sredi chuzhikh": mif ili realnost?* ["Among Strangers": Myth or Reality?]. Moscow: ITDGK "Gnozis".

Quine, W. V. O. *Uillard Van Orman Quine: Online Encyclopedia Krugosvet* [Electronic resource]. Retrieved from http://www.krugosvet.ru/enc/gumanitarnye_nauki/filosofiya/KUAN_UILLARD_VAN_ORMAN.html.

Kubryakova, E. S. (1992). Problemy predstavleniya znaniy v sovremennoy nauke i rol lingvistiki v reshenii etikh problem [Problems of Knowledge Representation in Modern Science and the Role of Linguistics in Solving These Problems]. *Yazyk i struktury predstavleniya znaniy*, 4–38.

Kubryakova, E. S. (1988). Rol slovoobrazovaniya v formirovanii yazykovoy kartiny mira [The Role of Word Formation in the Formation of the Linguistic Picture of the World]. *Rol chelovecheskogo faktora v yazyke: Yazyk i kartina mira*, 141–172.

Kubryakova, E. S. (1997). *Chasti rechi s kognitivnoy tochki zreniya* [Parts of Speech from a Cognitive Perspective]. Moscow: Institut yazykoznaniya RAN.

Kubryakova, E. S. (1991). *Chelovecheskiy faktor v yazyke: yazyk i porozhdenie rechi* [The Human Factor in Language: Language and Speech Generation]. Moscow: Nauka.

Kukharenko, V. A. (2002). *Interpretatsiya teksta* [Text Interpretation]. 3rd ed. Odessa: Latstar.

Kukharenko, V. A. (2004). *Interpretatsiya tekstu* [Text Interpretation]. Vinnytsya: Nova Knyha.

Kushnina, L. V. (2004). *Vzaimodeystvie yazykov i kultur v perevodcheskom prostranstve: geshtalt-sinergicheskiy podkhod*: avtoref. dis. d-ra filol. nauk: 10.02.19 "Teoriya yazyka" [Interaction of Languages and Cultures in the Translation Space: Gestalt-Synergistic

Approach: Author's Abstract of Doctor of Philological Sciences Monograph]. Chelyabinsk.
Lakoff, G. (2004). *Zhenshchiny, ogon i opasnye veshchi. Chto kategorii yazyka govoryat nam o myshlenii* [Women, Fire, and Dangerous Things: What Categories Reveal About the Mind]. Moscow: Yazyki slavyanskoy kultury.
Lakuna – Leksika – Ukrayinski entsyklopediyi ta slovnyky. Retrieved from http://leksika.com.ua/15800119/legal/lakuna.
Latyshev, L. K., & Semenov, A. L. (2003). *Perevod: teoriya, praktika i metodika prepodavaniya* [Translation: Theory, Practice, and Teaching Methods]. Moscow: Izdatelskiy tsentr "Akademiya".
Levy, I. (1970). Sostoyanie teoreticheskoy mysli v oblasti perevoda [The State of Theoretical Thought in the Field of Translation]. *Masterstvo perevoda*, 410–416.
Levi-Strauss, C. (1985). *Strukturnaya antropologiya* [Structural Anthropology]. Moscow: Glavnaya redaktsiya vostochnoy literatury.
Lysychenko, L. A. (1998). Movna kartyna svitu ta yiyi rivni [The Linguistic Picture of the World and Its Levels]. *Zbirka Kharkivskoho istoryko-filolohichnoho tovarystva, 6*, 128–144.
Likhachev, D. S. (1997). Kontseptosfera russkogo yazyka [The Conceptosphere of the Russian Language]. In V. P. Neroznak (Ed.), *Russkaya slovesnost. Ot teorii slovesnosti k strukture teksta. Antologiya* (pp. 280–287). Moscow: Akademiya.
Lotman, Yu. M. (2000). *Semiosfera. Kultura i vzryv. Vnutri myslyashchikh mirov. Statyi, issledovaniya, zametki* [The Semiosphere. Culture and Explosion. Within Thinking Worlds. Articles, Research, Notes]. Saint Petersburg: Iskusstvo.
Lotman, Yu. M. (1992). *Statyi po semiotike i topologii kultury: izbr. statyi. V 3 t. T.1: Tekst v tekste* [Articles on Semiotics and Topology of Culture: Selected Articles. Vol. 1: Text in Text]. Tallinn: "Aleksandra".
Lukin, V. A. (1993). Kontsept istiny i slovo ISTINA v russkom yazyke (Opyt kontseptualnogo analiza ratsionalnogo i irratsionalnogo v yazyke) [The Concept of Truth and the Word TRUTH in the Russian Language (An Attempt at Conceptual Analysis of the Rational and Irrational in Language)]. *Voprosy yazykoznaniya*, (4), 63–86.
Luhjenbrurs, D. (1996). Diskursivnyy analiz i skhematicheskaya struktura [Discourse Analysis and Schematic Structure]. *Voprosy yazykoznaniya*, (2), 141–155.
Lyubimov, N. M. (1988). *Nesgoraemye slova* [Non-burnable Words]. 2nd ed. Moscow: Khudozhestvennaya literatura.
Lyubchenko, T. N. (1991). Praktychni pidkhody do perekladu [Practical Approaches to Translation]. *Teoriya i praktyka perekladu, 17*, 89–97.
Maslova, V. A. (2001). *Lingvokul'turologiya: Ucheb. posobie dlya stud. vyssh. ucheb. zavedeniy* [Linguoculturology: Textbook for Students of Higher Educational Institutions]. Moscow: Akademiya.
Martynyuk, A. P. (2003). Hendernyy kontsept: prototyp i stereotip – denotat i konnotat [Gender Concept: Prototype and Stereotype – Denotatum and Connotatum]. *Nova filolohiya, 2*(17), 72–79.
Melnikova, A. A. (2003). *Yazyk i natsionalnyy kharakter. Vzaimosvyaz struktury yazyka i mentalnosti* [Language and National Character. The Interconnection of Language Structure and Mentality]. Saint Petersburg: Rech.

Minsky, M. (1979). *Freymy dlya predstavleniya znaniy* [Frames for the Representation of Knowledge]. Moscow: Energiya.

Mishina, E. V. (2003). Leksicheskie sredstva vyrazheniya kontsepta LOZH v sovremennom angliyskom yazyke [Lexical Means of Expressing the Concept LIE in Modern English]. In *Materialy mezhvuzovskoy nauchnoy konferentsii molodykh uchenykh* (pp. 211–213). Donetsk: DonNU.

Molchanova, G. G. (2001). Kognitivnaya stilistika i stilisticheskaya tipologiya [Cognitive Stylistics and Stylistic Typology]. *Vestnik Moskovskogo universiteta. Ser. 19, Lingvistika i mezhdunarodnaya kommunikatsiya,* (3), 60–72.

Nekryach, T. Ye., & Dovhanchyna, R. H. (2014). *Aysberh v okeani perekladu: Vidtvorennya idio-stylyu Ernesta Hemingveya v perekladakh ukrayinskoyu ta rosiyskoyu movamy* [An Iceberg in the Ocean of Translation: Reproduction of Ernest Hemingway's Idiolect in Ukrainian and Russian Translations]. Kyiv: Vydavnytstvo Lira-K.

Nekryach, T. Ye., & Chala, Yu. P. (2013). *Viktorianska doba v ukrayinskomu khudozhnomu perekladi* [The Victorian Era in Ukrainian Literary Translation]. Kyiv: Kondor.

Nesterova, N. M. (n.d.). Original i perevod: problema mezhtekstovykh otnosheniy [Original and Translation: The Problem of Intertextual Relationships]. *Language & Literature,* (1). Retrieved from http://frgf.utmn.ru/.

Nesterova, N. M. (2005). "Chuzhoye vmig pochuvstvovat' svoim": dialektika vtorichnosti perevoda ["To Feel Another's as One's Own Instantly": The Dialectic of Translation's Secondary Nature]. *Vestnik VGU, Seriya Lingvistika i mezhkulturnaya kommunikatsiya,* (1). Retrieved from http://www.vestnik.vsu.ru/pdf/lingvo/2005/01/nesterova.pdf.

Nikitina, S. E. (1991). O kontseptual'nom analize v narodnoy kulture [On Conceptual Analysis in Folk Culture]. *Logicheskiy analiz yazyka: Kulturnye kontsepty,* 117–123.

Nikonova, V. H. (2008). *Kontseptual'nyy prostir trahechnoho v p'yesakh Shekspira: poetiko-kohnityvnyy analiz* [Conceptual Space of the Tragic in Shakespeare's Plays: Poetic-Cognitive Analysis] (Doctoral monograph). Dnipropetrovsk.

Oparina, E. O. (1999). Lingvokul'turologiya: Metodologicheskie osnovaniya i bazovye ponyatiya [Linguoculturology: Methodological Foundations and Basic Concepts]. *Yazyk i kul'tura, 2,* 34.

Oryshak, O. V. (2009). *Faktory kulturnoy assimetrii v lingvisticheskom sopostavlenii i v perevode (na materiale russkikh i frantsuzskikh voyennykh i voyenno-politicheskikh tekstov):* avtoref. dis. kand. filol. nauk: 10.02.20 [Factors of Cultural Asymmetry in Linguistic Comparison and Translation (Based on Russian and French Military and Military-Political Texts): Author's Abstract of Candidate of Philological Sciences Monograph]. Moscow.

Pavilenis, R. I. (1983). *Problema smysla: sovremennyy logiko-filosofskiy analiz yazyka* [The Problem of Meaning: Modern Logical-Philosophical Analysis of Language]. Moscow: Mysl.

Perchi, M. Y. (2001). Kontsept, kontseptualizatsiya ta kontseptual'na kartyna svitu [Concept, Conceptualization and Conceptual Picture of the World]. *Problemy romano-hermans'koyi filolohiyi,* 78–82.

Pinker, S. A. (2004). *Yazyk kak instinkt* [The Language Instinct]. Moscow: Editorial URSS.

Pishchalnikova, V. A. (2000). Natsionalnaya spetsifika kartiny mira i yeye reprezentatsiya v yazyke [National Specificity of the Worldview and Its Representation in Language].

Yazykovoe soznanie: soderzhanie i funktsionirovanie. XIII mezhdunarodnyy simpozium po psikholingvistike i teorii kommunikatsii: Tezisy dokladov, 189–190.

Plank, M. (1966). *Yedinstvo fizicheskoy kartiny mira* [The Unity of the Physical Worldview]. Moscow: Nauka.

Ponomarenko, E. V. (2002). Lingvosinergika – novaya paradigma v nauke o yazyke i rechi [Linguosynergy – a New Paradigm in the Science of Language and Speech]. *Mova i kultura*, 5(2.2), 78–84.

Popovich, A. (1980). *Problemy khudozhestvennogo perevoda* [Problems of Literary Translation]. Moscow: Vysshaya shkola.

Potebnya, O. O. (1992). *Problemy suchasnoyi filolohiyi* [Problems of Modern Philology]. In V. Yu. Franchuk et al. (Eds.), Kyiv: Naukova dumka.

Pocheptsov, G. G. (2001). *Teoriya kommunikatsii* [Theory of Communication]. Moscow: Refl-buk.

Pocheptsov, O. G. (1990). Yazykovaya mentalnost: sposob predstavleniya mira [Linguistic Mentality: A Way of Representing the World]. *Voprosy yazykoznaniya*, (6), 110–122.

Protsenko, E. A. (2005). Vozmozhna li repatriatsiya pri perevode? [Is Repatriation Possible in Translation?]. *Vestnik VGU, Seriya "Lingvistika i mezhkulturnaya kommunikatsiya"*, (2), 124–128.

Radchenko, O. R. (2001). Lingvofilosofskie opyty V. fon Humboldta i posthumboldtiantsvo [Linguistic-Philosophical Studies of W. von Humboldt and Post-Humboldtianism]. *Voprosy yazykoznaniya*, (3), 96–125.

Reiss, K. (1978). Klassifikatsiya tekstov i metody perevoda [Text Classification and Translation Methods]. In V. N. Komissarov (Ed.), *Voprosy teorii perevoda v zarubezhnoy lingvistike* (pp. 202–228). Moscow: Mezhdunarodnye otnosheniya.

Rakhilina, E. V. (2000). O tendentsiyakh v razvitii kognitivnoy semantiki [On Trends in the Development of Cognitive Semantics]. *Izvestiya RAN, Seriya literatury i yazyka*, 59(3), 3–15.

Rebriy, O. V. (2012). *Suchasni kontseptsiyi tvorchosti u perekladi* [Modern Concepts of Creativity in Translation]. Kharkiv: Kharkivs'kyy natsional'nyy universytet imeni V. N. Karazina.

Retsker, Ya. I. (1974). *Teoriya perevoda i perevodcheskaya praktika* [Translation Theory and Translation Practice]. Moscow: Mezhdunarodnye otnosheniya.

Ryabinska, Yu. A. (n.d.). *Osoblyvosti adyekvatnoho spryynyattya tvoriv zarubizhnoyi literatury v oryhinali ta perekladi* [Features of Adequate Perception of Foreign Literature Works in the Original and Translation]. Retrieved from http://docs.google.com/viewer?a=v&q=cache:Wa6Wfz7CSFYJ:www.nbuv.gov.ua.

Rylov, Yu. A. (2003). Semanticheskie dominanty yazykovoy kartiny mira i perevod [Semantic Dominants of the Linguistic Picture of the World and Translation]. In *Perevod i perevodcheskaya kompetentsiya* (pp. 136–149). Kursk: Izdatelstvo ROSI.

Roshchupkina, E. V. *Diskurs globalizatsii: osnovnye problemy kontseptual'nykh postroeniy* [The Discourse of Globalization: Main Problems of Conceptual Constructs]. Retrieved from http://lib.socio.msu.ru/l/library.

Ryabtseva, N. K. (1991). "Vopros": prototipicheskoe znachenie kontsepta ["Question": Prototypical Meaning of the Concept]. *Logicheskiy analiz yazyka: Kulturnye kontsepty*, 72–85.

Samigullina, A. S. (2007). Kognitivnaya lingvistika i semiotika [Cognitive Linguistics and Semiotics]. *Voprosy yazykoznaniya*, (3), 11-24.

Safonov, I. A. (1993). *Chelovek i kosmos v istorii kultur* [Man and Cosmos in the History of Cultures]. Saint Petersburg.

Sdobnikov, V. V., & Petrova, O. V. (2006). *Teoriya perevoda* [Theory of Translation]. Moscow: AST: Vostok-Zapad.

Sevryugina, E. V. (2002). Kontsept "krasota" v poezii F. I. Tyutcheva [The Concept of "Beauty" in the Poetry of F. I. Tyutchev]. *Filologicheskie nauki*, (3), 30-39.

Selivanova, O. O. (1999). *Aktualni napryamy suchasnoyi linhvistyky (analitychnyy ohlyad)* [Current Directions in Modern Linguistics (An Analytical Review)]. Kyiv: Fitosotsiotsentr.

Selivanova, E. A. (2000). *Kognitivnaya onomasiologiya* [Cognitive Onomasiology]. Kyiv: Fitosotsiotsentr.

Selivanova, O. O. (2001). Kohnityvnyy aspekt kontrastryvnoyi onomasiolohiyi [The Cognitive Aspect of Contrastive Onomasiology]. *Movoznavstvo*, (1), 71-74.

Selivanova, E. A. (2002). *Osnovy lingvisticheskoy teorii teksta i kommunikatsii* [Fundamentals of the Linguistic Theory of Text and Communication]. Kyiv: Brama.

Selivanova, O. O. (2006). *Suchasna linhvistyka: terminolohichna entsyklopediya* [Modern Linguistics: A Terminological Encyclopedia]. Poltava: Dovkillya.

Sapir, E. (1993). *Izbrannye trudy po obshchemu yazykoznaniyu i kulturologii* [Selected Works on General Linguistics and Cultural Studies]. Moscow: Progress.

Serebrennikov, B. A. (1988). Yazyk otrazhaet deystvitelnost ili vyrazhaet yeye yazykovym sposobom? [Does Language Reflect Reality or Express It Linguistically?]. In B. A. Serebrennikov (Ed.), *Rol chelovecheskogo faktora v yazyke: Yazyk i kartina mira* (pp. 12-21). Moscow: Nauka.

Serebryanska, I. M. (2009). Etnokulturnyy kontsept "pryroda" yak skladova prostorovoho kodu [Ethnocultural Concept "Nature" as a Component of the Spatial Code]. *Filolohichni traktaty*, 1(1), 91-95.

Sysoyev, P. V. (2003). Kognitivnye aspekty ovladeniya kulturoy [Cognitive Aspects of Mastering Culture]. *Vestnik MGU. Seriya Lingvistika i mezhdunarodnaya kommunikatsiya*, (4), 110-123.

Slyshkin, G. G. (2000). *Ot teksta k simvolu: lingvokulturnye kontsepty pretsedentnykh tekstov v soznanii i diskurse* [From Text to Symbol: Linguocultural Concepts of Precedent Texts in Consciousness and Discourse]. Moscow: Academia.

Stepanov, Yu. S. (1997). *Konstanty. Slovar russkoy kultury. Opyt issledovaniya* [Constants. Dictionary of Russian Culture. Research Experience]. Moscow: Shkola "Yazyki russkoy kultury".

Stepanov, Yu. S. (2000). Kontsept kultury "v razreze" [The Concept of Culture "in Section"]. In *Kognitivnaya semantika. Materialy II mezhdunarodnoy shkoly-seminara* (Vol. 1, p. 8). Tambov.

Stepanov, Yu. S. (2001). Semiotika kontseptov [Semiotics of Concepts]. In Yu. S. Stepanov (Ed.), *Semiotika: Antologiya* (pp. 603-612). Moscow: Akademicheskiy Proekt.

Sternin, I. A., & Bykova, G. V. (1998). Kontsepty i lakuny [Concepts and Lacunae]. In *Yazykovoe soznanie: Formirovanie i funktsionirovanie* (pp. 9-17). Moscow.

Sukalenko, N. I. (1987). O granitsakh perevodimosti yazykovykh obrazov [On the Limits of Translatability of Linguistic Images]. In A. I. Cherednichenko (Ed.), *Teoriya i praktika perevoda* (Vol. 14, pp. 158). Kyiv: "Vysshaya shkola".

Terekhova, D. I. (2001). Pro movnu kartynu svitu ta obraz svitu [On the Linguistic Picture of the World and the Image of the World]. In *Problemy semantyky, slova, rechenya ta tekstu* (Vol. 6, pp. 224–228). Kyiv.

Ter-Minasova, S. G. (2000). *Yazyk i mezhkulturnaya kommunikatsiya* [Language and Intercultural Communication]. Moscow: Slovo.

Tymchenko, Ye. P. (1999). Vidobrazhennya pohodnykh yavyshch u movniy kartyni svitu (na materiali nimetskoyi ta ukrayinskoyi mov) [The Reflection of Weather Phenomena in the Linguistic Picture of the World (Based on German and Ukrainian)]. In *Movni i kontseptualni kartyny svitu* (pp. 81–85). Kyiv: KNU imeni T. H. Shevchenka.

Tokareva, N. I. (1999). *Etnokulturnye stereotipy kommunikativnogo povedeniya* [Ethnocultural Stereotypes of Communicative Behavior] (Doctoral monograph). Minsk.

Torop, P. (1995). *Totalnyy perevod* [Total Translation]. Tartu: Izdatelstvo Tartuskogo universiteta.

Ufimtseva, A. A. (1986). *Leksicheskoe znachenie (printsip semiologicheskogo opisaniya leksiki)* [Lexical Meaning (The Principle of Semiological Description of Lexis)]. Moscow: Nauka.

Ufimtseva, N. V. (2000). Soznanie, slovo, kul'tura [Consciousness, Word, Culture]. In *Kommunikativnaya lingvistika i kommunikativno-deyatelnostnyy podkhod k obucheniyu yazykam: Sbornik pamyati G. V. Kolshanskogo* (pp. 253). Moscow.

Fedorenko, L. V. (2003). Etnolingvisticheskiy aspekt issledovaniya individualno-avtorskoy kartiny mira [Ethnolinguistic Aspect of Studying Individual-Author's Worldview]. In *Materialy Mezhdunarodnoy nauchno-metodicheskoy konferentsii "Treti Karazinskie chteniya: metodika i lingvistika – na puti k integratsii"* (pp. 179–180). Kharkiv: KhNU imeni V. N. Karazina.

Fenenko, N. A., & Kretov, A. A. (1999). Perevod kak kanal vzaimodeystviya kultur i yazykov (k probleme yazykovogo osvoeniya "chuzhoy" deystvitelnosti) [Translation as a Channel of Interaction Between Cultures and Languages (On the Problem of Linguistic Assimilation of "Foreign" Reality)]. *Sotsiokulturnye problemy perevoda*, (3), 82–94.

Fenenko, N. A. (2001). *Yazyk realiy i realii yazyka* [The Language of Realities and Realities of Language]. Voronezh: VGU.

Fesenko, T. A. (2001). *Kontseptualnye osnovy perevoda* [Conceptual Foundations of Translation]. Tambov: Izdatelstvo TGU imeni G. R. Derzhavina.

Fesenko, T. A. (2002). *Spetsifika natsionalnogo kulturnogo prostranstva v zerkale perevoda* [The Specifics of National Cultural Space in the Mirror of Translation]. Tambov: Izdatelstvo TGU imeni G. R. Derzhavina.

Fillmore, C. (1983). Osnovnye problemy leksicheskoy semantiki [The Main Problems of Lexical Semantics]. *Novoe v zarubezhnoy lingvistike*, 12, 74–122.

Fillmore, C. (1988). Freymy i semantika ponimaniya [Frames and the Semantics of Understanding]. *Novoe v zarubezhnoy lingvistike*, 23, 52–92.

Filosofskiy slovar: Intertekstualnost [Philosophical Dictionary: Intertextuality]. Retrieved from http://mirslovarei.com/content_fil/INTERTEKSTUALNOST.

Fomenko, E. G. *Makrostrukturnyy uroven v obuchenii interpretatsii teksta* [Macrostructural Level in Teaching Text Interpretation]. Retrieved from http://web.znu.edu.ua/herald/articles/2369.pdf.

Frumkina, R. M. (1996). "Teorii srednego urovnya" v sovremennoy lingvistike ["Mid-Level Theories" in Modern Linguistics]. *Voprosy yazykoznaniya*, (2), 57–67.

Heidegger, M. (1986). Vremya kartiny mira [The Age of the World Picture]. In *Novaya tekhnokraticheskaya volna na Zapade* (pp. 93–118). Moscow: Progress.

Khayrullin, V. V. (1995). *Lingvokul'turologicheskie i kognitivnye aspekty perevoda* [Linguocultural and Cognitive Aspects of Translation] (Doctoral monograph). Moscow.

Kharitonchik, Z. A. (1992). Sposoby kontseptualnoy organizatsii znaniy v leksike yazyka [Ways of Conceptual Organization of Knowledge in the Lexis of Language]. *Yazyk i struktury predstavleniya znaniy*, 98–123.

Kharchenko, O. V. (2004). Tekst iz psykholinhvistychnoyi tochky zoru [Text from a Psycholinguistic Perspective]. *Naukovyy visnyk Chernivetskoho universytetu*, 188–189, 293–303.

Halliday, M. (1978). Lingvisticheskie funktsii i literaturnyy stil [Linguistic Functions and Literary Style]. *Novoe v zarubezhnoy lingvistike*, 9, 116–147.

Chomsky, N. (2000). *Logicheskie osnovy lingvisticheskoy teorii* [The Logical Foundations of Linguistic Theory]. Birobidzhan: IP "Trivium".

Tsvilling, M. Ya. (2003). Kognitivnye modeli i perevod: (k postanovke problemy) [Cognitive Models and Translation: (Towards the Problem)]. In *Perevod kak kognitivnaya deyatelnost* (p. 23). Moscow.

Chafe, W. L. (1983). Pamyat i verbalizatsiya proshlogo opyta [Memory and Verbalization of Past Experience]. *Novoe v zarubezhnoy lingvistike*, 12, 35–73.

Cienki, A. (1996). Sovremennye kognitivnye podkhody k semantike: skhodstva i razlichiya v teoriyakh i tselyakh [Modern Cognitive Approaches to Semantics: Similarities and Differences in Theories and Goals]. *Voprosy yazykoznaniya*, (2), 68–78.

Cherednychenko, O. I. (2007). *Pro movu i pereklad* [On Language and Translation]. Kyiv: Lybid.

Chomu amerykantsiv nazyvayut "yanki"? [Why Are Americans Called "Yankees"?]. Retrieved from www.verano.rv.ua/navkolishnij-svit/chomu-amerikanciv-nazivayut-yanki.

Shveitser, A. D. (1988). *Perevod i lingvistika: Status, problemy, aspekty* [Translation and Linguistics: Status, Problems, Aspects]. Moscow: Nauka.

Shveitser, A. D. (1988). *Teoriya perevoda: status, problemy, aspekty* [Translation Theory: Status, Problems, Aspects]. Moscow: Nauka.

Shevchenko, I. S. (2003). Germenevticheskiy aspekt perevoda kak vtorichnoy metakommunikatsii [The Hermeneutic Aspect of Translation as Secondary Metacommunication]. In *Problemy perevodovedeniya, kommunikativnoy i kognitivnoy lingvistiki: Visnyk Kharkivskoho natsionalnoho universytetu imeni V. N. Karazina* (Vol. 609, pp. 7–11). Kharkiv: Konstanta.

Shevchenko, I. S. (2000). Ob istoricheskom razvitii kognitivnogo i pragmaticheskogo aspektov diskursa [On the Historical Development of Cognitive and Pragmatic Aspects of Discourse]. In *Inostrannaya filologiya na rubezhe tysyacheletiy: Visnyk Kharkivskoho natsionalnoho universytetu imeni V. N. Karazina* (Vol. 471, pp. 300–307). Kharkiv: Konstanta.

Yazyk i natsionalnoe soznanie. Voprosy teorii i metodologii [Language and National Consciousness. Issues of Theory and Methodology]. (2002). Voronezh: Izdatelstvo VGU.

Alfarano, R. (n.d.). *Translators and Translations: Paintings and Shades in Their Frames.* Retrieved from http://accurapid.com/journal/34prof.htm.

Al-Shabab, O. S. (1996). *Interpretation and the Language of Translation: Creativity and Conventions in Translation.* London: Janus Publishing Company.

Bassnett, S. (1985). Ways through the Labyrinth: Strategies and Methods for Translating Theatre Texts. In T. Hermans (Ed.), *The Manipulation of Literature* (pp. 87–102). London: Croom Helm; New York: St Martin's.

Bell, R. T. (1987). Translation Theory: Where are we going? *Meta, 32,* 403–415.

Catford, J. C. (1965). *A Linguistic Theory of Translation: An Essay in Applied Linguistics.* London: Oxford University Press, 103–214.

Chomsky, N. (1991). Linguistics and Cognitive Science: Problems and Mysteries. In A. Kasher (Ed.), *The Chomskyan Turn* (pp. 26–53). Cambridge, Mass.: Basil Blackwell.

Downs, L. L. (1993). If "Woman" is Just an Empty Category, Then Why I am Afraid to Walk Alone at Night? Identity Politics Meets the Postmodern Subject. *Comparative Studies in Society and History, 35,* 414–437.

Dryden, J. (1992). On Translation. In R. Schulte & J. Biguenet (Eds.), *Theories of Translation: An Anthology of Essays from Dryden to Derrida* (pp. 17–31). Chicago-London: The University of Chicago Press.

Eco, U. (1894). *The Role of the Reader.* Bloomington: Indiana University Press.

Even-Zohar, I. (1990). Polysystem Studies. *Poetics Today, 11*(1), 1–268.

Even-Zohar, I. (1981). Translation Theory Today: A Call for Transfer Theory. *Poetics Today, 2*(4), 1–7.

Halliday, M. A. K. (1978). *Language as Social Semiotic: The Social Interpretation of Language and Meaning.* London: Arnold.

Halverson, S. (1999). Conceptual Work and the Translation Concept. *Target, 11*(1), 1–31.

Holubenko, N. I. (2015). Approaches to Reproducing Nominative Representatives of Cultural Concepts. *Science and Education a New Dimension. Philology, III*(8), Issue 39, 6–9.

Hönig, H. G., & Kußmaul, P. (1982). *Strategie der Übersetzung: Ein Lehr- und Arbeitsbuch* [Translation Strategy: A Teaching and Workbook]. Tübingen: Narr.

Hu, Y. (n.d.). *The Sociosemiotic Approach and Translation of Fiction.* Retrieved from http://accurapid.com/journal/14fiction.htm.

Iser, W. (2000). *The Range of Interpretation.* New York: Columbia University Press.

Jakobson, R. (1966). On Linguistic Aspect of Translation. In R. A. Brewer (Ed.), *On Translation* (pp. 232–239). New York: Oxford University Press.

James, K. (n.d.). *Cultural Implications for Translation.* Retrieved from http://accurapid.com/journal/22delight.htm.

Kade, O. (1971). Zum Verhältnis von Translation und Transformation. Studien zur Übersetzungswissenschaft [On the Relationship Between Translation and Transformation: Studies in Translation Studies]. *Beihefte zur Zeitschrift Fremdsprachen III/IV,* 7–26.

Karamanian, A. P. (n.d.). *Translation and Culture.* Retrieved from http://accurapid.com/journal/19culture.htm.

Kiraly, D. C. (1995). *Pathways to Translation: Pedagogy and Process*. Kent State University Press.

Koller, W. (1995). The Concept of Equivalence and the Object of Translation Studies. *Target, 7*(2), 191–222.

Kramsh, C. (1993). *Context and Culture in Language Teaching*. Oxford: Oxford University Press.

Krings, H. P. (1986). *Was in den Köpfen von Übersetzern vorgeht: Eine empirische Untersuchung zur Struktur des Übersetzungsprozesses an fortgeschrittenen Französischlernern* [What Goes On in Translators' Minds: An Empirical Study on the Structure of the Translation Process in Advanced French Learners]. Tübingen: Narr.

Lambert, J. (1994). The Cultural Component Reconsidered. In M. Snell-Hornby (Ed.), *Translation Studies: An Interdiscipline* (pp. 17–26). Amsterdam & Philadelphia: John Benjamins Publishing Co.

Langacker, R. W. (1968). *Language and Its Structure: Some Fundamental Linguistic Concepts*. New York: Harcourt, Brace & World, Inc.

Lefevre, A. (1985). Why Waste Our Time on Rewrites? The Trouble with Interpretation and the Role of Rewriting in an Alternative Paradigm. In T. Hermans (Ed.), *The Manipulation of Literature* (pp. 215–243). London: Croom Helm; New York: St Martin's.

Lewis, P. (1985). The Measure of Translation Effects. In J. F. Graham (Ed.), *Difference in Translation* (pp. 31–62). Ithaca: Cornell University Press.

Muñoz Martín, R. (2010). On Paradigms and Cognitive Translatology. In G. Shreve & E. Angelone (Eds.), *Translation and Cognition* (pp. 169–187). Amsterdam: John Benjamins.

Mossop, B. (1998). What is a Translating Translator Doing? *Target, 10*(2), 231–266.

Newmark, P. (2003). *A Textbook of Translation*. Longman.

Newmark, P. (1981). *Approaches to Translation*. Oxford: Pergamon Press.

Nida, E. A. (1975). *Language Structure and Translation*. Stanford: California.

Nida, E. A. (2002). *Contexts in Translating*. Amsterdam and Philadelphia: John Benjamins.

Nida, E. (1964). Principles of Correspondence. In *Toward a Science of Translating* (pp. 156–171). Leiden: Brill.

Pym, A. (1992). *Translation and Text Transfer: An Essay on the Principles of Intercultural Communication*. Frankfurt/Main; Berlin; Bern; New York; Paris; Vienna: Peter Lang.

Robertson, R. (2003). Globalization or Glocalization? In K. E. White (Ed.), *Globalisation: Critical Concept in Sociology* (Vol. 3, pp. 31–51). London.

Rosch, E. H. (1975). Cognitive Reference Points. *Cognitive Psychology, 7*, 532–547.

Samuelsson-Brown, G. (1998). *A Practical Guide for Translators*. Multilingual Matters.

Savornin, S. (n.d.). *Traduire l'intraduisible après les postcolonial studies* [Translating the Untranslatable After Postcolonial Studies]. Retrieved from http://e-lla.univ-provence.fr/pdf/article5.pdf.

Snell-Hornby, M. (1994). *Translation Studies: An Integrated Approach*. Amsterdam: John Benjamins Publishing Co.

Tannen, D. (2006). Language and Culture. In *An Introduction to Language and Linguistics* (pp. 343–372). New York: Cambridge University Press.

Thriveni, C. (n.d.). *The Indian Perspective: Cultural Elements in Translation*. Retrieved from http://accurapid.com/journal/19culture.htm.

Toporov, V. N. (1992). Translation: Sub Specie of Culture. *Meta, 37*(1), 2–49.

Toury, G. (1995). *Descriptive Translation Studies and Beyond.* Amsterdam and Philadelphia: John Benjamins.
Toury, G. (1980). *In Search of a Theory of Translation.* Tel Aviv: The Porter Institute for Poetics and Semiotics, Tel Aviv University.
Vermeer, H. J. (1994). Translation Today: Old and New Problems. In M. Snell-Hornby (Ed.), *Translation Studies: An Interdiscipline* (pp. 3–16). Amsterdam and Philadelphia: John Benjamins.
Wierzbicka, A. (1991). *Cross-Cultural Pragmatics: The Semantics of Human Interaction.* Berlin: Walter de Gruyter.
Wolfson, L. (n.d.). *The Contact Between Text, Mind and One's Own Word.* Retrieved from http://accurapid.com/journal/34workshop.htm.

Lexicographic Sources

ААЛР. (1996). *Americana: Anglo-russkiy lingvostranovedcheskiy slovar* [Americana: Anglo-Russian Linguistic and Cultural Dictionary] (G. V. Chernov, Ed.). Moscow: Pomiramma.
АРФР. (1984). *Anglo-russkiy frazeologicheskiy slovar: V 2-kh tomakh* [Anglo-Russian Phraseological Dictionary: In 2 Volumes] (4th ed., A. V. Kunin, Ed.). Moscow: Russkiy yazyk.
АУФР. (2006). *Anglo-ukrayinskyy frazeolohichnyy slovnyk* [Anglo-Ukrainian Phraseological Dictionary] (3rd ed., K. T. Barantsev, Ed.). Kyiv: T-vo "Znnnya", KOO.
VTSSUM. (2005). *Velykyy tlumachnyy slovnyk suchasnoyi ukrayinskoyi movy (z dod. i dopov.)* [Great Explanatory Dictionary of Modern Ukrainian Language (with Additions and Supplements)] (V. T. Busel, Ed.). Київ/Ірпінь: Perun.
КЛЭ. (1967). *Kratkaya literaturnaya entsiklopediya* [Brief Literary Encyclopedia] (A. A. Surkov, Ed., Vol. 5). Moscow: Sovetskaya entsiklopediya.
ЛСД. (1997). *Litaturoznavchyy slovnyk-dovidnyk* [Literary Dictionary-Reference] (R. T. Hromyak & Yu. I. Kovaliv, Eds.). Kyiv: Akademiya.
ПССУМ. (2008). *Praktychnyy slovnyk synonimiv ukrayinskoyi movy* [Practical Dictionary of Ukrainian Synonyms] (S. Karavanskyi, Ed.). Kyiv: BaK.
САМ. (1989). *Slovnyk antychnoyi mifolohiyi* [Dictionary of Ancient Mythology]. Kyiv: Naukova dumka.
СФСУМ. (n.d.). *Slovopedia. Frazeolohichnyy slovnyk ukrayinskoyi movy* [Phraseological Dictionary of the Ukrainian Language]. Retrieved from http://www.slovopedia.org.ua/49/53410/361916.html.
CDIEUS. (2002). *Chambers Dictionary of Idioms: English-Ukrainian Semibilingual.* Kyiv: Vseuvyto.
DCE. (2005). *Dictionary of Contemporary English* (D. Summers, Ed.). London-New York: Longman.
LDELC. (2003). *Longman Dictionary of English Language and Culture* (6th ed.). London: Pearson Education Ltd.
NWDTEL. (1993). *New Webster's Dictionary and Thesaurus of the English Language.* Danbury: Lexicon Publications, Inc.

OGBACLE. (2005). *Oxford Guide to British and American Culture for Learners of English* (2nd ed., J. Crowther, Ed.). Oxford: Oxford University Press.
RETS. (2001). *Routledge Encyclopedia of Translation Studies* (M. Baker, Ed.). London: Routledge.
AHDI. (n.d.). *The American Heritage Dictionary of Idioms* (2nd ed., Ch. Ammer, Ed.). Retrieved from http://www.books.google.ru/books?id=I_LxuR1jMVgC&pg.
WTNIDELU. (1961). *Webster's Third New International Dictionary of the English Language Unabridged.* London: Merriam Co. Publ.
YDBOD. (n.d.). *YourDictionary: The Best Online Dictionary.* Retrieved from http://www.yourdictionary.com.

Illustrative Sources

Mitrofanov. (2006). *Khatyna dyadka Toma* [Uncle Tom's Cabin] (H. Beecher-Stowe, Trans. V. Mitrofanova). Kyiv: Veselka.
Kuznetsova. (2012). *Khatyna dyadka Toma* [Uncle Tom's Cabin] (H. Beecher-Stowe, Trans. L. Kuznetsova, Ill. O. Poloskina). Kyiv: Krayina Mriy.
Nekryach. *Ydy, vartohoho postav* [Go Set a Watchman] (H. Lee, Trans. T. Nekryach). Manuscript.
Kharenko. (1997). *Ubyty peresmishnyka* [To Kill a Mockingbird] (H. Lee, Trans. M. Kharenko). Kyiv.
Nekryach. (2015). *Ubyty peresmishnyka* [To Kill a Mockingbird] (H. Lee, Trans. T. Nekryach). Kyiv: KMPublishing.
Dotsenko. (1992). *Zviyani vitrom: Roman: kn. 1* [Gone with the Wind: Novel: Vol. 1] (M. Mitchell, Trans. R. I. Dotsenko, Ill. V. I. Bariba & O. V. Shtramilo). Kyiv: Dnipro.
Dotsenko. (2004). *Zviyani vitrom: Roman: kn. 2* [Gone with the Wind: Novel: Vol. 2] (M. Mitchell, Trans. R. I. Dotsenko, Design by B. P. Bublyk). Kharkiv: Folio.
Steshenko. (1990). *Pryhody Heklberri Finna* [The Adventures of Huckleberry Finn] (M. Twain, Trans. I. Steshenko). Kyiv: Veselka.
Koretskyi. (1982). *Pryhody Toma Soyyera* [The Adventures of Tom Sawyer] (M. Twain, Trans. Yu. V. Koretskyi, Ill. V. I. Horyayev). Kyiv: Veselka.
Mitrofanov. *Use korolivske viysko* [All the King's Men] (R. P. Warren, Trans. V. Mitrofanov).
Dotsenko. (1972). *Kradiyi ta inshi tvory* [The Reivers and Other Works] (W. Faulkner, Trans. R. I. Dotsenko). Kyiv: Dnipro.
Beecher Stowe, H. (2006). *Uncle Tom's Cabin.* Saint Petersburg: KARO.
Lee, H. (2011). *To Kill a Mockingbird.* Saint Petersburg: Anthology.
Lee, H. (n.d.). *Go Set a Watchman.* US: Harper.
Mitchell, M. (2013). *Gone with the Wind.* London: Pan Books.
Twain, M. (1994). *The Adventures of Huckleberry Finn.* London: Penguin Books.
Twain, M. (1994). *The Adventures of Tom Sawyer.* London: Penguin Books.
Warren, R. P. (1996). *All the King's Men* (2nd ed.). Harcourt Brace.
Faulkner, W. (1962). *The Reivers.* New York: Random House.